VIRTUE AND HUMAN ENDS

VIRTUE AND HUMAN ENDS

POLITICAL IDEAS FROM INDIAN CLASSICS

VASANTHI SRINIVASAN

Orient BlackSwan

VIRTUE AND HUMAN ENDS: POLITICAL IDEAS FROM INDIAN CLASSICS

ORIENT BLACKSWAN PRIVATE LIMITED

Registered Office
3-6-752 Himayatnagar, Hyderabad 500 029, Telangana, India
e-mail: centraloffice@orientblackswan.com

Other Offices
Bengaluru, Chennai, Guwahati, Hyderabad, Kolkata, Mumbai, New Delhi, Noida, Patna

First published by Orient Blackswan Private Limited 2021

The artwork used herein is from the *Anwār-e Sohaylī* or the *Lights of Canopus*, a fifteenth-century Persian retelling of the Sanskrit *Panchatantra*, as available in the public domain.

ISBN 978-93-5442-049-8

041747

Typeset in
Minion Pro 10.5/13
by Manmohan Kumar, Delhi

Printed in India at
Avantika Printers Private Limited, New Delhi 110 020

Published by
Orient Blackswan Private Limited
3-6-752 Himayatnagar, Hyderabad 500 029, Telangana, India
e-mail: info@orientblackswan.com

To my dear friends, philosophers and guides
Professor Peter Emberley (1956–2016),
Professor Gurpreet Mahajan

CONTENTS

PREFACE AND ACKNOWLEDGEMENTS

The new education policy of the present Government of India explicitly invokes the need for liberal arts education alongside technical training to enable holistic cultivation of the intellectual, aesthetic, social, physical, emotional and moral capacities of students. In this context, it also lists many virtues such as commitment to liberal notions of freedom and equality, inclusivity, tolerance, diversity, and so on. More than preaching a standard table of values, a liberal arts education must endeavour to cultivate the mind and heart so that a student may reflect on her/his own interests and desires, life plans and choices, and learn to steer away from extremes. In this process, immersion into a culture's classics that deal with human ends, which essentially consist in deliberating about and acquiring pleasure, wealth, virtue and wisdom from the perspective of the rulers and the ruled, is imperative for both dialogue and criticism.

Indian classics such as Vishnu Sharma's *Panchatantra* (The Five Treatises), Vishakhadatta's *Mudrarakshasa* (The Signet Ring), Dandin's *Dasakumaracharita* (Adventures of the Ten Princes), Narayana Pandita's *Hitopadesha* (Beneficial Advice) and Shivadasa's *Vetala Panchavimshati* (Five and Twenty Tales of the Vetala) have been regarded as entertaining and edifying throughout the ages. But their discussions about the best modes of educating rulers in general, and princes in particular, in *niti*, or policy and propriety, their insights on the human ends of *artha* (acquiring wealth and worldly success) and *kama* (desire and erotic love), or their ironic affirmations of realpolitik have not been analysed in-depth, let alone comparatively. This book attempts to deepen the study of Indian political ideas by going beyond surveying concepts and ideas from canonical sources such as the epics and the *Arthashastra*, as is usually done. Drawing upon well-worn themes in Western political thought, such as the relationship between philosophy and politics, prudence in discerning friends and enemies, love and deception in politics, and so on, it lights up these narratives so that we may learn afresh about *niti*, or practical wisdom, in general.

While teaching the standard syllabi adopted in Indian universities on Western political thought, it became clear to me that without the attendant cultural aids (music, sculpture, paintings), both premodern and modern political thought seemed alien to many students, some of who are first-generation university wards. While *niti* or *dharma* (ethics and duties) found immediate resonance among students, terms like *phronesis* or *virtu* were all Greek and Latin! Of course, not all students in India are familiar with the content of *niti* or *dharma*, but they could draw upon their life-worlds, if only superficially. These terms are still a part of hallowed political rhetoric, albeit hollowed out. So while explaining phronesis, it was useful to delve into Kautilya's *Arthashastra* as well as the *Panchatantra*, which are imbued with practical wisdom. Students tend to miss thematic commonalities and connections between texts of different genres across time and space; they also compartmentalise what they know in terms of disciplinary boundaries, as if what they gleaned from comics and other popular narratives is 'literature' but not political 'thought'. More than stoking nationalist fervour or trendy cosmopolitanism, comparisons must aim at rekindling wonder about the diverse ways of reasoning about acquiring wealth, love and friendship, as well as war and peace. I am confident that students will recognise some of the *niti* stories analysed herein and realise that realpolitik need not exclude ethics.

As will become clearer, I chose this set of texts because they all fit the 'mirror of princes' genre of advice literature, and self-consciously carry on a debate with Kautilya's views. They explicitly allude to the *Ramayana* and *Mahabharata* epics and the *Arthashastra* when they pick up themes such as skilful intrigue in achieving ends (*Mudrarakshasa*), cultivating practical wisdom, especially regarding friends and enemies (*Panchatantra*), intricacies of war and peace (*Hitopadesha*), and the risks of educating princes (*Dasakumaracharita*). Admittedly, these were not self-styled commentaries on the *Arthashastra* and are works of fiction; however, they spell out the anxieties and difficulties only hinted at by Kautilya and simulate the contexts within which they must have been put to use, thus providing a window into popular as well as elite reception of political ideas. Though these are literary texts, I have focused on ideas and themes without being bogged down by stylistic analysis or historical minutiae. While they all address kings and courtiers of monarchies and oligarchies, their insights regarding rulers' aversion to learning and wisdom, untutored desire in high places, ordinary people's reasoning about war and peace, virtues and vices, and so on, are not regime-specific. I hope that scholars of comparative political thought and philosophy will gain from this broadening of sources in teaching and modifying the standard syllabi everywhere. Discussions on Aristotle's *Nicomachean Ethics*, Machiavelli's *Mandragola* or Giovanni Boccaccio's *Decameron* (which have been chosen here) can be deepened by seeing how similar concerns about friendship, infidelity and magnanimity were tackled elsewhere. As mentioned earlier, many liberal arts courses that engage with multicultural approaches to prudence, love, friendship and ethical excellence may also find this attempt to map out comparisons novel and useful.

The lurking danger of faulty translations and superficial assimilations, given our historicist piety, initially inhibited these pedagogical crossings and may not have been fully overcome. But I was inspired by my doctoral supervisor, the late Prof. Peter Emberley (to whom this book is dedicated), who taught me to go beyond polemical and politically correct posturing. Political thought, at its best, must peer into thought crystals—self, justice, prudence, sacred, virtues, love, friendship, revolution, utopia, and so on—until one sees how they circulate and morph in canonical texts and folk traditions, revealing similarities and concealing differences, or even incommensurabilities. If one asks questions of the Indian material using Western thought, or vice versa, one may find rough equivalences, he urged, fascinated by his travels to India and his work with Indian artisanal groups. Influenced by Eric Voegelin, Prof. Emberley showed that if only one probes the classics without succumbing to trendy historicist sophistry, scholarship could be absorbing and rewarding all the time. Doing so is neither easy nor popular, but the glowing embers he kindled continue to smoulder and crackle whenever I teach or write.

I am happy to also dedicate this book to Prof. Gurpreet Mahajan, who has encouraged me throughout, for being ever ready to listen to vague ideas, posing difficult questions and, above all, giving affectionate advice on many issues. Thanks to her, I saw that Francis Bacon was right in saying that an hour's conversation with a friend is more conducive to clearing the mind than a day's meditation.

I am grateful to the participants of the South Asia@Yale and National Institute of Advanced Studies, Benguluru, seminar on 'Indian Political Philosophy' held in July 2015, where a preliminary version of Chapter II, 'Friendship in *Panchatantra*' was presented. I am also indebted to the comments of Prof. Makarand Paranjpe and Prof. Sujata Patel, among others, at the Indian Institute of Advanced Study, Shimla, on another version of Chapter II, published as 'Friendship and Prudence in the *Pancatantra*', in *Studies in Humanities and Social Sciences* Vol. 25, No. 2, November 2018. I benefited from Prof. Aloka Parasher-Sen's comments on an initial draft of Chapter V, published as 'Seeing Beyond *Dharma*: Ethical Excellence in *Vikram and Vetaal* Stories', as part of the Working Paper Series, November 2009, of the Center for the Advanced Study of India, University of Pennsylvania. Prof. Sudipta Kaviraj showed his practical wisdom when he put my Sanskrit comprehension fears to rest by asking me to concentrate on the Telugu translations. I am grateful to Prof. J. S. R. Anjaneya Prasad for directing me to Pullela Ramachandrudu's work on the *Arthashastra*, and taking time out to check the translations of some key passages and terms in the *Dasakumaracharita*.

My students, Rajdeep Sarkar, who shared his insights on the *Hitopadesha* and found many online sources, and A. Sujana, who was always eager to help, deserve special mention. But for Sujana's painstaking efforts to fix the footnotes and bibliography, this book would not have been finished on time. I am grateful to the University of Hyderabad for granting me sabbatical leave for six months. I appreciate the Centre for Advanced Studies, Department of Political Science, University of Hyderabad, for providing a minor research assistance grant in January 2019. Thanks once again to Amma and family, who excused me from many duties and get-togethers with patience and affection. Blessings to fourteen-year-old Amrit, who wants to be an 'author' for his cover drawings.

Roopa Sharma of Orient BlackSwan prodded me to send a proposal in 2016, and when she kept nudging me every two months, I realised that I had to deliver, if only to redeem her faith in me! She was helpful and patient throughout in answering questions as I started getting anxious through the pandemic lockdowns. Lesley Esteves' copyediting queries and skills were both keen and subtle and she made the whole process a real pleasure. My heartfelt thanks to the entire team at Orient BlackSwan.

INTRODUCTION

> The science of politics is but the divine eye, the operation of which is never obstructed in giving insight into things, past, present and future, as well as hidden or far removed from sight...
>
> Surely, Your Majesty has got all this, viz. an exalted pedigree, unfaded youth, a lovely body and immeasurable prosperity. Don't you therefore render all these advantages vain by attention to statecraft, which is the source of all mistrust, an impediment in the way of the enjoyment of pleasures, and which is never without uncertainty on account of its having to have recourse to various kinds of tricks... (Kale 1986: 350, 354)

These contradictory views on the study of politics from the *Dasakumaracharita*, a seventh century CE Indian classic, ring as true today as they perhaps did at the time. After all, the study of politics evokes laughter and derision as a waste of time and resources. Politics, which is only about opportunism and expediency, is best left to politicians, and successful politicians do not study politics, let alone teach it. And yet, as the first quote shows, there were paeans of the 'lamp of political science' which enabled the intellect to shine and divine the meandering paths of worldly action. So, who were these teachers and how did they study and teach politics? What strategies did they devise to entice powerful but unwilling and/or dull patrons? What kinds of sentiments and virtues did they aspire to instil in the rulers and the ruled?

Impressed initially by the debates on friendship, war and peace in the *Panchatantra*, I soon realised that many literary classics were carrying on a serious dialogue with the great Indian epics *Ramayana* and *Mahabharata* in general, and Kautilya's *Arthashastra* in particular. Further inquiry led me to the *Mudrarakshasa*, *Dasakumaracharita* and *Hitopadesha*. While fusing edification and entertainment, I found that the compilers and authors of these texts saw themselves as contributing to *nitishastra*, which broadly means expert knowledge on propriety, policy and prudence in individual conduct as well as in public affairs. They deliberated on the three human ends of acquiring *artha* (broadly worldly success in gaining land, wealth, power or fame), *kama* (pleasure in general and erotic love in particular), and *dharma* (broadly virtues, ethics, duties). In the process, they wrestled with enduring political themes, such as the need for honing practical wisdom regarding means and ends, steering the sentiments so that rulers may rightly discern their friends and enemies, uncovering unexpected sources of virtues in society, identifying vagaries of action oriented to amassing wealth and fame, assaying the conundrums of political judgment when confronted with necessity and realpolitik, and so on. I pursued these themes through a series of literary classics that fall within what has elsewhere been categorised as the 'mirror of princes' genre of advice literature, namely the *Panchatantra*, *Mudrarakshasa*, *Dasakumaracharita*, *Hitopadesha* and *Vetala Panchavimshati*.

This choice might appear strange since conventional approaches to premodern Indian political thought focus on canonical sources such as the *Veda*s, the *Ramayana* and *Mahabharata* epics, the ethical and juridical corpus such as the *Manusmriti* and Kautilya's *Arthashastra*, as well as the manuals on practical wisdom such as *Chanakyaniti* (Guidance by Chanakya), *Shukraniti* (Guidance by Shukra), *Nitisara* (Essence of Policy) by Kamandaka, or Somadeva's *Nitivakyamritam* (Nectar of Practical Wisdom). While U. N. Ghoshal lays out these sources early on in *A History of Hindu Political Theories*, A. S. Altekar and others follow this path in *State and Government in Ancient India*, even as they include some more tracts (Ghoshal 1923: vii–viii, 5–7; Altekar 2001: 5–25). In doing so, these writers showcase the existence of a robust tradition of political thought (against the charge that India has only produced religious thought) and track the history of ideas on origins of the state, types of republics, cosmic and social order, divine kingship, law and customs, crime and punishment, war and peace, taxation and welfare, structure of administration, and so on. While providing valuable information about a glorious past, this approach tends to become antiquarian. Becoming aware of the manner in which indigenous sources broached the contractual obligations of the king or the state towards the people, long before these emerged elsewhere, may bolster nationalist pride, but may not enthuse non-specialists or students to plumb these ideas further. V. R. Mehta adopts a more thematic frame in *Foundations of Indian Political Thought*, delving into how the rules and principles of social order are derived from a cosmic and natural order in Vedic sources, how ideas of right order are simultaneously questioned and deepened in the epics, and how these are partly set aside in the realistic tract *par excellence*, the *Arthashastra* (Mehta 1996).

While these expositions are indispensable in kindling interest in Indian political thought, they also suffer from a few limitations. First, they restrict political thinking to a genre of texts by specialists. Thus, some portions of the epics and many *niti* (prudence/practical wisdom) manuals qualify, whereas popular literary and cultural narratives are barely mentioned. And yet, as we will see, the actual transmission and discussion of practical political wisdom is adumbrated in genre-defiant collections like the *Panchatantra*. Second, the epics, especially the *Ramayana*, are imbued with mythic rationale such that the notions of a divine king, and '*Ram Rajya*' as an ideal kingdom, cannot be isolated from a theological analysis. Also, the epics provide normative visions of the origins and sustenance of right order in the cosmos, society, kingdom and family, which have received extensive treatment in Indological literature. *Niti* is present but overshadowed by the prescriptive and legislative enterprise in the epics, and awaits future analysis. Third, the overemphasis on Kautilya's *Arthashastra* as the epitome of 'realist' thought has occluded internal debates regarding educating and advising rulers and ensuring that power is accumulated and wielded for welfare rather than self-aggrandisement. Fourth, the authors mentioned above themselves admit that the manual corpus such as *Chanakyaniti* or *Nitisara* are overtly didactic and tend to assert rather than argue; there is also an impression that they do not add to principles propounded by the *Mahabharata* or Kautilya, and are dubbed 'colourless summaries' (Altekar 2001: 19; Mehta 1996: 84, 128). For instance, the *niti* manuals advise seeking out equals as friends, but do not address the problem of false friends and unequal friendships, which nevertheless occur in ordinary life. There is no discursive engagement with the ideals espoused by canonical texts and thinkers, be it prudence or friendship or peace, as we will see in the texts chosen here. As a result, these approaches fulfil an archival agenda through which students are apprised of the rationale underlying divine kingship, or hierarchical social order, or the balance between spiritual and temporal powers. They do not provoke us to reflect on whether Kautilya's political realism, say regarding war and peace, was criticised by traditional teachers who might otherwise agree with his worldly wisdom, and what that might teach us about different kinds of realism. They do not enlighten us on the hope and despair about reconciling virtue, especially practical wisdom (*niti*), with human ends such as acquiring knowledge (*jnanam*), good friends, love (*kama*), wealth and kingdoms (*artha*), or doing one's duty (*dharma*), as do the narratives.

In the Greek context, Stephen G. Salkever has noted that traditional genre expectations must not inhibit political theorists from bringing narrative history, imaginative literature and self-conscious philosophising into dialogue with one another when delving into politics and human action (Salkever 2009: 4–5). Wherever there is *logoi*, or articulate speech about human nature and its relationship to nature as a whole, be it in imaginative literature or narrative history, it should be brought into dialogue with the *logoi* of our present institutions and practices to fine-tune the judgment of citizens about what constitutes 'the good life' and right political action. For political thinking must attend not only to modern concerns like securing equal liberty and a social minimum, but also to instilling practical wisdom in citizens and intellectuals on enduring political problems such as politicians who defy wise counsel, unbridled ambitions of the elite, or even erotic misadventures of the youth.

Apposite here is also Michael Freeden's advice that political thinking must move towards an 'interpretative realism' where the 'general nature of the political in all its intricate expressions, including vernacular forms' (Freeden 2012: 4), are explored. He counsels that the power aspect of politics, though permeating all of its forms as a core feature, does not offer a sufficient toolkit to decode the political, and that thinking politically should include, among others, 'discourses containing the ranking of collective priorities and the distribution of social significance, languages of social order and disorder and construction and critique of social visions, as well as the wielding of discursive power' (Freeden 2012: 4–5).

Love and Friendship, Allan Bloom's magisterial work on a series of Western literary classics starting from Rousseau through Stendhal, to Austen, Tolstoy, Shakespeare and Plato, provides a stunning rationale on why political thought must delve into literary classics. He argues that cultivating the imagination about the highest human ends such as love and friendship is best done not through pedantic explanations (which reduce them to power-play or utility), but rather through timeless plays and novels that bring these experiences alive and unveil their ambiguities and conflicts (Bloom 1993: 30). Political theorists must care about not only justice claims but also about forging social virtues and strengthening bonds of solidarity, which require that they attend to a whole gamut of human passions such as pleasure, revenge, love of glory, and so on. In love and friendship, humans discover their incompleteness, which propels them to seek exclusive relationships, wherein they learn to exercise courage, generosity, trust and sacrifice. As experiences, love and friendship compel humans to defy law and custom and resist being tamed by authority, be it of the family or state. Through them, humans are also lifted above self-interest to seek the good of the other and to accept the inequality, and even absence, of the benefits received. This makes love and friendship unlike political justice, where 'there is merely an attempt to induce through rewards and punishments the kind of association that friends and lovers have without the need for either' (Bloom 1993: 548–549). Moreover, love and friendship can often come into conflict due to the imperious demands they make on individuals for loyalty and exclusivity, which is best captured in literary works rather than avowedly political tracts.

Following these leads, I have plunged into 'imaginative literature' or 'vernacular discourses' and brought self-conscious philosophising to bear on the same. In the Indian context, while the narrative history of epics is plumbed for political ideas, the imaginative literature of the past has been largely neglected. This is particularly glaring since many of the literary classics avowedly concern themselves with educating the young and ambitious about the right means to acquiring the triple ends of pleasure, wealth and kingdoms, distinguishing between friends and enemies, circumstances conducive to the practice of virtues in war and peace, and so on.

TEXTUAL PRELIMINARIES

A brief overview of the selected literary classics is in order here. *Mudrarakshasa* (The Signet Ring) is a purely political play about diplomatic intrigue by Vishakhadatta (Dhruva 1923: x). As is the case with many classical Sanskrit texts, our knowledge of the author, date and context of composition remains sparse. According to Michael Coulson, Vishakhadatta mentions the titles of his father and grandfather, which lead us to believe that he came from the 'world of public affairs' (Coulson 1981: 165). Coulson also notes that estimates of the date vary widely, with Prof. A. L. Basham suggesting the sixth century CE, and internal textual allusions to king Chandragupta Maurya pointing to the fourth century CE. According to Coulson, the historical setting is about 700 years before the author's time and deals with Chandragupta Maurya, who seized the empire of the Nandas centred around Pataliputra (modern Patna), ably assisted by a minister called Kautilya or Chanakya (ibid.: 167). K. H. Dhruva surmises that it may be safely attributed to the second half of the sixth century. The names Chanakya and Kautilya have become synonymous with astute statecraft in Indian thought, and the *Arthashastra*, the most comprehensive treatment of a realist perspective on acquiring kingdoms, is attributed to him. *Mudrarakshasa* presents a shrewd Chanakya who has just secured a kingdom for his own sovereign Chandragupta Maurya, and is attempting to eliminate residual resistance from those still loyal to the defeated and deceased king, Dhana Nanda. Appreciative of the loyalty, valour and intelligence of Rakshasa, king Dhana Nanda's prime minister, Chanakya endeavours to win him over to the side of Chandragupta Maurya by hook or by crook. Seen as the most thoroughly political of Sanskrit plays, *Mudrarakshasa* simulates the entire panoply of *Arthashastra* techniques, such as a labyrinthine network of spies, deliberate rumour-mongering, fake arrests and escapades, mock quarrels and reconciliations. In the process, it juxtaposes Chanakya's ruthless and austere statecraft with Rakshasa's humane model, provoking us to ponder the connections between the two.

The *Panchatantra* is a well-known and popular compendium of tales on practical political wisdom. According to its composer, Vishnu Sharma, it was designed to awaken the intelligence of three dull-witted princes and make them fully adept at *nitishastra*. The five books or treatises (*tantras*) pertained to the estrangement of friends (*Mitra-bheda*), the winning of friends (*Mitra-samprapti/prapti*), crows and owls (*Kakolukiyam*, which deals with war and peace), the loss of gains (*Labdhapranasham*), and rash deeds (*Aparikshitakarakam*). According to Chandra Rajan in her translation, the *Panchatantra* must have been composed before 570 CE—the date of the Arabic version, which is the source of the foreign versions (Rajan 1993: xvi). Patrick Olivelle notes that Johannes Hertel, who brought out the earliest critical editions of the *Panchatantra*, listed about 200 versions in fifty languages in 1914, and concurs with Moriz Winternitz's observation that perhaps no book other than the Bible has had such extensive circulation. Hertel opined that the 'original' *Panchatantra* may have been composed in Kashmir around 200 BCE (Olivelle 1997: ix). Edgerton surmised that it may have originated in south India, given the prominent references to Mahilaropya, or Mylapore (Rajan 1993: liii–liv). It appears that the *Panchatantra* was composed, written and transmitted as a fixed text by experts of *nitishastra*, even though only fragments may have been in popular circulation (Olivelle 1997: xli).

The *Dasakumaracharita* (Adventures of the Ten Princes) by Dandin, a seventh-century court poet of the Pallava king of Kanchi, is about a deposed king's son and the sons of his various ministers who arrive in a forest and, having 'mastered all the arts, set out to conquer the world'. Soon after, the crown prince vanishes in the dead of night on a mysterious mission and, when he returns, he wanders about looking for his companions. On their part, they go in search of him and have adventures of their own in securing love, wealth and success. They all reunite fortuitously when they converge to aid an ally king, and recount their experiences. Robert D. DeCaroli surmises that Dandin probably came from a family that migrated to Kanchi from Vidarbha of the Vakataka kings after the latter were overthrown (DeCaroli

1995: 672). He claims that Dandin may have witnessed the alternation between pleasure-loving aesthete patron kings and energetic martial conquerors in the Pallava kingdom. The *Dasakumaracharita* deploys a comprehensive and fantastic use of fraud, adultery, murder, deceit and even identity theft to achieve *kama*, which is defined as the attainment of 'desired objects', including in its ambit wealth, pleasure and kingdoms. Understandably for a work on *artha* and *kama*, it plays upon the passions of lust, greed, treason and betrayal by close associates, wives and lovers. What seems like a ribald novel however takes an unexpected turn with a rhetorical discussion on the uses and abuses of Kautilya's *Arthashastra*.

Shivadasa's *Vetala Panchavimshati* (Five and Twenty Tales of the Vetala) was also compiled as a *nitishastra*, continuing the expert tradition of ethical and political wisdom. It is about the encounters between King Vikramaditya and the Vetala, a corpse-dwelling spirit. Through twenty-five delightful tales of resourceful courtesans, lusty hermits, cunning wives, jealous husbands, lovelorn youth, virtuous thieves, foolish brahmins, adventurous warrior-princes and wise kings, not to mention demanding gods and goddesses, Shivadasa poses ethical riddles requiring resolution through subtle reasoning and judgment. Like the *Dasakumaracharita*, this work also presents erotic misadventures wherein young men and women fall head over heels in love and pine for instant gratification. Vikramaditya often has to settle who is the right suitor or true father, thanks to the ingenuity of the lovers. While this is already a familiar motif in the *Dasakumaracharita*, what is unique in the *Vetala Panchavimshati* is the concern with ethical excellence. In striking contrast to the other texts, this work explicitly asks a king famed for his virtues 'who is greater' or 'which is nobler', showing that love's troubles do not exhaust the royal curriculum. Although the contents of these tales have an ancient provenance, they appear to have been committed to writing during the medieval period between the eleventh and fourteenth centuries (Rajan 1995: xix).

The *Hitopadesha* (Beneficial Advice), ascribed to Narayana Pandita and dated to 1675 CE, retells, embellishes and subtly modifies the *Panchatantra* in places (Chandiramani 1995: 1). Daud Ali places this text in the ninth or tenth century (Ali 2010: 33). The *Hitopadesha*'s author explicitly says that he has culled the ethical wisdom from the *Panchatantra* and other works (Chandiramani 1995: 14; Reddy 1994).

Ludwik Sternbach has calculated that of the seventy-one motifs of the *Panchatantra*, fifty-six were included in the *Hitopadesha*; 241, or nearly a third of the didactic stanzas, are traceable to various versions of the *Panchatantra* (Sternbach 1956: 118). It begins with the acquiring of friends, then moves on to the separation of friends, and war and peace, exhibiting an overt and coherent political purpose. Presently seen as children's fare, it is worth recalling that both the *Panchatantra* and *Hitopadesha* were compilations undertaken for the education of princes; while falling within the mirror of princes genre, they also became popular among ordinary people for mirroring society as a whole, and thus as a general source of entertainment and ethical wisdom. Extensively used for teaching both language and morals, there is scholarly consensus that though they specifically addressed kings and courtiers, they were also a source for reflections on practical morality and political wisdom for the general populace (Ali 2010: 36; Olivelle 1997: xix–xx; Rajan 1995: xxviii).

While the period and historical context in which these texts were composed, their authorship as well as the diverse sources they drew upon will continue to exercise scholars, there can be no doubt that these were *niti* texts, and hence warrant closer attention from political theorists. We need not worry unduly about their many versions since reliable critical editions have been used in this study, and my intent here is to learn about prudence for the present, rather than reconstruct what they meant in the past, or whether or not they were faithfully transmitted. These latter concerns are the domain of historians, Indologists and linguists. For my purpose, I have relied mainly on the available English and Telugu translations, while checking the Sanskrit sources to the extent possible. All the Telugu translations consulted carried the Sanskrit text alongside, which enabled me to authenticate and cross-check the English translations of key terms wherever relevant. The works of Pullela Ramachandrudu and G. Reddy Bala Chenna Reddy, used here, are considered to be definitive translations of the *Arthashastra* and *Panchatantra* in Telugu, respectively. For the *Dasakumaracharita*, I relied on M. R. Kale's Sanskrit text and extensive notes alongside the English translation. An English translation of Shivadasa's recension and an English translation alongside Jambhaladatta's Sanskrit text were used for the Vikram and Vetala tales (Emeneau 1934). While I was not able to marshal all the literary and stylistic nuances in these texts, there is sufficient argumentation upon the precepts of *nitishastra* to reward this emphasis on realism, friendship, and so on.

Even if one accepts the significance of the narrative genre, one may be inhibited by the sophisticated structural and linguistic analysis of folk tales to plunge into the kind of analysis attempted here. Nonetheless, I have been emboldened by Paul Ricoeur, who observed that

> narrative intelligence is closer to practical wisdom and moral judgment than to the theoretical use of reason in that it sets before imagination not abstract relations between virtues and happiness but situations by means of which we learn to join the ethical aspect of human behaviour to happiness and unhappiness, to fortune or misfortune. (Ricoeur, cited in Valdes 1991: 428)

Ricoeur has distinguished this first-order narrative intelligence from second-order narratological focus on the logic of structure and rules underlying narratives, an insight that is useful for our analysis. As will be clear, my interest is in extracting this first-order narrative intelligence as it pertains to practical political wisdom.

Chapter I lays out the great salience accorded to the study and transmission of *nitishastra* and *arthashastra*, the expert tradition of moral and political wisdom which deals with virtues and human ends systematically. Despite high repute, it was difficult to find teachers and patrons of practical wisdom and statecraft. It appears that political analysts were trying then, as now, to make studying public affairs easy, relevant, practical and 'realist' by distilling their wisdom into guidebooks, manuals, stories and plays, with mixed results. How far did they go in this effort and what challenges did they face in the process? Why do we find that even successful practitioners, after helping to recover lost kingdoms with panache, were eager to abdicate their responsibilities and retire to the forest? Given that the dialectic of contemplation and action has been probed by 'idealists' like Plato, among others, I explore how and why these texts, ostensibly more 'realist' in their assessment of political necessity, also affirm this tension.

Chapter II focuses on the *Panchatantra*, which was composed by Vishnu Sharma to educate three young princes in *nitishastra* or the art of ruling. As a compendium of prudence intended to 'awaken the intelligence of dull-witted princes', why does the *Panchatantra* deal with the estrangement of friends, the winning of friends, and false friends—all of which concern our often whimsical instincts in discerning and making friends? Why should friendship matter to *nitishastra* at all? What sense do we make of the repeated concern with equality in wealth (*samana dhanam*), lineage (*kulam*), and strength and power (*balam*) between friends in the *Panchatantra*? Given that friendship between equals epitomises practical wisdom for Aristotle (and many Western scholars), the *Panchatantra* compels us to revisit the imperatives of both friendship and prudence.

Chapter III picks up the quintessential political topics of war and peace as they are dealt with in the *Panchatantra* and *Hitopadesha*, respectively. Both texts show great familiarity with the sixfold strategies of Kautilya's *Arthashastra*. While Kautilya often justifies aggrandisement and glory from the standpoint of the conqueror, *niti* texts explore the right strategy for relatively weaker and roughly equal powers. What are the origins of war and peace from the standpoint of relatively weak powers? How do kings and courtiers deliberate over the sixfold policy and the niceties of intrigue in these texts? Does realism mean that expediency and opportunism alone matter, or is there room for goodness and peaceful coexistence?

That ends justify the means seems to be the overt message of the *Dasakumaracharita*, where *kama* (erotic desire and fulfilment) and *artha* (wealth/fame/success) are pursued by young princes through easy, cheap and sometimes desperate remedies. Adultery, deceit, fraud, impersonation, theft and murder are all justified to acquire princesses and kingdoms. Chapter IV analyses why a text that ostensibly depicts 'games of chance and strife' presents a gallery of rogues and rascals. What are the ingenious ways of desire and, is cunning resourcefulness everything? What do marriage and the pursuit of love (*kama*) have to do with the pursuit of *artha*? Why are a courtesan and a thief handpicked for voicing what it means to succeed at pleasure or wealth acquisition? What are the political risks involved in reining in untutored desire, especially erotic desire in high places? How does this compare with analogous realism elsewhere, say in Machiavelli?

Chapter V deepens the analysis of practical wisdom by venturing into an arguably quasi-mythic text, namely the *Vetala Panchavimshati*, popular as the 'Vikram and Vetala' stories. Once again, the compiler

Shivadasa meant this not as children's tales but as *nitishastra*, and the focus is on educating a ruler, King Vikramaditya, in ethical excellence. Presented with competing tales of generosity, deceit and vice in acquiring love or wealth, the king is asked 'who is greater or nobler or baser', and his answers compel us to probe what constitutes superlative proficiency in judgment. After a brief comparison with *Decameron*, which raises similar questions, I conclude with the ironies that are centre-staged in this text, making us reflect on the limits to ethical excellence in the pursuit of 'paramount sovereignty'.

REHABILITATION MATTERS

The above overview of chapters entails two methodological clarifications: one regarding comparison, and the second regarding historicism. Indian political thought has always been comparative, incubated as it was within colonial educational institutions. Earlier comparisons were geared to finding parallels for the philosopher-king, an ideal republic, the state of nature, contractual obligation or republican regimes. The emphasis was on showing that Kautilya is equal, if not superior, to Aristotle or Machiavelli, and that he anticipates not only the modern bureaucratic welfare state, but even contemporary management and accounting policies. To get a sense of the burdens of comparison, consider the following quotation from Benoy Kumar Sarkar, who was contesting the thesis of 'oriental despotism' way back in 1918:

> The number of republican states during the second half of the fourth century BC was large enough to draw the attention of Kautilya, the Hindu Bismarck...The method of *Artha-shāstra* is the same as that propounded about eighteen hundred years later in the *Prince* of Machiavelli, the first "nationalist" of Europe. The republics were, however, considered by Kautilya as very valuable assets...Before undertaking to destroy them by force of arms, therefore, the would-be *dominus omnium* or *sarva bhauma,* i.e., the imperialist nation builder should, says he, make it his duty to win them over to the cause of a unified empire state. (Sarkar 1918: 591)

Avoiding anachronistic apologetics, Mehta charts a thematic path, emphasising the nature of political reasoning, the relationship between spiritual and temporal powers, sources of law and visions of order. Still, he does not fully overcome modern Western prejudgements in looking for a 'contractual' basis of political obligation in the *Mahabharata*, or the 'autonomy' of the political in Kautilya (Mehta 1996: 71, 99). Preoccupation with doctrines of modern Western thought means that we must prove that Indian sources are *not* theocratic, religious, life-negating, tyrannical, inegalitarian, unscientific, and so on, before we can pay attention to their uniqueness. This doctrinal stress made the task of striking a balance between a narrow historicism and an ahistorical glorification difficult, if not impossible. For example, confronted with the 'divine king' idea, it appears safe and prudent to confine it to the historical context rather than extract the underlying rationale of the necessity of charismatic leadership in politics, since that is anathema to modern worldviews. In contrast, when we encounter Kautilya's rigorous discussion of offices and duties, he may be eulogised for anticipating the modern bureaucratic state or even the welfare state, thus leading to ahistorical exaltation.

Andrew March has observed that besides equivalence-based rehabilitation (of the above kind), there may also be an explanatory-interpretive motivation for comparison where we excavate and interpret new theoretical resources to contribute to practical theorising about norms and values (March 2009: 541–542).[1] Both these are critical in non-Western and non-Anglophone academies where Plato and Aristotle are seen as 'foreign'. Mehta observes that ignorance about one's traditions of thought 'is responsible for much of the alienation of the Indian intellectual from his own society' (Mehta 1996: 14). Diego von Vacano also makes a similar call to 'expand the archive of political theory that will permit comparative readings' (von Vacano 2015: 470).

As we discover new thinkers or texts, we may follow Fred Dallmayr's advice of 'reciprocal questioning' for a creative renewal of political thought in general, and Western political thought in particular. This entails moving between and within diverse traditions and thinkers, 'not to evolve fusion or synthesis but learning to address the right questions and be rewarded by answers truly adequate to our present situation' (Dallmayr 2010: 10).[2] Instead of asking whether the *Panchatantra* and *Dasakumaracharita* were patriarchal or democratic, and excoriating their prejudices, I have plumbed why a text on prudence deals with the vagaries of friendship, or why a work on erotic adventures actually has a long discourse on statecraft. In charting the premodern terrain for 'reciprocal questioning', I realised that I was, as Salkever puts it, 'interpreting texts that seem to deal with the most important and most disputed human problems, constructing from these texts dialogues that clarify these problems and participating in these constructed dialogues as we live our lives' (Salkever 2014: 2). I concur with Salkever that comparative work can enable us to rise above the powerful presuppositions of one's life-world and see that 'certain quasi-permanent political questions, such as the best life' cannot have universal answers (ibid.: 16). When we steer away from political doctrines to modes of reasoning about virtues such as prudence or friendship, or securing wealth and fame, we may be able to navigate better between historicism and a trans-historical understanding. Whether friendships should be between equals or based on utility, or whether expert knowledge is relevant at all for 'real-world politics', or whether we must settle for a hard-nosed realism impervious to ethics, are debates that are not confined to our time but have happened in other times. I try to show how some enduring dilemmas and difficulties can be revisited profitably by reconstructing some of these debates. In the process, whether I have succeeded in avoiding romanticist, historicist and anachronistic pitfalls is for readers to judge.

Notes

1. Of course, March pushes beyond this motivation, saying that a 'properly comparative' political theory must draw rigorous boundaries between different systems of thought and highlight radical disagreement on a common concern or criticisms of a dominant position, and explore the normative political implications for 'us' (Anglophone academics, as he admits) on specific value conflicts (March 2009: 541–542).

2. M. K. Gandhi's thought and practice has propelled such creative renewals for deepening liberal democracy beyond individual rights and interest group rivalries to include collective civic virtues and non-violent transformation, but the premodern material has garnered little attention (Pantham and Deutsch 1986).

I

STUDYING POLITICS VERSUS DOING POLITICS

Minding the Gap

Political thought is often accused of being theoretical, abstract and utopian, and hence irrelevant to political practice, which is messy, earthy and even dirty. It may appear as if normative political theory that focuses on 'what ought to be' rather than 'what is' may be guilty of the above more than realist political theory. The latter, being more attuned to strategic thinking regarding human interests and power equations, is usually admired as useful and worthwhile. Yet, the most realist of scholars often belabours the need for systematic study and reflection to act well in politics. In the *Arthashastra*, perhaps the most 'realist' tract on statecraft, Kautilya categorically advises a courtier that 'under no circumstances should one seek a position with a king who is depraved for such a king is likely to detest the study of polity (*nitishastra*) and thus good advice' (Rangarajan 1987: 203; Ramachandrudu 1999: 514; Shamasastry 1919: 352).[1] The aspirant is advised to have a discussion on political teachings with the king and ensure that the latter does not hold opinions contrary to *nitishastra*. Conversely, he must also convince the king that he is well-versed in *nitishastra* to secure his position. In the context of deliberations about undertaking tasks, Kautilya reiterates that one must not include those ignorant of *arthashastra* in secret councils. Lest we misunderstand, Kautilya also cites a prevalent view that a king should not appoint those with merely theoretical knowledge and no practical experience, since such persons will commit serious blunders in politics (Ramachandrudu 1999: 31; Shamasastry 1919: 19). The *Panchatantra*'s frame story also affirms the role of *nitishastra* in 'awakening the intelligence' of three dull-witted princes who were averse to learning. The *Dasakumaracharita*'s encomium on *arthashastra* as that which enables the intellect to shine in its proper sphere has already been cited.

Though definitions cannot be exhaustive, they do provide a starting point. *Niti* broadly connotes guidance, direction, conduct, course of action, propriety, policy and prudence, and narrowly a contrivance or scheme. *Naya*, which is less frequently used, also denotes policy, political wisdom, prudence and foresight, as well as, at times, a plan, design or scheme (Apte 1987: 280, 301; Naik 2016). *Artha* refers to worldly success in gaining land, wealth, power or fame, and thus, may encompass the activities of merchants, labourers, entrepreneurs, heads of households, political officials and whoever seeks influence and wealth, though in scholarly treatises it sometimes tends to be restricted to statecraft (McClish and Olivelle 2012: xxxiv). According to Thomas Trautman, *artha* in Vatsyayana's *Kamasutra* includes acquiring and increasing even intangible things like learning and friends besides land, gold, cattle, grain, household goods and furnishings (Trautman 2016: 2–3). He also notes the more dynamic definition of Kautilya, who begins with *artha* as the creation of wealth by humans through their pursuit of livelihood, then expands it to include the earth inhabited by such beings, and finally calls it the art by which a king acquires and protects such an inhabited and productive earth. Ashay Naik has emphasised that *niti* or *naya* are concerned with conduct in daily life, while *artha* refers to general prosperity and economic and political governance, although *nitishastra* and *arthashastra* may be used synonymously by Kautilya, an interchange that is also evident in our narratives (Naik 2016).

Scholars such as A. S. Altekar have appreciated the high regard for political studies in traditional Indian sources under various terms such as *rajadharma* (duties of kings), *dandaniti* (proper application of force), *nitishastra* (expert knowledge on propriety, prudence and wisdom), *arthashastra* (expert knowledge on acquiring wealth and success) and *nayashastra* (expert knowledge on policy and prudence) (Altekar 2001: 2). D. Mackenzie Brown has observed that politics was the 'master science' and *rajadharma* was pre-eminent and supposed to contain all *dharma*, thus encompassing the whole of society (Mackenzie Brown 1953: 244). Incidentally, there is a predilection to translate *arthashastra* as the 'science of politics', as does R. P. Kangle, or as the 'science of wealth', as does Trautman. D. D. Kosambi prefers the 'science of material gain', and Roger Boesche uses 'science of political economy' (Boesche 2003: 14). This, however, can be misleading since Kautilya is not value-neutral, though he is certainly unsentimental about means and ends. He is categorical about the use of state power for the welfare of subjects; the long list of virtues to be cultivated and vices to be avoided by an ambitious king is one proof. Hence it may be apt to follow Patrick Olivelle's translation of *shastra* as a 'tradition of expert knowledge', rather than a science. While emphasis varied, all the above terms referred to expert traditions of knowledge regarding broadly political topics, such as origins of kingship and a ruler's education and conduct; duties vis-a-vis dependents and subjects; acquisition of kingdoms and wealth; proper uses of physical force; law and customs in maintaining justice; policies for augmenting wealth and securing all-round progress and welfare; and the conduct of war and peace. Altekar has surmised that while *rajadharma* and *dandaniti* may have been preferred in the early stages of development of the 'science', *nitishastra* became the most popular over time (Altekar 2001: 4).

Undoubtedly there was a vibrant tradition of discussion on the nature, scope and uses of *nitishastra*. We may be justified in wondering whether and how this expert knowledge was taught, transmitted, criticised and modified. While Kautilya's treatise is full of references to experts and their contrarian views, literary texts like the *Panchatantra* and *Dasakumaracharita* centre-stage the scepticism regarding expert knowledge with great irony and humour. It appears that the theory–practice dichotomy was often voiced then, as it is now, and compelled teachers to distil and transmit their wisdom in easily accessible and jazzy formats. What were the strategies adopted to attract readers and audiences to the pleasures and profits of *nitishastra*? Despite such exciting efforts, why do we find that successful practitioners often wished to quit the stage? Could it be that the dialectic between contemplation and action is insurmountable, after all?

ABRIDGE AND ALLURE

A common fear regarding knowledge acquisition is that one might grow old just studying, forgetting to live well in the bargain. This fear is particularly accentuated with respect to politics, which, both in the sense of acquiring wealth and establishing a just order, requires timely action in the world rather than endless cogitation. In the *Shanti Parva* of the *Mahabharata*, Bhishma details how a gargantuan treatise of 100,000 chapters on *dharma*, *artha* and *kama* (virtue, profit and pleasure), composed by Brahma, was studied and abridged by divine editors, starting with Shiva and Indra and ending with seers, until it was condensed into 1,000 chapters. Bhishma explains that this abridgement was necessary, given 'the period of men's lives and the general decrease (of everything)...' (Ganguli 2004: 125–126). The tension between the comprehensive urges of knowledge-seeking and the short lives of mortals, and even shorter windows of opportunity for worldly success already announced in this 'originary' moment, is repeated often.

Kautilya reassures us in his *Arthashastra* that he is presenting a compendium of *all arthashastras* of the ancient teachers. Following an elaborate listing of contents of the fourteen books, he closes the first chapter claiming that his work, comprising fifteen books, 150 chapters, 180 topics and 6,000 stanzas, 'is bereft of *undue enlargement, easy to grasp and understand, and composed in words the meaning of which has been definitely settled*' (Shamasastry 1919: 8; emphases added)! The *Arthashastra* was so successful that it killed off the earlier sources, which ceased to be copied thereafter (Trautman 2016: 17). And yet, its appeal was limited among aspiring rulers and courtiers, as we will see presently.

The *Panchatantra* eloquently unravels the predicament in its preamble. Amara Shakti (Eternal Power), a king who was like a wish-fulfilling tree for all supplicants, adept in many arts and worshipped by many able vassals, ruled from Mahilaropya, a jewel among cities. He was looking for a suitable tutor who would 'awaken the intelligence' of his three sons so that they became fit to rule. His three sons were

Bahu Shakti (Great Power), Ugra Shakti (Fierce Power) and Ananta Shakti (Endless Power) (Rajan 1993: 3; Reddy 1989).[2] Amara Shakti summoned his ministers and complained, 'Honourable counsellors, you well know that my sons, all three of them, have set their faces against learning. They lack proper judgment. When I see them, my kingdom, though free of thorns, brings me no happiness' (Rajan 1993: 3). He lamented at length that it is better to have no sons at all, or even to lose sons than have sons who are foolish and stubborn, for the first two only cause temporary sadness, whereas the last brings life-long misery. Even merits such as good looks and wealth cannot compensate for a lack of intelligence. So some suitable means had to be devised to impart practical wisdom to these dullards.

Some obtuse ministers helpfully inform Amara Shakti that it takes only twelve years to learn grammar, after which one must study treatises of law and statecraft for the mind to truly shine. Impatient with this advice, a wise minister recommended that it was better that the king entrust the charge to an accomplished brahmin called Vishnu Sharma, who had mastered several fields of learning. The king summoned and requested the revered pundit to teach his sons and offered him a hundred grants of land. Vishnu Sharma replied that he was not interested in wealth since he was eighty years old and beyond passion; he then accepted the task, boasting that he would make the princes experts in the *nitishastras* within six months (Olivelle 1997: 4). If he failed in making them unsurpassable masters, he would forsake his reputation, and the king may show him his 'bare royal bottom' (Rajan 1993: 5).

Vishnu Sharma then devised the five *tantras* (treatises): Book I, *Mitra-bheda* (Estrangement of Friends), which details the blossoming of friendship between a lion-king, Pingalaka (Tawny) and a grass-eating bull, Sanjivaka (Lively), undone by a cunning jackal, Damanaka (Wily); Book II, *Mitra-samprapti/prapti* (Winning of Friends), which details the bonds forged by a mouse, Hiranyaka (Goldy), a turtle, Manthara (Slowcoach), a crow, Laghupatanaka (Lightwing) and a deer, Chitranga (Speckled) that secures them against the wiles of a hunter; Book III, *Kakolukiyam* (Of Crows and Owls), which details the war between a crow, Meghavarna (Cloud-hued) and an owl-king, Arimardana (Foe-crusher) through intrigue; Book IV, *Labdhapranasham* (Loss of Gains), which details the ordinary vices of friends; and Book V,

Aparikshitakarakam (Rash Deeds), which details erratic instincts in judging friends who are unequals (Rajan 1993).[3]

As prologues go, there cannot be a more humorous laying out of the indifference of youth and the need for innovative teaching methods. The *Hitopadesha* embroiders this frame story with minor variations. The place is Pataliputra (rather than Mahilaropya as in the *Panchatantra*), the king is Sudarshana and the teacher is Vishnu Sharma, but the problem is the same; a king sighing about his ignorant and stupid sons and grieving over 'what is the use of a son being born//who is neither learned nor religious? What is the use of a defective eye//it is merely painful' (Chandiramani 1995: 14–15). Out of despair, he calls for a council of the learned and asks, 'is there anyone of such calibre who will give my sons, who are constantly straying on the wrong path and who have not studied the scriptures, a second birth now, through the instructions of the science of ethics?' (ibid.: 20). Vishnu Sharma rises and says, 'in this royal family, a child devoid of merits cannot be born…therefore I shall make your sons conversant in the science of ethics in six months' (ibid.: 21).

What is striking is the awareness that those devoted to reflection may have all the time in the world, whereas those who are committed to worldly action must be instructed in a short time. Since the latter may shun learning, wise teachers are not only compelled to distil their knowledge and offer crash courses, but also make it all lively to leave a lasting impression. Abounding in hypocritical brahmins, stupid kings, duplicitous ministers, adulterous wives, dumb husbands, acquisitive sages, wise merchants and, topping it all, resourceful animals, the *Panchatantra*'s allure remains unparalleled. Talking birds and animals have accounted for the assessment that the *Panchatantra* is meant for children; however, popular folklore has always instructed through allegories and images. Uma Chakravarti has noted that the narrative use of animals in folk traditions may have served to enliven sleepy audiences; they may also reflect the close relationship between the domestic/human and the wild forest in the distant past. But their most significant contribution may have been to distance audiences from the human world in order to make social and political comments (Chakravarti 2004: 221). Many animals are presented as being guided by the same anxieties and emotions afflicting humans, such as female birds concerned about the safety of their eggs, or male birds being cocky and ignoring sound advice. Olivelle, while listing various animals' character traits in the *Panchatantra*, notes that the lion is always a king; the jackal is often greedy and a minister; the snake and crocodile symbolise danger lurking in unexpected places; a monkey is playful, fickle and foolish; herons are greedy, cunning and heartless; hares are crafty and smart; crows and crabs are curious, and so on (Olivelle 1997: xxii; Totton 2003: 11–13). Thus, as Chandra Rajan notes, non-human characters are often human actors wearing masks (Rajan 1993: xxxvii). Also, there are many signposts in the text itself which show that these stories are about human beings, such as when Sanjivaka, a bull, is described as learned in many branches of knowledge, or when a mole, crow, turtle and deer are all described as scholars who regularly meet to discuss *dharma*, *artha*, and so on (ibid.: xi).

While luring the ambitious to study and reflect, wise men must administer learning in just the right measure and not endanger themselves in the process. This is evident when we probe the first book of *Panchatantra* concerning the estrangement of friends, which showcases a powerful lion-king, Pingalaka, befriending a wise bull, Sanjivaka. The immediate context is that the lion-king, 'sovereign by sheer prowess', saunters to the river to drink water and, startled by loud, thunderous bellowing, retreats and stands rooted to the ground. Pingalaka reigns supreme without any pomp, such as a 'royal white umbrella or parasol, jewelled flywhisks or entourage of bards and wanton women, or even elaborate fortifications...beaming from sheer pride and innate majesty, born of indomitable daring and uncompromising honour' (Rajan 1993: 13). We learn that Pingalaka is 'noble, disdaining flattery, small-mindedness, intrigue, above suspicion but easily aroused to anger due to an overabundance of valour and uncommon appetite for power' (ibid.). Having espied the lion's present discomfiture, the jackal Damanaka, a hereditary courtier who has been sidelined, sees an opportunity for regaining favour and offers to investigate the source of the fearsome sounds. Gladdened, the lion-king greets him and asks about his long absence, whereupon Damanaka reminds him that hereditary ministers are bound to attend to their masters in crisis, even though their worth may not be recognised. He then lectures the lion, quoting sayings to the effect that 'servants and ornaments are to be placed each in the position right for them; to say, "I can do this, so I shall", and fasten a crest jewel on the foot—that is not done', and further that, 'once retainers see the master treat//all alike, and no distinctions make//the persevering zeal for service there//of the diligent and skilled among them wanes' (Rajan 1993: 25–26).

Damanaka finds that Sanjivaka, a bull whose bellowing caused such fear, has been abandoned in a forest due to a broken limb; freed thus from man's yoke, it recovered and, feasting on Yamuna's green banks, grew sleek and plump like Shiva's bull (Rajan 1993: 12). Impressed, Damanaka introduces the bull to the lion-king after extracting suitable promises from the bull that it would be loyal in future. The lion-king was so besotted by the wisdom of the grass-eating bull that it turned away from governing and lost its prudence altogether. Based on contextual hints, Naik observes that the transfiguration of an ordinary bull into a magnificent creature that first induces fear in a mighty lion-king and then impresses the king with its erudition harks back to itinerant Indian *rishi*s, or seers, who acquire such powers through ascetic ardour in forests and return to edify kings (Naik 2016). Ananda Coomaraswamy has shown that canonical texts such as the *Brahmana*s articulated this in terms of the subordination of temporal authority to spiritual power. While recasting this ideal bond in terms of a friendship between a grass-eating bull and a meat-eating lion, the *Panchatantra* also depicts the conflicts and suspicion from hangers-on in a political context. As Rajan puts it:

> Now, Lively (Sanjivaka) possessed great intelligence and had developed profound wisdom, having studied and mastered various branches of learning. He spent much time instructing Tawny (Pingalaka) so that in a short while, even a blockhead like the King of beasts became wise and intelligent. ...The two friends were so close that they spent all their time together, talking and discussing between themselves, in private and unattended...Lacking the strength of the lion and his skill in hunting and foraging, the animal community, including our two jackals, were unable to forage for themselves as needed. (Rajan 1993: 44)

Left out in the cold, Damanaka sows dissension between the two friends and gets the king to assassinate the bull, thereby restoring the 'right order' of things. As will be shown later, the ease with which the jackal accomplishes this exposes the learned bull's complete lack of prudence and the lion-king's momentary loss of judgment. Mirroring as it does the situation of Vishnu Sharma (and others like him), who, like Sanjivaka, instil learning in those endowed with power and energy, this story sounds a note of caution. One must not go to the extreme of inducing an excessive thirst for learning in daring and ambitious dullards, blunting their natural urges and street-smart wisdom. Thus, Vishnu Sharma is also warning those immersed in erudition to be mindful of the extremes that they are pulled to: solitary contemplation in a forest, or thoughtless sharing of wisdom with apparently favourable patrons. They must be prudent both in what they impart and to whom, lest they are blindsided by trust in powerful patrons. Sanjivaka, the wise bull, cuts a sorry figure in that despite knowing several stories of conniving jackals, he fails to see that the one he is conversing with is one such, and must be suspect.

RHETORIC OF FLATTERERS

While Vishnu Sharma hints very little at what kind of knowledge the bull imparted to the lion, except that it is 'other-worldly', he leaves his wards and us in no doubt about the rhetorical and opportunistic uses of the knowledge of *arthashastra*. Damanaka, the wily and ambitious courtier-hero of this book, puts it aptly when he says that one must enter royal service to 'help friends and harm enemies'. This raises questions about who is a true friend and whether *nitishastra* can help us in discerning friends and enemies, the topic of the next chapter. For now, we should note that Damanaka's spirited defence of *arthashastra* is true to the letter. As Damanaka discusses how to regain the king's favour, his friend and sounding board Karataka reminds him that dependence entailed by political life is a wretched thing, the duties of one who serves are more difficult than that of yogis, and that one must be content with 'leavings' that suffice for self-preservation. Damanaka counters by saying that the wise do not serve kings only for food; even birds fill their bellies and crows, too, survive by scavenging on sacrificial offerings. One must not be contented like a dog that wags its tail and grovels for a mere bone (Rajan 1993: 16).

Damanaka asserts that what distinguishes man from beast is the ability to discern the good and the proper from the bad and the mean. One by whose wealth and well-being many lives are sustained and flourish is one who truly lives (Rajan 1993: 16). A 'good life' is one where practical knowledge, bravery and prosperity shine at least for a short while. One must be deemed famous for generosity and compassion, like the rain clouds that shower their bounty (Reddy 1989: 19). As Daud Ali notes, moral cultivation and pecuniary and political success were not mutually contradictory in courtly societies (Ali 2010: 27).

But subordinating the former to the latter was an ever-present danger. Resolved to drive a wedge between the lion and the bull, Damanaka declares: '[H]aving studied deeply every text on policy// grasped the essential meaning in its entirety//but to his advantage not turning all that vast learning—what use are texts so demanding?' (Rajan 1993: 146). When his friend Karataka protests that personal advantage amounts to little, Damanaka retorts: '[Y]ou are totally ignorant of statecraft' (ibid.; Reddy 1989: 197). Damanaka's textual knowledge on statecraft is quite impressive since he reels off the rules of etiquette for a courtier, the seven constituents of the state (*saptanga*), and the vices of a king, as elaborated by Kautilya, at appropriate moments. A courtier should always know the right time and place for addressing the king, discern the king's moods from mere signs, not antagonise the king's favourites, not laugh or talk loudly, not consort with the master's enemies, not associate with harem intrigues, and so on (Rajan 1993: 21). As for the constituents of state, excluding the king, they are: ministers, land and subjects, fortresses, treasury, allies and the army. Echoing Kautilya, Damanaka holds that the king has seven vices—four stemming from excessive desire, and three from anger. Due to great desire, one falls for women, dice, hunting and drink; due to anger, one indulges in abusive speech, harsh physical torture and plundering another's property. Further, there are six policy expedients (*shadgunya*), namely peace or alliance, war or expansion, advance or pursuit, halting and holding position, falling back or seeking shelter, and the use of deceiving tactics (Rajan 1993: 60–61; Rangarajan 1987: 137).

Indeed, all this comes in handy when Damanaka consoles the lion-king, who grieves over the hasty killing of his 'second self', saying, that *rajniti* or the 'policy of princes is protean, assuming many forms, appearing true but actually false, appearing sweet but often harsh, appearing compassionate but really cruel', and so on. He reminds the lion-king that there is nothing wrong with slaying a traitor-foe, and that a state cannot be governed by the nature and norms of commoners (Rajan 1993: 187). He even quotes the *Bhagavad Gita* (Book II, Verse 11): 'while speaking learned words, you are mourning for what is not worthy of grief. Those who are wise lament neither for the living nor the dead' (Reddy 1989: 237; Prabhupada n.d.). Incidentally, John B. Alphonso-Karakala has documented several translations of this story floating about in southern Europe by the Renaissance period, and surmises that it may be the source of Machiavelli's famous lion and fox metaphor in *The Prince* (Alphonso-Karakala 1975: 83).

Damanaka's friend Karataka attacks him for perversely focusing only on intrigue and dissension oriented to narrow self-interest, and endangering the king in applying *nitishastra*. Karataka bemoans that the lion-king did not consult all his retainers, got carried away by persuasive speeches, and did not have a mind of his own that could weigh the consequences of his action (Rajan 1993: 189). This is apt advice to the princes, coming as it does after illustrating how a noble Pingalaka is prone to extremes, swayed by contemplation to neglecting his duties at one end, and falling for a wily scheme hatched by a selfish courtier at the other.

A hilarious debate on the rhetorical uses and abuses of knowledge of statecraft occurs in the climactic book of *Dasakumaracharita*. It details the restoration of order in a kingdom racked by licentiousness and chaos due to the neglect of *nitishastra*. An old and wise courtier laments the pitiable state he is in due to the king Anantavarman's disdain for *arthashastra*. Lest we think Anantavarman is a brute, we are told that he was endowed with 'every excellence but unluckily held the science of politics in low esteem' (Kale 1986: 349). Apparently, this king is a dilettante, and his old minister tries to convert him to the study of statecraft. He impresses upon the king that the intellect only shines when it is refined by a study of *arthashastra* rather than just music, painting and poetics. Through *arthashastra*, one is trained to discern the proper means and ends of action. Lacking this, one acts injudiciously, and quickly earns the contempt of one's subjects. One's projects are then undermined by subjects who refuse to obey the king's orders and do whatever they like, thus paving the way for ruinous anarchy. To quote the wise minister:

> *When the path of action is seen by the lamp of political science (nītishāstra), the course of worldly affairs proceeds smoothly on.* The science of politics is but the *divine eye*, the operation of which is never obstructed in giving insight into things, past, present and future, as well as hidden or far removed from sight. Devoid of that eye, a man, although having large eyes, is no better than a blind creature, owing to his inability to penetrate into political ends. Abandon, therefore, the attachment to mere external accomplishments, and study the science of government (*daṇḍanīti)*, your family inheritance. (Kale 1986: 350; emphases added)

This wholesome praise of *arthashastra/nitishastra* is a rare piece, not to be found even in Kautilya's work. Dandin's minister is unequivocal in claiming that the study of *arthashastra* sharpens the intellect's discriminating capacity in judging proper means and ends, and thus aids action. If the king undertakes actions injudiciously, then he is despised and disregarded, leading to general disorder. Unlike in other areas such as poetics, politics requires a 'divine eye' that can see not only the past, present and future but also hidden things, and this eye opens from studying *arthashastra*.

But this paean is no match to the oratory of a sophistic courtier, Viharabhadra, who overhears the interchange, and parodies Chanakya/Vishnugupta/Kautilya's *Arthashastra* to dissuade the king from taking political thought seriously. This courtier was a royal favourite and a childhood friend who excelled in 'acting, dancing and enigmatic speeches, was libidinous, clever, of licentious tongue, devoted to finding the weak points of others, delighted in scandal, expert in the art of receiving bribes, professor of all wicked acts' (Kale 1986: 350). Viharabhadra begins by warning that clever rogues always surround and manipulate a person blessed with prosperity, promising mirages through chicanery. Either they delude him about felicity in the afterlife and get him to shave his head, goad him to wear a string of holy grass and drug and rob him, or entice him to leave his wife and children. Or, they recommend the 6,000 stanzas of Vishnugupta—composed for the use of the Mauryan king, and said to yield rich fruit—but warn that *kings would grow old reading and hearing it* since it is connected to other *shastras*, and unless these are also known, nothing is truly known![4] Once the principles are grasped, the first lesson to be learnt is *not to trust one's* wife or child. Another lesson is to measure out everything, including rice and firewood!

The schedule of a *rajarishi* (sagely king), which Kautilya presents, is exposed for what it is: exacting, vain and sad; adept at sophistry, the courtier picks up exactly what Kautilya presents in bare outline and caricatures the details. Consider the following samples. Kautilya advises that 'during the first watch of the day, the king shall receive reports on revenue, defence and expenditure'. Dandin's courtier spells it out thus:

> [A] king, on rising, when he has scarcely washed his mouth fully, must devote the first watch to the examination of receipts and expenditure, admitting a handful or half a handful [of anything]; and yet even while he hears, the clever superintendents will defraud him of twice as much. By the force of their own ingenuity, they multiply a thousand-fold the forty modes of defrauding set forth by Cāṇakya. (Kale 1986: 352)

Kautilya advises that during the second watch of the day, 'a king must give public audience and receive petitions', which, according to Dandin's courtier, means that 'the prince, with his ears assailed by the squabbles of contending subjects, lives a most wretched life and the judges, disposing of suits according to their whims increase the sin and infamy of the sovereign' (Kale 1986: 352). In the third watch, when the king has personal time for bathing, meals and study, Dandin reminds us of the king's dread of poison until the food is digested! In the fifth watch of the day, the king shall 'correspond in writs with the assembly of his ministers and receive the secret information gathered by his spies' (Shamasastry 1919: 51). For Viharabhadra, this means that the king

> has to suffer great *mental strain* on account of the consideration of political schemes. In presenting these too, the *counsellors, appearing to be neutral*, enter into mutual agreement, and pervert at will merits and defects, misstate the reports of the ambassadors and spies, misrepresent possibilities and impossibilities, confound all distinctions of place and time, and live upon [i.e., seek their own ends through] the friends of

> their own partisans or enemies; and secretly stirring up internal and external factions, and then appearing to allay these openly, they bring their helpless master into their power. (Kale 1986: 352; emphases added)

After spending his forenoon thus, the king is allowed some time for amusements for an hour and a half, and then he must review his troops and proceed to consult with his chiefs of defence. He is to receive emissaries in the first watch of the evening and must study after meals, while in the third watch of the night, he is sent to sleep with the sound of trumpets for the next couple of hours. But Dandin wryly observes that the king is supposed to study like a *brahmana* (person from the scholarly class), and how can the poor man sleep given that his mind is constantly distracted by anxious thought (Kale 1986: 353)? In the seventh watch of the night, Kautilya recommends that the king consider administrative measures and send out spies, while in the final eighth watch of the night (an hour and a half before sunrise), he shall consult his priests and teachers and receive their benedictions. Dandin's courtier expands that

> in the seventh, he must consult with his ministers regarding the dispatch of *agents and emissaries*; and these fellows, as is well known, increase the money obtained from both sides by saying sweet things, by trading on the road, being free from the fear of having to pay taxes; and making work even in slight degree where there is none, they wander about at all times. (Kale 1986: 353; emphases added)

In the eighth, the *purohita* (royal priest) and others are said to dream up bad omens that require grand rites with golden implements and rich presents to brahmins. The so-called wise counsellors who say that the senses must be subdued, that the six natural foes should be shunned and all time should be spent in discussing war and peace, themselves spend money on harlots and sense pleasures. And then there is the uncertainty of results, in that even the stern dictators of policy such as Shukra, Angirasa, Vishala, Akshabahu, Dantiputra and Parashara were confronted by failures in undertakings they had set afoot, and could not guarantee success (Kale 1986: 354).

The courtier sums up his case by saying that *state-craft is the source of all mistrust and anxiety*, an impediment in the way of pleasures, and is never without uncertainty on account of having recourse to various tricks. He concludes that the sage-king leads a life that is not the least happy, in dread of poison even in private, and always looking out for deception and fraud. Besides, the course of worldly existence requires no policy, just as a suckling babe knows how to get milk from the mother by various means. Since life is short and the time for enjoyment even shorter, the king must not be devoted to acquiring more but leave that burden to others, abandon restraint and enjoy the pleasures of the senses with heavenly damsels (Kale 1986: 353). The courtier then prostrates before the king, touching the ground with the five parts of his body, and the king raises him up, calling him his own 'true guru'. This leads to the kingdom falling prey to the designs of a neighbouring king 'adept in policy', who sends a shrewd sophist, Chandrapalita, to deliver encomiums on gambling, hunting, drinking and womanising.

Viharabhadra's diatribe about the mental strain and confusion initially appears unfair, in that Kautilya himself had considerably abbreviated the *Arthashastra*, leaving out mythic and contractual accounts of the origins of state and divine kingship in ancient India. He also did not emphasise studying other branches of knowledge, including the *Veda*s and other philosophical studies. He directly addressed practical problems of government and provided a ready-to-use treatise on administration (Altekar 2001: 11; Mehta 1996: 95). Kautilya explicitly assures potential kings and courtiers thrice that 'whoever is well versed in the science of polity wrests friends, wealth and territory and overreaches enemies' (Ramachandrudu 1999: 611, 615, 617; Shamasastry 1919: 412, 414, 444). All three instances occur in the book on *shadgunyam*, or six strands of policy, and at the close of their respective chapters; hence their rhetorical status cannot be gainsaid. The first emerges in the course of a discussion on an agreement for peace in return for land, and an elaborate analysis of whether it is better to acquire land by putting down a powerful or a powerless enemy; whether it is better to acquire land from a fortified enemy; whether it is better to acquire land close to a powerful or powerless enemy; whether one must prefer fertile land close to a powerful enemy or sterile land close to a powerless enemy; whether it is better to acquire a small piece of land not far or an extensive land very far; whether it is better to acquire land from a stupid or wise king, etc. It appears that being well-versed in the science of polity (*arthashastra*) will enable one to acquire land and outshine allies and enemies. The second emerges in the context of a discussion on colonising wasteland, and delves into whether one should choose watery or plain land; watery land that is conducive to producing grains or to producing medicinal plants and spices; cultivable land or land with mines; forest land with timber or elephant forest, and so on. The third pertains to managing one's circle of friends and enemies against the initiatives of a *madhyama*, or intermediary king, and concludes the discussion on the six strands of policy thus:

> Whoever is acquainted with the science of polity (*arthashāstra*) should clearly observe the conditions of progress, deterioration, stagnation, reduction, and destruction, as well as the use of all kinds of strategic means. Whoever thus knows the interdependence of the six kinds of policy plays at his pleasure with kings, bound round, as it were, in chains skillfully devised by himself. (Shamasastry 1919: 444)

Despite such guarantees, Kautilya could not simplify beyond a point or fully suppress the demanding nature of *nitishastra* studies. As L. N. Rangarajan admits, the *Arthashastra* is not just a rulebook, for it gives logical arguments about how the rule may be adapted to specific circumstances. In the above sample, we see that acquiring land is good, but many factors have to be balanced in order to choose the lesser evil. It is clear that courtiers had to be well-versed in weighing available options, such as ease and expense of acquisition and maintenance, security of possession, long-term and short-term uses of land and resources so acquired, and so on. The encyclopaedic nature of the *Arthashastra* is forbidding even for experts; the ways in which topics are ordered and the discussion of different possibilities is so exhaustive that it does not yield its secrets easily. Kautilya often cites the views of his predecessors and proceeds by considering their opinions; he then lays out the logic of his preferences, albeit cryptically. Kautilya's presentation is largely devoid of humour and is designed to evoke awe, and not love, of the subject in a hearer. As Ali has observed, the *Arthashastra* is not a textbook but a multi-centric treatise; the knowledge traditions contained therein would rarely have been mastered by any one person, and it appears to have been designed for high-ranking counsellors rather than kings themselves (Ali 2004: 86). But the king's daily instruction included the recitation of some parts of the *Arthashastra* (Trautman 2016: 21).

Even for the committed few, acquiring felicity in the *Arthashastra* required devoting time and effort, and was hardly easy. In the course of an interview with a king, the courtier is advised to reply to the king's questions in accordance with *artha* and *dharma* without '*being afraid of those present*' (Rangarajan 1987: 203; emphasis added). It is possible that there were open debates between rival counsellors on matters of policy, not to mention tests and conferral of honours (Ali 2004: 93). Given the thirty-two devices of exposition and argumentation at the end of the *Arthashastra*, J. C. Heesterman has argued that the practical value of the text consists not in its being a manual of statecraft, but a guide for methodical argumentation and the proper handling of discussion on questions of statecraft (Heesterman 1985: 130). It is also possible that responding honestly in critical moments without being cowed down by flatterers was unnerving to even the most devoted counsellors. Robert Goodwin has also noted, in the context of *Mudrarakshasa* where Chanakya countermands Chandragupta's orders to celebrate the full moon festival, that the strategic work of shoring up the authority of the king often required thwarting his inclination toward sensual pleasures or vigorous military action, and incurring his wrath (Goodwin 1998: 121).

The cultivated pleasures of winning contests cannot subdue the feeling among detractors that studying *arthashastra* causes mental strain, confusion and anxiety. The joy of outshining friends and enemies through the skilful use of policy is no match for the immediate, palpable pleasures of wine, women and song that Dandin's courtier recommends. Further, Kautilya's methodical argumentation itself can spawn self-serving and perverse interpretations. Like Damanaka arguing for the crooked ways of statecraft, Dandin presents a sophist called Chandrapalita (a counsellor of a powerful enemy adept in policy, who had gained influence over the king through Viharabhadra), who could make the weaker argument appear stronger. Quoting almost verbatim from Kautilya, he argues that

> no sport other than hunting can do much good to the body which is the best kind of exercise that generates swiftness of foot, removes phlegm, improves the appetite, the sole root of health; destroys the fat as limbs become firm, hardy and exceedingly active; it hardens one to endure cold and heat, thirst and hunger and one becomes acquainted with the thoughts and action of various animals as well as with wild forest environs and the inhabitants therein. (Kale 1986: 356)

Except that Kautilya highlighted these 'merits' while debating whether hunting is worse than gambling! Chandrapalita argues that

> gambling reveals incomparable largeness of one's mind on account of the abandonment of a heap of wealth as so much straw; one learns not to yield to joy or sorrow [good or ill luck], owing to the instability of victory or defeat; besides, it kindles high spiritedness which is the mainspring of manliness; it endows one with infinite acuteness of intellect, on account of marking of subtle tricks, difficult to be observed, used in the handling of dice and moving the pieces in squares; it also promotes one-pointed concentration and teaches one self-respect and maintaining the body in noble dignity. (Kale 1986: 356)

Similarly, the enjoyment of beautiful damsels 'reveals pride in manhood, skill in knowing the inner sentiments, and cleverness in all the arts, eloquence and ingenuity, as measures have to be constantly devised for gaining the damsel loved, preserving her when acquired, enjoying her when preserved, pleasing her when enjoyed and pacifying her when offended' (Kale 1986: 356), not to mention other benefits of taking care of one's body and appearance (for her sake)! Besides, erotic desire leads to affection for friends, high regard for attendants, sweetness of address, behaviour marked by courtesy and, above all, generation of progeny (ibid.: 357). Finally, drinking

> preserves youth, dissipates anxiety, engenders a sense of self-sufficiency, removes darts from the mind, blots out memory of crimes committed, increases a sense of confidence inspired by the free talks that indicate candour, enables uninterrupted enjoyment of all sense objects, induces the habit of distribution and thus enlarges circle of friends, and makes the man fit for battlefield as it takes away all sense of fear. (Kale 1986: 357)

There is no better parody of Kautilya, who also discusses these as vices (*vyasanas*) and ranks them according to their bad consequences. Kautilya regards gambling as worse than hunting, lusting after 'outside' women to be worse than gambling, and drinking to be the worst, and regards all these as vices stemming from excessive desire (Rangarajan 1987: 138). Kautilya concedes the relative 'merits' of hunting, such as physical exercise and skill, in comparison to gambling, wherein the gambler never knows how much wealth he has, tries to enjoy the wealth he hasn't got, and loses it all before he enjoys it, not to mention the irregularity of habits and stomach disorders (ibid.: 139). Chandrapalita also conveniently exaggerates the benefits of drinking, such as enjoying sense pleasures, honouring followers, overcoming fatigue and showing affection to others, which Kautilya attributes to Vatavyadhi, an earlier *arthashastra* expert (ibid.). The adverse effects such as 'loss of one's senses, acting like a madman, looking like a corpse, shamelessness in exposing oneself, separation from good people, association with harmful people, throwing away one's wealth as well as loss of learning, intellect, strength and good friends' (ibid.) are shown up to be strengths through rhetorical sleight of hand. For example, what Kautilya considers a weakness of consumption, i.e., shamelessness in exposing oneself, is twisted into the 'confidence emanating from candour'. Association with harmful people is dressed up as 'enlarging the circle of friends'. Thus Chandrapalita manages to convert all vices into virtues so that the pleasure-loving king is lulled into self-destruction.

MYSTERY OF STATECRAFT

Besides the disdain of kings and competition from sophist-sycophants, a wise statesman may also be deterred by the exasperating demands and vicissitudes of statecraft from plunging headlong into active service. Service under a king is described as worse than living in a fire, for the latter only burns one part of the body and, at worst, all of it, whereas a displeased king may get one's whole family killed; as such, a wise man must make self-preservation his 'first and constant concern'

(Rangarajan 1987: 205). On this point, the literary works also concur; in the *Panchatantra*, Karataka bemoans that service under kings can be thankless and dangerous for they are like serpents, 'cruel, tortuous in movement, menacingly fierce, savage, yielding only to magical arts' (Rajan 1993: 24). Kautilya therefore advises the aspirant to stipulate the preconditions of appointment to the king, such as not seeking the advice of those who have not mastered the study of *dharma* and *artha*, as well as agreeing not to harm his livelihood, not to divulge his secrets, or punish those associated with him (Rangarajan 1987: 203).

Once appointed, the courtier must always be by the king's side, neither too close nor too far, not talk slyly against other advisors, not say untrue or uncultured or unknown things, speak only what has been well thought out, not laugh loudly, not spit or break wind, not be quarrelsome in public, not talk secretly with another counsellor, not dress clownishly, not ask for gems or special favours, not indulge in winking or biting or frowning, not interrupt another when he is speaking, not antagonise the powerful, and not associate with enemies or disreputable people. He must try to turn the king away from saying evil things about others and himself, not use evil words against anyone or tolerate evil spoken to him, and be as forbearing as Mother Earth herself (Rangarajan 1987: 204). He must always endeavour, when asked, to give advice that is good and pleasing, but never that which is harmful though pleasing to the monarch. A wise courtier must never say anything unwelcome or likely to provoke the king, but remain silent even when asked his opinion (ibid.: 205). The *Panchatantra* instructs that a courtier, 'even if lacking in learning and wisdom and of humble birth, may ensure royal favour is his if he stays close to the king in constant service, for kings and women and slender climbing vines cling to whatever they find close to them' (Rajan 1993: 20). Damanaka (in Book I of *Panchatantra*) embroiders this further, saying that a courtier must walk in the forefront of battle, walk behind the king in the city and be at the royal chamber door, endear himself to royal favourites, swear enmity to his foes, never return insolent words even when chided, and above all, be adept at scotching anger by bending low, singing the master's praises, extolling his largesse, and so on (ibid.: 23–24).

However, even if he succeeds in all of this, it is likely that he will fall out of favour, and may be deprived of wealth and honour. The

Panchatantra and *Dasakumaracharita* highlight courtiers who have fallen out of favour and are awaiting return to court. One reason for this tension is the fact that power was shared and wielded by powerful ministers, which rendered them both indispensable and suspect in the eyes of kings (Ali 2004: 59). A wise courtier in the *Dasakumaracharita* actually quotes Chanakya, observing that,

> Counsellors (even though undesirable), if they follow the bent of the king's mind, ingratiate themselves into his favour; while on the other hand, such as are wise and just come to incur his hatred, if they fail to minister to his whims (or if they are ignorant of the fitful tendencies of the King's mind). (Kale 1986: 355)

Having served both the father and grandfather, this courtier languishes at his post, urging the king to matters distasteful to him, humiliated by the king who accords him unworthy duties. Early Jaina literature mentions a Chanakka, a minister of Chandragupta who, being on hostile terms with Chandragupta's son Bindusara, retired from ministership and retreated to the forest (Burrow 1968: 22).

Besides these vicissitudes of patronage, the very nature of statecraft might make its experts reluctant to continue at their posts for long. This is hinted at in the *Mudrarakshasa*, which presents a Chanakya who unleashes Kautilyan techniques to dizzying effect to entrench a new conqueror, Chandragupta Maurya.[5] He has a formidable opponent in Rakshasa, the prime minister of the defeated and deceased Nanda king, whose services Chanakya wishes to secure for his sovereign, Chandragupta. To this end, he is portrayed as deploying 'fate like strategies' which are 'myriad shaped', 'sometimes comprehensible, sometimes too intricate, at times displayed in all their magnitude and at times shrink to a vanishing point, at times their very clue is lost while at other times, they present the goal in all its vastness' (Dhruva 1923: 63).

Chanakya begins by thundering, '[W]ho while I am still here dares try to overthrow Chandra Gupta? Who is that doomed fool… so little able to measure his strength and mine that he invites his own destruction?' (Coulson 1981: 181). He boasts that he is 'Kautilya' who 'vowed before the whole world to slay the Nanda race and then fulfilled that impossible vow'. He has already 'uprooted' the Nanda forest and continues in office only to secure his prince. But his work is not finished until he wins over Rakshasa, who is still loyal to the deceased Nanda king, and is busy gathering forces for a discontented ally, Malayaketu, whose father has been killed by Chanakya. Ali has commented that loyalty, not only to the king but also to his family, was prized because it helped to ensure continuous sovereignty (Ali 2004: 106). Appreciative of the loyalty, valour and intelligence of Rakshasa, Chanakya will go to any length to secure him. To this end, he has already extirpated the entire family of the Nandas, including a renunciate, for fear that Rakshasa would not defect if even a single member was alive (Dhruva 1923: 5). He praises Rakshasa for being loyal to a master even after his death, and resolves that he will trap this wild elephant through guile and make him fit for service under Chandragupta (Coulson 1981: 181).

He has already infiltrated Rakshasa's intimate circle with his spies so that many of the latter's confidantes are indirectly reporting to Chanakya. He has caused many of Chandragupta's allies to defect and join the opposite camp. He is presently inquiring into the whereabouts of Rakshasa's family and his best friends from a spy who has procured Rakshasa's seal-ring. By the end of Act One of *Mudrarakshasa*, Chanakya has sent out a forged letter and has Chandanadasa, a friend of Rakshasa, arrested for shielding Rakshasa's family.

For his part, Rakshasa has fled the capital Pataliputra, which was under siege, and is plotting secretly. He laments that the fickle Goddess of Fortune is ignoring merit and favouring the upstart Maurya, while he goes on painting pictures on a non-existent canvas (Coulson 1981: 200)! A chamberlain arrives to present him with a necklace, ostensibly given by Malayaketu for his services. Then a spy arrives with bad news: every move of his has misfired; the poison girl engaged to kill Chandragupta has ended up killing Parvataka, an ally of Chandragupta. This is convenient for Chanakya since Parvataka was promised half the kingdom for his assistance. Further, Chanakya gives out that Rakshasa has intentionally killed Parvataka to hurt Chandragupta. Other attempts to assassinate Chandragupta, by causing a gateway to collapse on his coronation procession, or burning his bedroom, are also foiled by Chanakya in such a manner that the agents themselves got killed or burnt by their acts. Rakshasa bemoans that 'the Mauryan reaps the benefit of every plan I make', and that Chanakya sows one seed of policy and harvests many fruits (Coulson 1981: 212). To add to his woes, he hears that his trusted aide Jiva Siddhi has been banished and another, Shakatadasa, has been imprisoned for treachery. As he was being led to be impaled, Chanakya's agent Siddharthaka saves Shakatadasa, and thus endears himself to Rakshasa, who adorns him with the necklace received just that day. Siddharthaka pleads that he cannot safe-keep the same and requests that a ring in his possession, along with this gift, be stored in Rakshasa's strongroom. Discovering that the ring is his own seal, Rakshasa is content when Siddharthaka clarifies that it was found at the gate of Chandanadasa's house. Impulsively, he buys some more precious jewellery brought in by a courtier. At the close of Act Two, Rakshasa instructs his agent at Chandragupta's court to deepen an emerging rift between Chandragupta and Chanakya.

Act Three opens with a proclamation that the river palace balconies will be decorated for the full moon festival, and Chandragupta Maurya enters, musing that a kingdom brings little comfort if the king is intent only on doing his duty towards others, and forgets his own pleasure. How can he be a 'master' if he disregards his interests, and how can a bonded slave know what pleasure means (Coulson 1981: 219)? He is presently worried also because Chanakya has just instructed him to feign a quarrel. Expecting a decked-up city, Chandragupta is furious to find that his orders for a festival have been rescinded by Chanakya. Summoned to clarify, Chanakya lectures the king on three types of government, monarchical, ministerial or both, and adds that since Chandragupta is dependent on his ministers, he need not bother about reasons! Observing the king's rising temper, a bard present fans the fire, saying that 'it is not luxury and pomp that distinguish a king but that his orders are never disobeyed' (ibid.: 227). As the king is about to reward the bard, Chanakya admonishes him on his extravagance, and the king retorts that he feels more like a prisoner than a king! Chanakya then produces a list of traitors who have joined the rival forces, including a superintendent of elephants, a superintendent of horses, a former tutor and some key allies (ibid.: 229). He then says that some have defected out of greed, some out of resentment at being punished for addiction to women, drinking and hunting, and the consequent neglect of duties, a few due to fear of being caught for treachery, and some others out of envy at the favours other kinsmen received.

Asked why he did not take action against them, Chanakya expatiates on the futility of acting either through reward or punishment. Incompetent ones cannot be reinstated without endangering the foundations of government. Those who are given to greed cannot be satisfied even with a whole empire, and rewarding those who have run away for fear of being caught would be irrelevant. By the same token, punishing erstwhile allies and supporters harshly would have cost the confidence of the subjects of the new conqueror. Thus, all the disaffected elements have been allowed to go and join forces with Malayaketu, who is plotting to overthrow Chandragupta. When Chandragupta asks Chanakya why he let Malayaketu escape, he retorts that arresting him would have confirmed that they had killed his father, and befriending him would have meant giving him half the kingdom, but without any gain. On why he let Rakshasa escape, Chanakya clarifies that citizens were still loyal to Rakshasa, and that he had only to be distanced so he could not stir up trouble; using force against him would have made him kill himself or rout their own forces. Admitting defeat in the argument, the king changes tack by saying that it is Rakshasa who is admirable, incensing Chanakya, who—threatening to untie his topknot once again—lashes out that it was indeed he, Chanakya, who overthrew Nanda, to which the king coolly responds that it was destiny! Chanakya storms out, saying that he is relinquishing his sword of office, and Chandragupta proclaims that from now on he will rule in person, without reference to him. This charade, staged for the benefit of Rakshasa's spies in the Mauryan court, has the intended effect of convincing everyone present that there is a rift between the king and Kautilya. Nonetheless, it also voices some genuine problems facing a new conqueror, who can never rest on his laurels and must act ceaselessly to consolidate his victory by acting judiciously towards friends and enemies.

As Act Four opens, Rakshasa is musing about how, despite winning many of the disaffected, he is unsure of his chances, for Chanakya skilfully plants tiny germs of whatever he undertakes, then develops them, makes them bear remote fruit hidden from the eyes of others, deepens the dubious aspects, and then winds up his scheme successfully like a playwright (Dhruva 1923: 50). As an agent arrives to give him the news of the fall-out at the Mauryan court, we see that Malayaketu has also arrived with his close advisor (who is Kautilya's spy), and eavesdrops on the conversation. As Rakshasa probes the extent of the breach (did they fall out just over a festival or was there more, did Kautilya take the insult lying down etc.), the dim-witted Malayaketu is given to believe by the newfound advisor that Rakshasa wants to ensure the success of their mission by knowing these details. When the next act opens, we have another agent wondering about how Kautilya's strategy is a fertile vine that yields rich fruit, even as he hastens to show a forged letter that would seal Rakshasa's fate for good. Malayaketu's trust in him is wholly shattered by a monk who insinuates that Rakshasa killed his father. Adding to the overall effect, there arrives another spy with a coded letter alleging that Rakshasa is plotting Malayaketu's downfall. Mindful of the fact that Chanakya wanted Rakshasa alive, the advisor dissuades Malayaketu from hasty reprisal. Realising he has been completely outwitted by Chanakya, and that his protestation would yield no result, Rakshasa departs in disgrace. When he finally surrenders, thinking that he might at least rescue a friend who has been condemned to death for shielding his family, Kautilya appears and convinces him to switch loyalties and serve the Mauryan king. As Ali comments, 'Cāṇakya has thus won over his opponent without compromising the very virtue which makes him so desirable a servant, his loyalty' (Ali 2004: 106).

Vishakhadatta's Chanakya plays with the six strands of policy mentioned in the *Arthashastra*, namely reconciliation, hostility, indifference, attack, protection and duplicity, with superlative felicity and single-mindedness. He is also artful like a playwright in knowing his characters thoroughly and adapting actions to suit them. As Goodwin observes, Chanakya is the author of the play in which the average man may take any of the roles according to his capacity: sacrificial beast (Nanda), misguided rebel (Rakshasa), student and protégé (Chandragupta Maurya), and so on (Goodwin 1998: 118). Rakshasa is shown as an equally astute adversary whose plans fail partly because he is more trusting, vulnerable and generous than the omniscient Chanakya. In fact, it is his loyalty, first to the deceased sovereign and then to the best friend about to be executed, that is in stark contrast to Chanakya, who seems to have no family or friends, only obedient pupils. Revered as he is, he is also seen as ruthless and cursed by his opponents. Goodwin highlights Chanakya's affinity to the powerful and irascible sages of Hindu mythology, whose *tapas* or ascetic ardour makes their intellect and will capable of steering the course of destiny. Even though the transcendental Chanakya looms large, Goodwin notes that the *Mudrarakshasa* also recognises that the man of feeling is the mainstay of the world, without whom it would be merely the scene of a heartless power struggle or empty ritual formalism (Goodwin 1998: 123), a view also echoed by the translators Michael Coulson and K. H. Dhruva.

Why is the successful Chanakya eager to abdicate his premiership at the height of his glory? Is it due to the exacting demands of the role? He may complain that his sovereign Chandragupta takes no interest in the affairs of state and throws all the burden on himself, but there is no doubt that Chanakya enjoys the responsibility. Rakshasa also admits that he sleeps little due to the cares of the state and the uncertainty of fate. He has 'enslaved' himself to another king not for sense pleasures or self-preservation or personal greatness, but solely to avenge his dead king (Dhruva 1923: 20). Ali has noted that counsellors often had to bear the burden of rule through generations (Ali 2004: 87). It is not surprising that they may want to abandon it all at some point, especially when, like Chanakya, they are 'renouncers in disguise' (Goodwin 1998: 116).

However, I think that Chanakya's hastening to the 'penance forest' is also necessitated by the founding violence he has engaged in. It appears that skill in intrigue may be useful in winning a kingdom, but the sinfulness of what one must do to achieve that end is not absolved. Betraying and assassinating allies, spreading rumours and manipulating pious beliefs, and treachery towards the good, though justified and known only to a few, must induce discomfort and remorse even in the toughest of counsellors. In the *Dasakumaracharita*, too, this is spelt out, wherein another *niti* expert named Vishruta, through many questionable machinations involving deceit, murder and fraud, rescues and enthrones the legitimate prince. Vishruta, though supremely successful, is also eager to depart, partly for fear that his deceitful deeds may come to light someday. Though these are imaginary heroes, the authors express a real problem faced by politicians and statesmen of all stripes, but particularly the realists who elevate political necessity over abstract morality. For all practical appearances, the beneficent counsellor is indistinguishable from a self-interested minister in the instrumental use of others.

ENDURING MISGIVINGS

These misgivings of 'theorists' about political action are not unique to the Indian context. Its full-blown articulation in Athens around the fifth century BCE, culminating in the tragic execution of Socrates, is well known. The inaugural moment of political philosophy in the Western tradition played out the tension between those who study, teach and reflect on politics, and others who 'do' politics, in the tragic figure of Socrates. Through his dialogues on everything ranging from piety to justice, Socrates exposed that Athenians were led by demagogues who were substituting reality with appearances of truth, justice and piety. Accused of ignorance regarding the highest things, the city's powerful charged him with corrupting the young, inquiring into things in the heavens above and below the earth, impiety towards the old gods and introducing new gods (West and West 1984: 17–23).

Going beyond the cliché of the ineluctable gap between theory and practice, Leo Strauss has highlighted the specific dilemmas of political philosophy in this context (Strauss and Cropsey 1987: 56). First, the uncomfortable philosophical questioning regarding populist views of justice or piety is bound to evoke deep suspicion in politicians. The relentless search for truth regarding law, justice or piety in contrast to mere opinions can upset entrenched power structures and settled customs. It appears that there is no way to permanently allay these fears, though the political thinker may prudently uphold some customs while questioning others. Plato's Socrates is the archetypal figure here, in that he shows how to preserve both political philosophy and the city. For, he does not retreat from the city but conducts his dialogues in the open, and is not interested in truths above or below the earth but in all-too-human opinions.

Second, when students come calling, the political philosopher must assess how far he should go in turning them to philosophy without thwarting their ambition to act on the world stage. By adapting speeches to the souls of the interlocutors, by steering young students away from sophistry, by taming their zeal for wholesome change, by appealing to their noble spirit, he tries to make budding politicians open to philosophy and its pleasures. Far from being unworldly and impractical, political philosophy seems to be training them to act moderately in politics, resisting both status quo and radical overhaul.

Third, the sobriety of the Socratic philosopher may not attract the young as much as the rhetoric of the sophists, who teach them how to win arguments and wrest power and success. As such, the Socratic philosopher may be compelled to dazzle and entice the young, at least initially, by choosing topics such as love or friendship rather than justice. And he may flatter the few through noble lies about their chosen mission, as in the case of philosopher-kings. But this move is beset with many dangers, in that the youth may literally and selectively interpret the teachings, as some students possibly did, say by imitating Socrates' method of questioning everything, or simply by abandoning the enterprise and becoming tyrants. Learning from the experience, Plato would moderate the claims of the wise man as well as the radical activists eager for wholesome change through the figure of the statesman and the rule of law. But Plato himself could not resist the fatal attraction to 'convert' rulers to philosophy (as with Dion of Syracuse), only to return to the academy when they turned tyrants, impatient with the rigours of pursuing wisdom (Lilla 2001).

Fourth, the forms of argumentation, couched in the dialogue form in Plato, do not lend themselves to easy reading by the uninitiated, which further fuels doubts about the enterprise. Multiple layers of meaning in Plato's dialogues and Socrates' averring that he only knows that he does not know, may not inspire confidence in many; even the few who are captivated by the charm of Socrates, like Alcibiades, may be unable to resist the lure of fame; the rarest of the rare, like Plato, may withdraw to the academy, seduced by the rewards of reflection on the human condition. But bereft of the ordinary pleasures of family and fame, the political philosopher appears 'unhappy' to the many.

In sum, Plato's dialogues already hint that the reconciliation may never be final or perfect; political philosophers may never fully endorse the city, and vice versa. Practising politicians may never overcome their suspicion that political philosophers are teaching impractical things and being too critical, if not irreverent, towards existing structures and practices. Moreover, political philosophers may themselves appear like sophists when they deploy rhetoric and try to charm young aspirants. Political philosophers may also wish to distance themselves from direct political engagement, given the many compromises dictated by political necessity. Even if circumstances were favourable, they may not be willing to rule for long because they regard contemplation as the most pleasant and blessed possession, and become impatient with human affairs.

CONCLUSION

What the Indian material shows is that the scepticism about studying *nitishastra* or *arthashastra* persists even when thinkers opt to be concise and practical, as did Kautilya. Sloughing off the normative aspects, such as the nature of the soul or cosmos or ideal regime, and speaking effective truths need not endear political thought to wielders of power. Neither Kautilya nor Vishnu Sharma upset established customs or practices. They did not make the exaggerated claims for reason or truth that mark Socratic inquiry. They even deigned to deliver their lessons in enticing formats, as with Dandin artfully masking political education in romantic adventures.

But simplifying the lessons or presenting them attractively could not eliminate the intrinsic complexity of political affairs, which by their very nature involve a variety of actors and interests. As such, their cognitive and ethical demands were faulted for causing 'mental strain, mistrust and uncertainty' by Dandin's courtier. Expertise does not insulate one from the anxiety and uncertainty of results. Nor does it engender happiness for the king, who must forego peace and sleep, held Dandin's courtier. These may not be as weighty as the charges against Socrates; but they are serious charges against the claim of practical wisdom of the Indian thinkers.

Unlike Plato's experience with Dionysus of Syracuse, which ended in failure, Indian political thinkers seem optimistic about finding kings who are amenable to wisdom, at least once in a while. The historical fact of Chanakya advising Chandragupta Maurya may have inspired the *Panchatantra* and *Dasakumaracharita*, which show wise and able teachers being sought after by kings. But the shadow of tyranny and sophists who prop up tyrants do not cease to haunt the experts. Strauss observed that politics is coeval with tyranny and, extending that, one can say that sophistry is coeval with political speech (Strauss and Kojeve 1991: 22). Political thought, even when it is realistic, cannot overcome the problems of tyranny and sophistry that mock thinking per se. Moreover, by making allowances for political necessity, realism in political thought may even appear to support both tyranny and sophistry. For these reasons, even experts who achieve great success may wish to periodically go into exile and wait for a propitious time to re-enter the world stage.

Notes

1. While Rangarajan and Shamasastry translate *nitishastra* as 'political science' and 'science of polity', respectively, I have used more generic phrases like 'the study of politics', 'the systematic knowledge of politics' and 'expert tradition on statecraft'. I have borrowed the last from Mark McClish and Patrick Olivelle (McClish and Olivelle 2012: x).
2. Rajan translates Bahu Shakti, Ugra Shakti and Ananta Shakti as 'rich energy', 'fierce energy' and 'endless energy', respectively, but considering the royal context, I think *shakti* as power is more apt.
3. I have mentioned Rajan's translation of the animal names to enhance access, while sticking to Sanskrit names in the remaining text.
4. Ludwik Sternbach opines that the text by Vishnugupta referred to here might be Chanakya's *nitishastra* (available in different versions), which is in verse, rather than Kautilya's *Arthashastra*, which is in prose, though he does not deny the latter possibility altogether (Sternbach 1956: 119).
5. Vishakhadatta alternates the names of Chanakya and Kautilya, and tradition has it that Chanakya, Kautilya and Vishnugupta refer to the same person—the minister of Chandragupta. Coulson uses Kautilya throughout in his translation to distinguish him from Chandragupta and Chanakya for English readers. Dhruva uses Chanakya in his translation, and I have followed him. Some argue that Chanakya may have been different from the author of *Arthashastra*, ascribed to a Kautilya alias Vishnugupta, while admitting that Chanakya may also have been famous for his prowess as a practitioner of politics (Burrow 1968: 24; Trautman 2016: 24).

II

DISCERNING FRIENDS AND ENEMIES

Prudence in the *Panchatantra*

Vishnu Sharma, in the *Panchatantra*, has a resourceful mouse, Hiranyaka, wondering about 'a chalice of trust and affection//a sanctuary from sorrow, anxiety and fear//who created this priceless gem, a friend? A word of just two syllables, Mitra?' (Rajan 1993: 263). This encomium to friendship comes after a long book on the 'Estrangement of Friends' (*Mitra-bheda*, Book I), where a great friendship between a noble bull and majestic lion is undone by a jealous jackal. As mentioned earlier, the *Panchatantra*, a compendium of prudence intended 'to awaken the intelligence of dull-witted princes', deals with the estrangement and the winning of friends, natural enemies and false friends, the ordinary vices of friends, and rash or impulsive deeds reflecting our erratic instincts in judging friends. Why should friendship matter to politics or the art of government—'*nitishastra*', as Vishnu Sharma puts it? Why should people in power value friendships? What kinds of friendship are contracted by the weak? What pitfalls are intrinsic to the practice of friendship and how can we sharpen our practical wisdom in this regard? Through these questions, I examine the role and contours of *niti*, or practical wisdom, in analyses of friendships, especially as it pertains to equality between friends. Given that friendship is extensively debated in Western political thought, is there anything unique in the *Panchatantra*'s discussion of the same?

FIRST IMPRESSIONS

Recall that the *Panchatantra*'s preamble narrates of a glorious king, Amara Shakti (Eternal Power), who was looking for a suitable tutor to 'awaken the intelligence' of his three sons so that they become fit to rule. His three sons were called Vasu Shakti (Great Power), Ugra Shakti (Fierce Power) and Ananta Shakti (Endless Power). To educate them, Vishnu Sharma, who vowed to make them masters of practical wisdom, devised the five *tantras* (books), all of which deal with the pleasures and perils of friendships between unequals. Patrick Olivelle and Chandra Rajan are among the few who have noted the primacy of friendship in the *Panchatantra*. Rajan highlights how friendship is singled out for high praise and expected to flourish only between equals and with noble minds, cherished for their learning, refinement and discipline (Rajan 1993: xlvi). However, as Olivelle notes, 'the Sanskrit term mitra signifies both political ally and personal friend, and the *Panchatantra* cleverly plays on this ambiguity, using aspects of the latter, especially its emotional content, to support its advocacy of the former' (Olivelle 1997: xxxix). Bhikhu Parekh distinguishes three levels of friendship in Indian epics: friendliness (*maitri*), based on mutual interest and reciprocity; bonding of hearts (*suhrd*), manifest in instinctive and immediate understanding and feeling for one another; and, finally, greater intimacy and total mutual commitment (*sakhya*) (Parekh 2008: 156). However, the use of '*mitra*' in the title of *Panchatantra*'s second book, *Mitra-samprapti* (Winning of Friends), which deals mainly with the bonding of hearts, suggests that the above three types/possibilities were seen as overlapping rather than mutually exclusive. Interestingly, the *Hitopadesha* uses the term '*suhrd*' in the title of the book on the estrangement of friends (*Suhrd-bheda*), and sticks to '*mitra*' for the book on the winning of friends (*Mitra-samprapti*). As we will see, dealings with all kinds of friends loom large, especially with unequals who come calling. In a full-length analysis of the first book, *Mitra-bheda* (Estrangement of Friends), Ashay Naik has noted that the *Panchatantra* is a *nitishastra* not because it dishes out didactic verses in the midst of stories but because it 'represents political situations and actions of political agents' (Naik 2016). He observes that even though it deals with the internal dynamics of monarchy and oligarchy (*gana-sanghas*), it contains insights that are relevant for all time.

So far, only select aspects of *niti* (prudence/practical wisdom), namely expedient opportunism and cleverness, have been highlighted in *Panchatantra* scholarship. The *Panchatantra*'s most popular stories, whether of the hare and the elephant or the sparrow that gets rid of a predator serpent, often involve strategic outwitting of the powerful by the powerless. Johannes Hertel translated '*tantra*' as cases of trickery, and set the tone for dominant readings by regarding the *Panchatantra* as a Machiavellian treatise of deceit, cunning and ruthlessness in achieving political aims (Olivelle 1997: xxxi). Franklin Edgerton regarded the stories as generally amoral and positively immoral (ibid.: xxxii). Olivelle declares that 'it is clear to me, therefore, that the central message of the *Panchatantra*, with the possible exception of Book II, is that craft and deception constitute the major art of government' (ibid.: x, xxxv). It is not clear why the rather large Book II, 'Winning of Friends', dealing with the wonderful experiences of greeting one another, eating together and meeting to share witty stories, must be treated as an 'exception'.

Furthermore, the contextual ambiguity embedded in the so-called craft and deception thematic has not been given its due in the above readings. As Uma Chakravarti has pointed out in the context of the *Jataka* tales, several stories deal with unequal characters in a hierarchical situation, where the inferior resorts to deception and cunning to subvert the stronger party's threats. At the same time, there are also alliances suggesting an ambiguity in handling the master–servant relationship as merely hierarchical (Chakravarti 2004: 220).

From the *Panchatantra* preamble, while it is obvious that *shakti*, or 'power' (suffixed to the names of the three dim-witted princes mentioned above) must be tamed by practical wisdom, it is not so apparent why that would involve learning about friendship. It is because *niti* lessons regarding who should be befriended must be imbibed by prospective rulers, especially as many unequals may come calling. Maxims such as 'make friends with those who are similar or equal in wealth, strength and lineage' are often expounded and problematised with wit and irony. Conversely, it is also because we learn about *niti* in general, i.e. deliberating about the right means to attain wealth or pleasure or virtues with and through friends. Interpreting Aristotle, Robert Sokolowski has argued that friendship is the finest way in which we exercise practical reason, and that practical reason finds its highest employment in friendship in that it affords room for practising courage, temperance, justice, and so on (Sokolowski 2002: 452). Here, I flesh out the nuances of *niti* as pertaining to prudence, propriety and policy, and not just as a contrivance or scheme. While there is a good dose of cunning involved, there is also a sense that prudence is not just cleverness or expediency; it involves judging right and wrong after due deliberation and acting judiciously. For instance, cleverness in the service of greed and lust is less prudent compared to cleverness in the service of compassion, especially towards friends. While recognising that friendship enhances our virtues, the *Panchatantra* also shows how the diverse and compelling ways of friendship may disrupt practical wisdom.

THE LURE OF STRANGERS

As mentioned before, the *Panchatantra*'s first book tells of a cunning and ambitious jackal, Damanaka (Wily), working his way back into royal favour by engineering a friendship between a lion-king, Pingalaka (Tawny) and a learned bull, Sanjivaka (Lively). Once they meet and seal their mutual regard, they spend all their time in esoteric discussions, shutting out all others. Engrossed in this exclusive relationship, Pingalaka neglects his royal duties, causing much hardship for his dependents. Instead of hunting energetically to provide for his retinue, Pingalaka is busy gathering 'wisdom' from the 'grass eater.' It appears that he also elevates him to chief ministership (in the *Hitopadesha*, the post is that of chief treasurer), sidelining the two jackals (Reddy 1989: 197). In fact, the *Hitopadesha* is much more forthcoming, in that the bull also alerts the lion-king to the jackals' pilfering and depleting the treasury, thus compelling the lion to work hard to procure wealth (Chandiramani 1995: 124).

Pinched by hunger, Damanaka begins consulting his friend Karataka, who blames him for introducing the grass-eating bull to the lion-king. Damanaka admits his fault and narrates some stories of how go-betweens are inevitably hurt, especially if they are stupid. Unlike the greedy jackal who steps in between two fighting rams to lick the blood and is killed, or the barber's wife who substitutes for her friend so she could go on an adulterous date, only to be mutilated by the latter's enraged husband, Damanaka is far-sighted. Never one to give up, Damanaka resolves to devise some clever means to sow mutual suspicion (*bheda*), so that the lion and bull are estranged. He believes that where sheer prowess cannot succeed, a clever ruse might; in support, he narrates some famous stories. One is about a mother crow which loses all her eggs to a black serpent until, following a jackal's advice, she carries away a queen's gold chain and drops it into the serpent's hollow; the royal guards pursuing her notice this, kill the serpent and retrieve the chain. The second story is about a smart hare which incites a dimwit lion, that was devouring all the animals, to kill a powerful rival mirrored in a lake. A third, lesser-known story is of a lazy crane which beguiles the fish in a lake into believing that danger is imminent and agrees to transport them to another lake, only to leisurely eat them all up.

Karataka is not convinced by these stories and says that it is not advisable for the weak to stoop to deceive the powerful, lest they be caught (Rajan 1993: 75). Nevertheless, our enterprising and unscrupulous Damanaka plots and succeeds in creating mutual suspicion. Damanaka enters Pingalaka's den, feigning great concern for the king's well-being, and seeks his leniency for bringing bad news. He reminds the lion-king that flatterers are many, but frank courtiers who speak wholesome though unpleasant truths are hard to find. He confides in the king that Sanjivaka was plotting to usurp the throne for himself. When the lion looks stunned, he quotes texts which say that a single minister must never be made all-powerful, especially when there are hereditary retainers around. Damanaka expends all his rhetorical prowess to persuade the lion-king, now appealing to his interests, now warning him against soft feelings, all the while lamenting that good advice is wasted on naive rulers. He rues the fact that well-meaning and truthful courtiers like himself often come to ruin! He dares to suggest more than once that the lion may know maxims of practical wisdom but lacks the ability to act in time due to misplaced affection or compassion for strangers (Rajan 1993: 97). He poisons Pingalaka's mind about how the latter has placed all his trust in one friend, that too a stranger, and allowed him to become powerful.

To hammer the point home, Damanaka narrates some stories of betrayal by men and animals. One story is about a *brahmana* who rescues a snake, tiger and monkey from a well, all of whom advise him not to save a man who has also fallen into the same well, saying he is ungrateful. Moved by the man's pleas, the brahmana helps him out, after which he is promptly betrayed. A second story is about a bedbug which deigns to share its home, the king's couch, with a selfish wasp-guest, and the latter, unmindful of when and where to bite the king, stings him early one morning, causing a massive hunt that ends in the host-bedbug being killed. A third story is about a jackal that falls into an indigo vat and, when it returns to the forest, is mistaken for a new beast and made king, only to howl (on hearing other jackals) and thus reveal its true colours. Trusting a stranger against one's better judgment, helping and elevating him is the theme that unites these tales, and Damanaka hammers at it, using suitable wise sayings (*subhashitas*) on statecraft, posing as the 'true friend' who is risking his life to protect the king.

Damanaka is an expert in sheer opportunistic prudence. Expediency, rooted in narrow self-interest, is all that he cares about. He knows what is good but uses that knowledge only rhetorically to further his creed of 'helping friends and harming enemies', which is why he is in royal service. More sympathetically, Naik has characterised this as the classic '*kula-jāti*' (kinship-clan) morality of the *Panchatantra* world, wherein elders, impoverished brethren, servants and others are to be cared for. He also adds that these categories still hold, albeit applied within an 'ideological community' wherein we consider those who are original thinkers as 'elders', those who live by its code but are impoverished as 'brethren', etc. (Naik 2016). But Damanaka's own friend Karataka is not convinced that Damanaka is helping anyone other than himself through his actions (Rajan 1993: 172).

Initially, Pingalaka does not subscribe to a narrow notion of friends and enemies. He demurs, saying that Sanjivaka has been a good retainer, that he is dear to him like his own 'body', that a virtuous one like him cannot turn against a benefactor, and so on. Pingalaka reminds the jackal that he promised safe passage to the bull in court, praised him as virtuous and elevated him, and that therefore killing the bull would compromise his public standing (Reddy 1989: 134–137). In the *Hitopadesha*, the lion says that he has great affection for the bull and that he would like to ascertain the facts on his own before jumping to conclusions based on the complaints of others (Chandiramani 1995: 147). When he is somewhat inclined to believe the courtier, noble as he is, Pingalaka wants to warn Sanjivaka first, which Damanaka brushes aside, saying, '[W]hat kind of policy is that? For it is known that: you caution a man, and straight out of fear he dissembles, or, he decides to strike. Have no doubt; it is most impolitic to caution a foe by word or act' (Rajan 1993: 104). Pingalaka repeatedly maintains that Sanjivaka is only a grass-eater and cannot do much harm. Damanaka boldly hints that that may be so, but Sanjivaka could be instigated by some disgruntled elements at court. Pingalaka asserts that nobility consists in doing good not only to the virtuous, but even to those who harm you, at which point Damanaka lectures the lion on the crux of *rajadharma*, i.e. the duty of kings, which is to punish the wicked. The bull had caused harm by distracting the lion from hunting and providing for his retinue, as a result of which they were deserting him (Reddy 1989: 138). If traitors were not punished, talented servants would leave. When Pingalaka asks how he could confirm the bull's treacherous intent, Damanaka tells him to watch out for the bull's demeanour, which, far from being humble as usual, would be cavalier, as if the bull was ready to thrust horns.

Pingalaka begins by showing some prudence in doubting the goodwill of the courtier who sneaked in and volunteered to find out the cause of a fierce sound (that turned out to be a bellowing bull), and wondering whether he 'may not play one against the other and that he may well do me an ill turn for he bears a grudge for having been turned out of office previously' (Rajan 1993: 32). The king recalls sayings to the effect that those who were once honoured and then slighted will work towards one's downfall, and that the mighty who are foolish and trusting may be overthrown by the weakest. The irony is that even when Damanaka quotes similar sayings to make Pingalaka suspect his dear friend, and openly alludes to intrigue stemming from discarding hereditary retainers, the lion does not see through the jackal's motives, and hacks his friend to death. Could it be that Pingalaka's friendship with the urbane Sanjivaka had dulled his native aristocratic prudence forged in the wilderness?

NAIVETE OF THE LEARNED

Sanjivaka epitomises someone who is learned but displays no practical wisdom at all. He knows many stories of manipulative jackals, but cannot recognise one staring him in the face. On being told that the lion-king harboured ill-will towards him, he rants about how kings often cultivate the unworthy, how they are easily deluded and distrustful and cannot appreciate sincerity and truth, surrounded as they are by flatterers and con men. They are like the 'silly wild goose which, searching in a pond for white lotus shoots at night pecks at reflected stars and thereafter does not even peck at the white lotus shoots in daylight assuming them to be stars' (Rajan 1993: 113; Olivelle 1997: 41). He quickly jumps to conclusions about the lion-king as being a 'false friend' who drips honey but is all poison. He also regrets not exercising proper judgment in assessing the lion-king, and choosing an inopportune course and wrong company. He compares himself to a greedy honey bee that forsakes blooming lotuses and jasmines to go after the sap trickling from the temples of elephants, only to be crushed by an elephant's winnowing ears (Rajan 1993: 119; Olivelle 1997: 44). He recalls ethical adages that proclaim that virtues themselves cause one's undoing, if carried to 'lofty heights'.

Sanjivaka then relates a story that closely mirrors his own predicament. A rich merchant set off with a caravan of a hundred camels with valuable textiles; one of his camels buckled under the load and was abandoned in a forest, where it recovered and regained its health. A lion that chanced upon this camel found it quaint and offered it protection. Soon, however, the lion was gored by an elephant and could not hunt, at which point the royal attendants, a crow, a panther and a jackal, consult among themselves and connive at doing away with the camel. At first, the lion baulks at the idea of slaying the camel, saying that it is sinful to harm those to whom one has granted protection. The jackal convinces the lion that there is no harm if 'out of devotion' the camel offers itself. In the meeting that ensues, the camel, deluded by the speeches of the crow, jackal and panther offering their own lives to quench the master's hunger and gain spiritual merit, fame and the 'other world', hastens to make a similar speech, thinking that since the others have come to no harm, he might as well follow suit, as the occasion demanded, and is promptly killed.

Another story of a king with evil counsellors pertains to that of a chariot-maker Devagupta, who, faced with a lion, quickly offers him his own lunch. Being in a benign mood, the lion-king says that it cannot be satisfied with boiled rice and vegetables. The chariot-maker strikes a pact to ply the lion with sweetmeats and candies in exchange for safe passage, on the condition that the lion comes alone every day. In time, they become good friends, the lion gets used to being provided with food and gives up hunting; when its retainers, the crow and the jackal, get to know about this, they insist on joining the party. The chariot-maker, on seeing them approach, realises the danger and climbs up a tree, saying that he cannot trust the lion anymore. Sanjivaka does see that the lion may have been set up by someone, but overlooks the jackal standing right in front of him as the culprit (Reddy 1989: 154, 165; Rajan 1993: 128). He also forgets that the same jackal, before securing the bull's safety and the friendship of the lion, had extracted a promise that it would always act in agreement with the jackal and not be carried away by royal favour. Then, Damanaka had narrated a tale of an able minister who slights a royal sweeper, who then poisons the king's mind, causing estrangement until the minister figures out the mischief and makes amends. Trusting and naive, Sanjivaka thunders that he shall fight the lion bravely, since he has everything to gain if he were to win, including the throne, or attain heaven if he were to lose and die (Reddy 1989: 167).

Recalling sayings which state that 'victory is uncertain in wars even for mighty warriors', and anxious that the lion may be struck down by the bull, the jackal hastens to deflate the bull's pride. He narrates a tale of a male lapwing which, to save its eggs from the ocean, tried along with other birds to empty the ocean and, when that proved futile, began to fill the ocean with sticks and stones! It is only through divine intervention of the eagle mount, who complains to Vishnu about the plight of his bird subjects, that the ocean is humbled. Damanaka also accosts Sanjivaka with another hilarious story of a weaver who pretends to be the great Vishnu himself, riding every night on a wooden bird to a princess' bedchamber, until one day the secret is discovered. The 'blessed' king and queen then entreat the 'weaver-god' to save them from the impending rout by an invading army. Vishnu, watching the goings-on and anxious that, should the weaver be killed, rumours would spread that Vishnu had been killed, and performances of sacrifices and worship would cease, decides to infuse the weaver with divine energy (Rajan 1993: 88; Reddy 1989: 111)! This superb satire reminds us that success requires not just bravado but also divine assistance when faced with powerful enemies. Sanjivaka is easily mollified (just as he is easily excited), and decides to wait and watch and not attack first. When Sanjivaka shows up, ready to surrender and fight only if needed, having been coached by the jackal, the lion-king misunderstands his distant demeanour. He lunges and, in the ensuing battle, hacks the bull to death.

Sanjivaka's application of his wisdom is wanting on several counts; as noted before, he cannot recognise Damanaka's villainy staring him in the face. His speeches reveal that he is easily swayed by appearances and takes unnecessary risks. Upon learning about the lion-king's wrath, he bemoans that he was deceived by the latter's sweet speech, bowing and rising, praising and gifting, and so on. He regrets flouting the famous truth that marriage and friendship work well only where lineage (*kulam*), wealth (*dhanam*), virtue (*silam*) and strength/power (*balam*) are roughly equal or similar (*samanam*) (Rajan 1993: 117; Reddy 1989: 153). He repeatedly laments that he ignored the disproportion between himself and the lion-king. Olivelle highlights the frequent instructions in the *Panchatantra* that there can be no friendship between meat-eaters and grass-eaters, and between the wild and the domestic spheres (Olivelle 1997: xxv). Naik also argues that this book reflects the tensions between meat-eaters, signifying the imperatives of power (the belligerent, close-fisted, realistic factions), and the grass-eaters, signifying the pull of righteousness (the peaceable, compassionate, idealistic, munificent mob). Thus, the fragile balance between the meat-eating Kshatriyas and the lion's retinue of ministers is threatened by the entry of the civilian community, represented by the bull or camel or man (Naik 2016).

HELPING FRIENDS AND HARMING ENEMIES

But this is not the last word, for the princes also listen to a long valedictory lecture from Karataka about his friend Damanaka's short-sightedness, as well as the lion's lack of judgment in killing a great friendship. Here, the friendship between the two jackals Damanaka and Karataka, who are equals, deserves analysis. Their relationship is full of intimate sharing and frankness. Their exchange on statecraft and the qualities of a courtier is quite serious and scholarly. When Damanaka is enthusiastic about gaining the favour of the king through some clever ploy, Karataka reminds him that they were doing well enough on Pingalaka's leavings and must be contented. Damanaka mocks him, saying that filling the belly must not be one's sole concern and that the 'wise embark on a journey of serving kings in order to help friends and harm enemies' (Rajan 1993: 14). But does Damanaka truly know how to distinguish between friends and enemies, and does he have what it takes to be a true friend in general, and a king's friend in particular?

When Karataka probes him about his proficiency in statecraft, Damanaka alludes to the epic of the Pandavas, especially their stay at Virata's court, which revealingly is all about masquerading in exile. Damanaka knows how to choose the right time and place, assess the royal mood, desist from intruding when the king is in secret counsel, or occupied in intimate activities, or is being attended to by a physician or barber, etc.; he knows when and how to address the king, how to treat his well-wishers and favourites, and so on. Karataka warns him that princes are like 'mountains with hearts of stone, sought after by the low and vile and murderous and cannot be trusted' (Rajan 1993: 23). But when his friend insists upon trying out his luck, Karataka relents, wishes him good fortune and urges him to act with due circumspection. Later, when Damanaka sets out to deceive the lion and the bull, he remonstrates, in vain, with Damanaka about the myopic gains of such policy. For Naik, Karataka represents a wise counsellor who is timid and afraid that his superiors may laugh at his advice (Naik 2016).

But when Karataka sees the ghastly spectacle of the lion and the bull goring one another, he forcefully counters Damanaka's notion that statecraft is inherently crooked and protean. Unsentimental to the core,

Damanaka boasts that one must achieve success, if necessary through another's ruin, and gloats that they will now feast on the bull's flesh. Damanaka's *rajniti* is not shared by his friend and alter ego, Karataka. Disgusted, Karataka fulminates that the test of a minister's political sagacity is in cementing rather than breaking friendships that sprang up spontaneously, and that Damanaka is a minister only in name for he has denuded and endangered the king (Rajan 1993: 152–153). Conciliation is the choice-worthy expedient rather than war, which is hazardous and uncertain and should never be engaged in for paltry gains. In the process, Karataka calls Damanaka a fool, a perverse blockhead and a low-bred courtier, and accuses him of bringing about disorder and confusion in the realm to further his own ends. Karataka mocks Damanaka, saying that the latter's textual knowledge of statecraft is useless, for it had neither shaped his passions nor his intelligence; his bravery is unfair, his pride is overweening and his jealousy is vicious. He tries to gain friends through deceit and profits through others' afflictions, and is devoid of good feeling and good sense. Friendship, thus, has an unpalatable component in that genuine friends speak frankly and fearlessly. Rajan rightly notes that the two jackals Damanaka and Karataka represent the politician and the statesman, respectively (Rajan 1993: xxvi).

Lest we think that Karataka is just an armchair critic who analyses things post facto, we must note that he is equally prudent. Incidentally, Olivelle translates Karataka as 'the prudent' and Damanaka as 'the daring' one (Olivelle 1997: 7). It is not as if Karataka expects the world to be all nice and noble. He is aware of the precariousness of a minister's position, the unreliability of kings' patronage and their susceptibility to chicanery. He knows of greedy sons who endanger their families for ill-gotten wealth, and of false friends who appropriate what has been entrusted to their custody.

And yet, Karataka advises contentment, not meddling in other's business, acting within the bounds of trust and duty, avoiding deceit to trap the powerful and not risking the king's life for small gains. Naik has noted that Karataka's plaint is not that one must not engage in intrigue, but that one must mitigate the risks involved, and Damanaka had no plans to forestall the violent escalation. A minister like Damanaka, who engages in continuous intrigue, would scare away competent people (Naik 2016). Karataka also bewails that Pingalaka listened to Damanaka without proper scrutiny and deliberation. Above all, an expert in *nitishastra* must know how to discern true and false friends, in order to help friends and harm enemies.

Karataka proceeds to tell stories which show that good advice is wasted on unfit people, and that one must not make friendships with fools and rogues. In a certain wooded region lived a troop of apes, who on a cold evening noticed a firefly, thought it to be fire, lifted it up, placed it in dry grass and leaves, and started enjoying what they believed to be its warmth. A tailor bird flew down and admonished them, saying that the 'fire' was in fact a firefly and, when it did not stop giving out advice after being rebuffed, was dashed against a rock (Rajan 1993: 165). Then there is the story of a king who made friends with a monkey and made it his personal sword-bearer; once, while wandering in his delightful garden, the king goes to sleep, instructing the monkey to guard him; the monkey, on seeing a bee settle on the king's head, draws the sword and kills the king (Rajan 1993: 184). While it is clear that Damanaka is a rogue, Karataka seems to suggest that he is also a fool for his ways bring destruction for his friends and family. Thus, here is a friendship between equals that turns sour on principle. This book ends on an ambiguous note; in some versions, Pingalaka survives and the wily jackal becomes the chief minister. Rajan points out that it is not clear in some versions whether Pingalaka survives the battle (Rajan 1993: xxx). In the *Hitopadesha*, Pingalaka wins and, with Damanaka's advice, reoccupies the throne.

Through Karataka's powerful critique (which is also the last word in some recensions), it appears as if the book acknowledges the power of ethical prudence over opportunistic prudence.[1] Naik notes this when he says that *niti* need not be opposed to *dharma* (broadly virtues), though he tends to justify Damanaka's ambition, boldness and rightness from the standpoint of meat-eaters. Political necessity might require that rules be broken for a just outcome in a given set of circumstances. As he puts it, if the jackals were not dismissed, or if Damanaka had been rewarded by the king earlier on for bringing about his friendship with the bull, or if Sanjivaka had not adversely influenced Pingalaka, etc., it would not have been necessary to separate the two. Naik then goes on to say that Karataka's concluding note is an appeal to competent and compassionate people to take up public service. Naik sums up *niti* counsels thus: do not meddle in work outside your jurisdiction, do not surrender to verbal threats, be respectful of the lowest worker, reflect on your own faults, employ strategic thinking to defeat a stronger rival, excess leads to downfall, deception (if well-crafted and well executed) works, do not give refuge to those whose conduct is unfamiliar to you, do not fall prey to stereotypes, outsiders cannot become insiders, know your true friends, and so on (Naik 2016).

While this is all valid for individual stories in the first book, it does not capture the ambiguity and despair about *niti* pertaining to friends, in particular. Conventional wisdom has it that one must make friends with those who are roughly equal or similar, as Sanjivaka puts it. And yet, this is not what is affirmed in the book; no simple rule is put forth that one must form friendships only with equals and avoid unequals. Karataka never condemns the friendship between the lion and the bull as an inappropriate match. True, friendship with unequals is risky, in that it attracts hostility from hangers-on who may feel excluded from the charmed circle. It is also difficult, since inequality lurking in the background makes such friends easily succumb to misunderstanding. It appears that one must form friendships after careful scrutiny; friendship with one who is resourceful and straight is advisable over friendships with fools and rogues (Rajan 1993: 172). There is no algorithm by which such discriminating judgment can be taught or assessed; only through experience can one gain some maxims and the courage to test these in action.

TAKING RISKS FOR THE VIRTUOUS

This is the leitmotif of *Panchatantra*'s second book, 'Winning of Friends', which opens with a verse that asserts that despite a lack of resources and wealth, wise men possessed of knowledge and insight are quick to accomplish their desired aims.[2] It closes with a verse that says when dumb beasts can form firm friendships welded through worldly wisdom, is it any wonder that humans do the same (Rajan 1993: 193, 264)? The Telugu translation closes with a verse that reminds us that he who gains friends and acts without crookedness (in Sanskrit, *kautilyena*, linking crookedness to Kautilya), will not be defeated or let down by them (Reddy 1989: 335). The main story is about a pleasant friendship between a mouse, a crow, a turtle and a deer, who achieve their aims by acting in concord.

Once again, *niti* regarding who should be chosen as a friend is raised here, as if the conventional wisdom spouted by Sanjivaka earlier is found wanting. The first debate occurs when a crow called Laghupatanaka seeks out a mouse Hiranyaka for friendship, thinking that 'though a person is self sufficient, a person should still have friends to raise his standing' (Rajan 1993: 201). Laghupatanaka has just witnessed the mouse freeing his friend Chitragreeva, the pigeon king, and his retinue from a hunter's net. On this occasion, there is an exchange between Hiranyaka and Chitragreeva, where friends are portrayed as not only trusting one another but also playfully testing one another. When Hiranyaka, delighted to help his friend, starts nibbling away at the fetters, the pigeon king exhorts him to free his retainers first. Hiranyaka says that masters come first, and Chitragreeva counters by saying that as a king, he is bound to show concern towards those who have attached themselves to him (Chandiramani 1995: 36; Rajan 1993: 199). He cites wise sayings which state that a master who heaps honours on servants constantly and far beyond their due will never be forsaken by them. This reply pleases Hiranyaka, who says he only wanted to test his friend (Rajan 1993: 200).[3]

Though 'capricious by nature and generally distrustful', the crow admits that one must have a trusted friend (Rajan 1993: 201). Impressed by the mouse's fortress with its hundred entrances, as well as by its astute intelligence, Laghupatanaka beseeches Hiranyaka to become his friend. Hiranyaka, however, refuses, saying that there can be no friendship between food and its eater, and that 'one who is fool enough to make friends with a person not his equal, be he inferior or superior, merely becomes the world's butt of ridicule' (ibid.: 202). The operative word (in both Sanskrit and Telugu) is *samana*, which connotes 'same, equal, like, similar' in the first instance (Apte 1987: 587). In this context, the mouse refers to equality of wealth (*dhanam*), of lineage (*kulam*) as well as strength (*balam*) and intelligence (*jnanam*) (Reddy 1989: 252–253). Sanjivaka also referred to the same parameters. Olivelle has noted that different social groups and strata are regarded as different species, and thus inequality and hierarchy are 'natural' rather than cultural and malleable (Olivelle 1997: xxxvi). He also points out that the text almost always shows 'brahmins' in a poor light and it is most positive about merchants, who are shown as wise, ambitious and virtuous (ibid.: xxx). While it presupposes *varna-jati* (category-caste) as a given, it is not obsessed with caste identity. In one story, a rich weaver who falls in love with a princess and becomes obsessed with possessing her is asked by his best friend, 'are you not afraid of transgressing the Law [*jati dharma*, or caste-specific conduct]? You are an artisan, belonging to a class of traders and merchants—those who carry on business; the king belongs to the class of warriors…' To which the weaver replies, 'The Law allows the warrior a third wife. Who knows if the princess is not the daughter of a lady of my class, belonging to the business community…' (Rajan 1993: 80). Needless to say, he goes on to seduce the princess through subterfuge and, with some divine help, even marries her and inherits the kingdom. Thus, caste inequality is not so pronounced as inequality of physical strength, wealth, lineage and intellect.

The crow threatens to go on a hunger strike; but the mouse cites well-known ethical precepts that say that friendship and marriage work well only where there is parity (*samanam*) of wealth and lineage (Reddy 1989: 252). Alliances between the strong and the weak seldom work. Moreover, aligning with foes is imprudent and, when they happen to be 'natural enemies', positively dangerous. To the crow's queries, the mouse replies that incidental enmity springing from specific injuries can be remedied, but natural enmity is permanent and inborn. Natural enmity—such as that between grass-eaters and meat-eaters, dogs and cats, rival wives, fire and water, gods and titans, snakes and mongooses, lions and elephants, crows and owls, scholars and dunces, chaste wives and harlots, saints and sinners—ends only with death. As Rajan points out, it is not that someone gets killed all the time, but they all strive to fight the other to death (Rajan 1993: 203).

The crow, like a constructivist, argues that one makes friends or enemies for a reason, and that one must not seek enmity without reason. In its view, 'we make friends with people because they help; with beasts and birds for some special reason or other; with fools out of fear or greed but with *the good* [*sajjan*], we make friends at first sight' (Rajan 1993: 204; emphasis added). Unconvinced, Hiranyaka says that it would be foolhardy to think that because one is virtuous, none shall harm one. The crow offers to bind itself with oaths and remonstrates that friendship with the virtuous is difficult to break, easy to mend and sweet altogether. The mouse says that one must not trust a foe and cites Indra, king of the gods, who smote Vritra after binding himself with strong oaths (Rajan 1993: 204). Trusting an enemy and an indifferent wife is fatal; besides, one must not trust anyone too much. The crow is even more struck by the wisdom of the mouse and ups the ante, saying that it will give up its life if friendship is not granted.

Hiranyaka finally relents, won over by Laghupatanaka's persistence and frankness. He clarifies that he was only testing the intent of the crow, and rushes out to meet him. Halfway out of the fortress, he is assailed by doubt—how can one be sure about the crow's friends? Once again, the crow displays its good heart, saying that it would not sacrifice a virtuous friend. In the Telugu version, the mouse agrees to be a friend but, ever cautious, it bars the crow from ever entering its home (Reddy 1989: 259). At last, the mouse emerges from the fortress and embraces the crow.

It appears that when faced with someone who seeks out one's friendship, even a natural enemy, calculations of equality and utility must be deferred, if not abandoned. One must recognise that 'friendships arise spontaneously and are a blessing of good fortune', and make friends with the good (Rajan 1993: 261). One must take a risk, though it need not be a leap in the dark; all these stories have long exchanges where truthfulness in speech and cleverness is tested; however, maturity and steadiness cannot be gauged without experience (Chandiramani 1995: 56). Of course, not all friendships are based on chance encounters and good fortune; a friend's friend may become one's friend. This is how the mouse is befriended by Manthara, the turtle, who is introduced by the crow. 'Winning of Friends' concludes with a deer, Chitranga, that seeks the friendship of the mouse, crow and turtle. Running from hunters, the deer chances upon the forest where the three friends are assembled; charmed by the sweet speech of the turtle and seeing that they do not pose a danger to him, the deer proposes that they be friends. The turtle demurs, saying that there cannot be any friendship since they are small and cannot help in times of need (Rajan 1993: 251). The deer tells them the story of an elephant herd freed by mice, reminding them that size need not inhibit the virtuous from coming together, and reiterates that one must make friends not only with the powerful, but also with the powerless.

SHARING WIT AND WISDOM

It may appear as if utilitarian calculations dominate the formation of such bonds between unequals. Olivelle has observed that the *Panchatantra*'s second book demonstrates the alliance of the weak in response to external threats. In his words,

> ...[T]he four animals are all weak: a tiny mouse, a slow turtle, a crow who is more a scavenger than a predator, and a deer who is the ultimate prey, the typical object of the hunt. They are also very different, possibly representing the four different habitats: the turtle in the water, the mouse underground, the crow in the air, and the deer on land... Working together, these four unlikely friends with very different skills and coming from diverse backgrounds are able to outwit the greatest threat to an animal, a human hunter who is here represented as death and evil incarnate. (Olivelle 1997: xix)

However, this is to overlook the great joys of friendship which shape and sustain these bonds. Once friendship is struck, it grows with the activities of 'giving and receiving, each other's secrets sharing, dining and entertaining'; the affection between friends is often physically manifest; 'seeing a friend sends shivers of joy, body quivers with delight, eyes tear up with joy' (Rajan 1993: 209). Even when one is dying, the sight of a dear friend is said to bring happiness (ibid.: 255). In fact, it is far better to give up one's life than be parted from dear friends, since life can be regained through rebirth, but not friends (ibid.: 259). A trusted friend is even elevated above one's relatives, such as mother, wife, son and brother. Genuine friendship is not diminished by constant enjoyment, unlike wealth (ibid.: 261).

But the greatest happiness seems to come from exchanging '*subhashitas*', or wise sayings, on *dharma*, *artha*, and *karma*, or fate, etc. 'For the wise, poetry and science suffice to keep the mind occupied// it is only for fools that time passes in sleep, squabbling and hatching mischief// their skin tingles, their limbs thrill, relishing the savour of witty, well turned phrases; men of intellect experience pleasure though they lack the company of women' (Rajan 1993: 254). Whether it is the pigeon Chitragreeva who laments about karma and fate, or the turtle Manthara who also holds forth on fortune, or Hiranyaka who expounds on wealth, friendships are sustained not just by utility, but with shared wisdom, or *subhashitagoshti*.[4] In collective gatherings (*goshti*s) one recalled, traded, polished and modified 'wise sayings' or *subhashita*s, according to the context. They were the fees (*dakshina*) to be collected and given in mutual conversation (Reddy 1989: 322–323).

In this sense, Daud Ali has argued that *subhashita*s constitute a genre of ethical practice; as such, they reflect codes of self-fashioning, aesthetics of virtue, and the collective shaping of ethical discourse through public dialogues of 'well spoken' maxims (Ali 2010: 24). Besides reflecting the prestige of poetry, the ubiquity of poetic verses lent authority to the tales and pithily summed up moral essence, and were thus extremely useful in moral guidance and instruction (Ali 2004: 84). They function as parts of larger moral arguments in narrative contexts, and, as sayings, travelled across genres and contexts into vernacular literary cultures. Instead of dismissing these as just legitimatory or utilitarian, we must see them as a communicative idiom in which there is critical reflection on ethical values, aspirations and resultant tensions (ibid.: 95). They tell us about processes of ethical self-formation, which moves through inner monologues as well as dialogues with friends, wherein fragments of received wisdom are recalled, their ambiguous meanings and contradictory demands are exposed, and the conflicting pulls we experience in specific action contexts are sounded out.

Consider, for instance, the pigeon king Chitragreeva who sees grain spread out in an unlikely spot and is driven towards it by greed, only to get trapped, after which he recalls various sayings about 'being fettered by doom's deadly coils, the feeling heart fate-burdened, the judgment of even the great goes with twisted crooked gait' (Rajan 1993: 195). Similarly, when the hunter sees the birds carry away his net and all in flight, he muses, 'what one is not destined to have is lost even as it lies in the palm of one's hand' (ibid.). That greed can undo one's gains and even be fatal is repeatedly emphasised. There is the jackal which chances upon a dead deer, a dead hunter and a dead boar struck with an arrow and, unable to believe its luck and greedy to save the meat for the future, starts nibbling at the flesh in the bowstring, which comes unstuck and pierces the jackal's head; finally, there is the hunter who, not satisfied with a turtle in hand, decides to also pick up a dead deer and loses both.

Most of all, the four friends discourse on the effort to earn and preserve wealth, especially in the face of adverse fate and wheeling fortune. When the mouse Hiranyaka loses its hoard and is rendered homeless, it gets obsessed with what was lost and tries to regain wealth, in vain. It bewails, 'when a man is penniless, his kinsmen find no time to give him the time of day; his pride takes a beating// his moon of good conduct wanes, vanishes, leaving no trace; in cold indifference his friends turn away//misfortunes swell and burgeon and soon, others' misdeeds are imputed to him' (Rajan 1993: 222). Thus, poverty appears to be the root of all evils, causing shame, depression and dullness. On the one hand, deserted by retainers, Hiranyaka broods upon ways of regaining wealth and honour. On the other, it considers retreating to a forest, thinking that 'men whose heads are held high in honour should choose adversity rather than prosperity'. Then it contemplates begging, thievery and charity to regain wealth. Begging, however, appears as terrible as death, since it requires cringing before the mean and wicked, and destroys a proud spirit. As it is said,

> it is better for the penniless to offer their lives up to the flames than cringe for help before the niggard who has brushed aside the duty to help others//it is better to roam with wild beasts over the mountains and gorges than importune in an abject voice: 'Give', a mean despicable word. (Rajan 1993: 224)

Thievery is pernicious, and charity is also dreadful and a door to death. Thus, the mouse bravely returns to pillaging the grain hoard of the monk who had driven it out, only to be beaten up. Finally, spurning desire as the root cause of all misery and contentment as the highest prosperity, it reconciles itself to destiny and leaves for another land with its friend, the crow, which had also fallen upon hard times.

Manthara the turtle chimes in with another set of wise sayings, which assert that wealth is not everything and that its joys are 'ephemeral like the shade of clouds, cooked food, women and youth'. It is troublesome to acquire and even more trouble to keep, and thus it causes continuous anxiety and sorrow. Moreover, one who is rich is a milch cow that everyone tries to live off, if not defraud and denude. Then, the turtle encourages the dispirited mouse by saying that fortune favours 'a man of mettle, brave and prompt in action', and not one who is lazy and irresolute, trusting in fate. Manthara asserts that Hiranyaka's virtues of hard work, loyalty, gratitude and skill will attract wealth and allies. It adds that an intelligent and resourceful person must not make too much of the difference between native and foreign lands (Rajan 1993: 235), for warriors, scholars and beautiful women make a home wherever they go.

However, wealth must either be used for charity or promptly for one's enjoyment (Rajan 1993: 236). 'No treasure like giving to others, no wealth like contentment, no jewel like good conduct and no gain like health', postulates the turtle (Rajan 1993: 237; Reddy 1989: 318). The miserliness of the industrious is a common occurrence, since everyone is tempted to hoard wealth without enjoying it or giving it away. Saying that the miser in fact hoards for others, the turtle takes a gentle dig at the mouse; the *Hitopadesha* explicitly says that the mouse had accumulated too much (Chandiramani 1995: 71).

Manthara then narrates the story of a weaver who was destined to get no benefit from wealth; he nevertheless labours and hankers for it, until he realises that there is greater benefit in giving away than in guarding over wealth (Rajan 1993: 247). This lesson is hammered home through a discussion between Karta, or doer, and Karma, or deed. Whenever the weaver earns a handsome amount, Karma accosts Karta for giving him more than his due. Karta retorts by saying that he is bound to reward effort and that it is up to Karma to apportion enjoyment or deprivation according to merit. What appears as 'one's fortune' or 'fate' are unveiled as what is 'due' to one, or karmic retribution. Though one may be aware that one's actions bear fruit over time, one may still experience them as 'fate' and get discouraged. Unlike Job's comforters, friends empathise with one's plight and inspire us to act rightly in difficult moments.

Manthara's discourse exemplifies how friends console and persuade, encouraging one another, understanding and forgiving, and mocking and nudging, through a mixture of flattery and gentle threats. There is no straightforward moral lecture, but a tossing about of competing ideas drawn from a range of sources, all of which may not cohere. For instance, there are sayings that counsel being contented and staying put in one place, but also sayings which decry lazy reconciliation and extol exertion. For every adage that elevates destiny, there is another that exhorts effort. Secular sayings drawn from *nitishastra* are mixed with spiritual sayings drawn from hoary texts like the *Bhagavad Gita*. More than reeling out virtues or vices, they unveil how we reason out right action in fits and starts; harkening to our desires and weaknesses, weighing costs and benefits, wondering about fate and destiny, oscillating between the noble and the base passions, vacillating between resignation and enthusiastic action, counting blessings and cutting losses, recalling stories of epic figures and folk tales, and so on. As such, it is strange that Parekh claims that intellectual friendship, where there is a shared pursuit of truth and knowledge, mutual exploration of common problems, and delight in the exchange of ideas and arguments, is absent in the Indian context (Parekh 2008: 164).

Inequality of wealth, lineage or might is nullified by the compatibility in learning and wit that we may find in so-called 'unequals'. As we share our weaknesses and confusions, good friends help strengthen one's virtues and wisdom. Given the unreliability of fortune, sharing one's good fortune with friends, enjoying the company of friends and offering sanctuary to those seeking help distinguish the noble. However, this is not easy, since friends often do not heed good advice and take huge risks. The turtle disregards the advice of his friends and lands up in search of the missing deer, when a hunter, seeing a turtle crawling on land, traps it. Of course, the turtle's resourceful friends, the aforesaid mouse, crow and deer, free him through quick wit by first having the deer feign death, with the crow appearing to peck at its eyes. The hunter, as expected, drops the turtle to chase after the deer, only to have the mouse cut away the turtle's cords and, in the nick of time, the deer runs away. Thus, as Parekh has noted, *sahaya* or mutual help in calamity is an enduring touchstone of Indian friendship (Parekh 2008: 160).

All this analysis should not detract us from the fact that these stories have flourished due to their comic flavour, and show that shared laughter nourishes friendship as much as mutual aid. Lee Siegel has shown that the satiric and humorous constitute the two modes of the comic in India, with the former exposing the gap between the ideal and the real, and the latter exulting in the paradox of wisdom in folly and virtue in vice (Siegel 1989: xviii, 52). It may be seen that both these modes are at work in the frame stories as well as in the didactic stories.

While the *Panchatantra*'s first book was all about intrigue (*bheda*), the second book elevates conciliation and gifts (*sama* and *dana*, respectively) as choice-worthy political virtues (Reddy 1989: 260–261). The overall message of this book is that received maxims such as 'do not make friends with the powerful, especially a natural enemy', or 'do not make friends with someone who shows up all of a sudden', are not to be applied mechanically. In fact, the mouse expresses periodic disaffection (*virakti*) with *nitishastra*, as when he and his friends land in trouble (ibid.: 327). The mouse, eminent in *nitishastra*, is initially repulsing a natural enemy seeking friendship based on these adages, until it is satisfied that they are worth setting aside, judging the crow to be genuine in intent. The next two books pick up on how one could go wrong in such judgments, especially when a former enemy comes as a friend.

THUS FAR AND NO FURTHER

Varying the theme of natural enemies coming as friends, the most critical advice regarding war and peace in the third book is imparted through a story of a former enemy seeking friendship. In this context, an owl-king who had been humiliated in the past by a busybody crow, raids the crows' habitat, pushing the latter to fight or flee. Finding a wise crow minister abandoned, the owl is inclined to grant refuge. Despite an astute minister warning him that 'an enemy who comes as a friend' must be killed right away, the owl-king chooses to be compassionate, and is ruined. Misplaced hospitality is also the theme of the next book of the *Panchatantra*, where a monkey befriends a crocodile resting under its tree by sharing some pleasant fruit and conversation. The crocodile's wife, pleased but not content with the sweet fruit sent by the monkey every day, persuades her dull husband that the monkey's heart may be even sweeter, and beseeches the crocodile to bring him home. While transporting the monkey, the foolish crocodile confesses the wife's bright plan; the monkey quickly befuddles the crocodile, saying that he left his heart in the hollow of the tree and they must go back to fetch it, and thus saves itself. Dumb and hopeful, the crocodile waits and appeals to the monkey, only to be regaled with stories of woes that befall henpecked husbands. Titled 'Loss of Gains' (*Labdhapranasham*), this book drives home the ubiquity of false friends and the pitfalls of trusting a friend who has betrayed one before.

It must be admitted that there are many 'misogynistic' stories portraying women as dull, greedy, self-centred, lusty, myopic, credulous, and so on. Reading against the grain, Naik has argued that the prominence of the adulteress may be interpreted as female resistance to male ordering and control in general, especially in the realm of sexuality (Naik 2016). I am concerned with stories that present them as quick-witted, practical, content and, above all, as equally interested in ethical discussions as males. A shining example is that of a female lapwing who pleads with her husband to migrate since the ocean was devouring all her eggs; her husband refuses, saying that their home on land near the ocean is inherited from their forefathers, and that the ocean is a friend and dares not be hostile. Laughing off his bravado, the female lapwing tells stories of those who do not heed good advice, lack forethought and ready wit, and are thus blind to their own strengths and weaknesses (Rajan 1993: 133). Another striking example is that of a sparrow which faced a similar predicament of losing her eggs to a wild tusker, and set upon revenge. Her best friend, a woodpecker, consoles her and takes her to another friend, a gnat, which then enlists her dear friend, a male frog, and together they devise a trap to kill the elephant. Interspersed in their discussion is the question of 'who is a true friend' and whether helping a friend expecting the return of favours is friendship at all (Reddy 1989: 185). While male bonding dominates the stories, as Olivelle has noted, female friendships are not altogether absent (Olivelle 1997: xli).

Not heeding a good friend's advice is another recurring theme in all five books of the *Panchatantra*, but especially in the last book entitled

Aparikshitakarakam (Rash Deeds). The frame story is a well-known, heart-rending tale of a woman who rears a son and a mongoose with love until, one day, she leaves her husband in charge of her sleeping son; when the latter also takes off, the mongoose slays a snake that had entered the house and, blood-smeared, rushes to meet the mother, who immediately harms it, thinking that the mongoose has killed her son. In this final book, friends often advise one against excessive greed, while in the former books, friends advise against self-interested intrigue (Karataka to Damanaka), excessive craftiness, sentiments, compassion, complacency, naiveté, and so on.

One may ignore a friend's advice because one is moved by the other's plight and thus land in danger oneself, as does the turtle Manthara. Or, because one's wife overrules the friend's advice, as with the crocodile that betrays the monkey's friendship. Or, it may be that one is too confident about overcoming hurdles and ignores dangers staring one in the face. Or, it may be that one assumes that one's present good fortune would continue forever, like the lucky ass clothed in tiger skin and left alone to graze, until it sings.

While friends may ignore good advice, it is binding on us to help them in their calamity. That this may not always be possible is the last lesson of the *Panchatantra*, where four friends set out in search of wealth and meet a magician who gives them each a quill, saying that wherever it falls on their journey, they will find their treasure. Where their respective quills fall, the first three find copper, silver and gold, respectively, and return contented. The fourth one decides that he would continue further on to find gems, and on his journey sees a man standing with a wheel whirling on his head. As soon as he asks the man about his plight, and whether he could find some water to drink, the wheel lands upon his own head. It appears that the lord of wealth had devised this torture to prevent humans from stealing the divine hoard. The third merchant prince, who found gold, waits for his friend to return and, when he does not, goes on to find him in this tortured state. Saddened, Suvarnasiddhi (Gold-finder) tells him stories of imprudent greed and requests permission to leave, while Chakradhara (Wheel-bearer) counters with stories that show fate triumphing over prudence. What is touching is that exchanging stories provides solace even in extreme adversity, such as the torture borne by the wheel-bearer. Unable to help him further, Suvarnasiddhi finally takes his leave with a heavy heart, while Chakradhara waits for some other greedy person to come along to be freed from the torture. In the Telugu version, the wheel-bearer ironically cautions the friend on the perils of travelling alone, even as he is left alone (Reddy 1989: 294). Despite these difficulties, why does the *Panchatantra* espouse the charms of friendships with unequals and strangers?

IF A MAN COMES AS A FRIEND, HOW CAN I REJECT HIM?

Before the *Panchatantra*, the two Indian epics the *Ramayana* and the *Mahabharata* repeatedly play with friendships between unequals, and the attendant joys. Rama's friendship towards Hanuman, and Krishna's friendship towards Arjuna as well as towards Sudama/Kuchela exemplify some aspects of a perfect relationship. Rama, the epic hero of the *Ramayana*, when approached by Vibheeshana, the brother of his arch-enemy Ravana, 'seeking service and sanctuary', asks 'if a man comes as a friend, how can I reject him?' (Rajagopalachari 1980: 270). In fact, Rama is committed to granting refuge to whoever comes to him; if Ravana himself were to come, he says, he would not reject him.

Rama's friendship with Hanuman is fascinating, for it shows the dependence of a god-man on a monkey. Hanuman's sweet and apt speech, miraculous acts and superlative astuteness pave the way for Rama's victory over Ravana. In not knowing his own strength and delivering more than was asked of him, Hanuman is like god himself. Rama is glad when Hanuman agrees with him that Vibheeshana must be accepted as a friend, for 'a good man is glad when a friend's opinion supports his decision on a question of duty' (Rajagopalachari 1980: 270). Rama is saddened that he could not reward Hanuman adequately for the supreme joy he brought through his success. It is a simple pearl necklace that Sita garlands him with that Hanuman regards as a supreme gift. In all this, it is not at all clear that Rama, the god-man, is superior to his devoted friend, even though appearances favour such an assumption.

Throughout the *Mahabharata*, the question of whether friendship is possible only between equals is explicitly thematised and subtly negated in the Duryodhana–Karna, Drona–Drupada, Krishna–Arjuna and

Krishna–Kuchela relationships. In the Drona–Drupada story, Drupada refuses to acknowledge his childhood friend Drona after becoming king, saying that only equals can be friends. An offended Drona gets his disciples to defeat Drupada, conquers his kingdom, spares his life, and returns half his kingdom, so that they can be friends as equals! Duryodhana, an heir-apparent, adopts Karna, who was humiliated for being a charioteer's son after he had matched Arjuna's skills, by instantly enthroning him as the king of Anga (Rajagopalachari 1999: 45).

The crowning jewel is, of course, Krishna's friendship with Arjuna, which is celebrated as the archetype of the divine–human relationship. As J. L. Mehta has noted, Krishna seeks Arjuna first, makes gestures of friendship, advises him to abduct his own sister, and is delighted when Arjuna freely chooses him over his army (cited in Jackson 1992: 123–124). Parekh notes that Krishna tells occasional lies and even breaks his vows in order to protect Arjuna, such as when he fears that Arjuna may not be able to kill Jayadrata by sunset the following day, and decides to break his pledge not to engage in active combat (Parekh 2008: 159). Hence, Krishna's friendship with Arjuna at once moves and troubles discerning minds. Balarama openly says that Krishna's affection for Arjuna has misled him into approving the war (Rajagopalachari 1999: 263). Even so, what is striking here is the Indian penchant for unequal friendships and the transcendence, if not inversion, of who-needs-who issues.

Devotional lore played up the same in the celebrated friendship between Krishna and Sudama (or Kuchela). Sudama was a childhood friend, with whom Krishna had studied the *Veda*s in the *gurukul* (teacher's residence). Racked by poverty, Sudama's wife suggests that he go and see Krishna, who is ruling over Dwaraka. Desirous of seeing his Lord, Sudama wonders aloud what he could take to give to a king, when his wife packs some flattened rice she had begged from the neighbours. Sudama goes to the palace of Rukmini and, sighting him from a distance, Krishna rushes to embrace him and 'felt instant ecstasy upon touching the body of his friend and shed tears of love' (Prabhupada 1977: Canto 10, Chapter 80, Verse 19). Not only does the Lord wash Sudama's feet, he also sprinkles some of the water with which the feet were washed on his own head. He worships Sudama with incense and lamps, and fondly recalls how they held hands and wandered about in childhood, having lost their way in a forest where they went to fetch firewood for their teacher. Praising Sudama for his knowledge of the *Veda*s and aversion to sense pleasures, Krishna proceeds to inquire after his wife and, when Sudama is reluctant to offer what he had brought, grabs the flattened rice and eats a handful! Ecstatic that his friend had not forgotten him despite his opulence, Sudama returns home, only to find that it had been transformed beyond recognition by untold riches bestowed by the Lord.

Again and again, the epics suggest that friendship has little to do with equality of wealth or usefulness. In Rajaji's words, 'the hearts of good men meet and instantly come together. As the Kural says, the spontaneous mutual attraction of two hearts and not long acquaintance creates friendship…' (Rajagopalachari 1980: 178). In his view, the art of friendship was governed by a spiritual law that was both simple and taxing. Neither effort nor mutual advantage but openness to the unexpected sources that nourish and provoke us to give freely seems to be at the heart of friendship. The helping forces, be it a bird, or a monkey, a humble boatman or even a *rakshasi* (demoness) compel humans and gods to respond with generosity. These are what Friedrich Nietzsche calls 'star friendships', the association of those whose orbits make contact briefly, but will part again. Alphonso Lingis explores this other 'solar economy' of expenditure without recompense in his work. Here, the sun, as that which gives forth freely to one and all, is the paradigm (Lingis 1983: 149).

To an extent, the *Panchatantra* also affirms the epic imperative of responding to the appeal of one who comes seeking friendship, and the sheer nobility of accepting even an enemy who comes as a friend.

But it is also attuned to the risks posed by 'natural' as well as 'accidental enemies', and aspires to train the young princes in handling the consequences if things go awry. Prudence suggests some thumb rules: as Hiranyaka demonstrates, one must first test a natural enemy coming as a friend and not assume that no harm will befall one just because one is virtuous. If a weak former enemy who is shrewd and loyal to his king comes as a friend, one must reject his overtures, unlike the owl-king who readily took in the 'defector' crow. Another rule is that a friend who is loyal but foolish is more dangerous than an enemy who is noble and intelligent. The monkey which kills the king trying to save him from a bee, or the singing ass which endangers its jackal friend instead of grazing quietly, are foolish and hence avoidable. Book I leaves us in no doubt that even among natural friends, such as the two jackals Karataka and Damanaka, there is a need to avoid rogues and rascals.

EQUALISING FRIENDSHIP

All this resonates with the Stoic view that loyalty, frankness, sociability, sympathy and goodwill were the marks of friendship. Friends are to be cherished because they give counsel, encouragement, comfort and reproof (Cicero 1991: 24). Conversation among friends 'redoubleth the joys and cutteth griefs in halfs', as Francis Bacon put it (Bacon 1965: 114). Bacon also noted that it conduces to the clearing of one's mind, such that one gains more by an hour's discourse than by a day's meditation (ibid.: 115–116). Besides, a friend's admonition works better than a good book in preventing gross errors. The *Panchatantra* demonstrates all this and more.

But what is strikingly different in Western thought is the dominant idea that friendship flourishes best between equals, and that too much disproportion in wisdom, virtue or wealth will destroy the basis of friendship (Cropsey 1977: 267). Arguably, this is first shown by Plato, who depicts Socrates as a 'friend' of Athens who is beneficial to the city, but its powerful and wealthy politicians charge him with treason because he exposes their ignorance of real justice. By persuading the young to seek *sophia* (wisdom) about justice or piety, Socrates shows that the highest type of friendship cares for the soul. While Plato and Xenophon turn out to be good friends, Alcibiades brings a bad reputation to Socrates due to his lacking the discipline needed to pursue wisdom. This raises the question of whether there can be genuine friendship between those who are wise and those who are politically powerful and ambitious, due to the disproportion in wisdom and virtue.

Still, the political significance of friendship was recognised by Aristotle, who is famous for noting that where there is friendship, there may be no need for justice, but where there is justice, there is still need for friendship. It is in the process of educating potential rulers in *phronesis*, or practical wisdom about justice, that Aristotle links friendship and equality. Aristotle believes that friendship can hold cities together, and legislators must be even more earnest about it than justice (Irwin 1985: 208). Justice is partly corrective, restoring to everyone what is his own, and partly distributive, giving to each what he deserves (Cropsey 1977: 265). In friendship, humans fulfil the demands of justice without exhortation or punishment (Bloom 1993: 413). For this reason, Aristotle also holds that lawgivers must foster friendships between citizens. For this to happen, they must experience great friendships themselves. Friendship means liking or loving others for some good that they control, or that resides in them, and can be had from, with or through them. He also knew that this liking need not be for what is good in itself, or what is truly good for one, but what *appears* to be good, and thus classifies friendships to be based on pleasure, utility or virtue (Irwin 1985: 210). Because it involves exchange, Aristotle writes:

> Within each type, some friendships rest on equality, while others correspond to superiority. For equally good people can be friends, but also a better and a worse person; and the same is true of friends for pleasure or utility, since they may be either equal or unequal in their benefits. Hence equals must equalize in loving and in the other things, because of their equality; and unequals must make the return that is proportionate to the types of superiority. (Irwin 1985: 232)

Joseph Cropsey clarifies that equality in friendship means equality primarily regarding quantity, and secondarily according to merit, in contrast to equality in matters of justice, where it is first according to merit and then quantity (Cropsey 1977: 267). If there is a wide gap in virtue, vice, wealth or something else, then people find that they are friends no more, just as there is no friendship with gods or kings. Aristotle asserts that 'worthless people do not expect to be friends with the best or wisest' (Irwin 1985: 221).

Of course, disputes nevertheless arise 'only or most often' in utility friendships, as compared to pleasure or virtue relationships. In friendships between the virtuous, friends want to benefit one another, while friends who come together for pleasure also benefit from each other. Whereas in utilitarian relations, one who has received benefits thinks that it was a small thing for the benefactor, while the latter thinks that this was the biggest thing he had. The fair thing here would be a return proportionate to the utility that the recipient received, though it would be finer if it were more (Irwin 1985: 235). The benefit received by the first beneficiary according to the worth he put on it before he got it must be the measure of repayment.

Similar disputes also arise in friendships between unequals and those with dissimilar aims. In the former, a better or a more beneficial person always thinks he deserves more from the friendship, while the inferior thinks that it is no use to be a friend of an excellent or powerful person if you are not going to gain anything by it. Aristotle says it is right for each to expect more, but not more of the same thing; the superior should get more honour and the inferior, more profit (Irwin 1985: 236). More intriguing is the following:

> In all the friendships corresponding to superiority, the loving must also be proportional, e.g. the better person, and the more beneficial, and each of the others likewise, must be loved more than he loves; for when the loving reflects the comparative worth of friends, equality is achieved in a way, and this seems proper to friendship. (Irwin 1985: 226)

Lorraine Smith Pangle has explained that the inferior should bestow more affection than he receives (Pangle 2003: 57). This kind of 'distribution equalises and preserves' the friendship. Even in the 'best' friendships between the virtuous, there is an expectation and obligation of equal return. To quote Aristotle, 'when a good person becomes a friend, he becomes a good for his friend…and repays in equal measure the wish and pleasantness of his friend; for friendship is said to be equality' (Irwin 1985: 217). After an exhaustive analysis of Aristotle's views, Pangle concludes that ordinary friendship thrives on a rough equality of benefits, and in mature friendships, equal merit is needed for partners to share their most important activities of philosophising and being virtuous (Pangle 2003: 198). Prudence requires that we gather around us, in the most thoughtful way, people to make one's own because, and to the extent that, they are suitable companions in life's most important activities (ibid.). Michel de Montaigne's friendship with Étienne de La Boétie, where he tells us about the mysterious consonance of their wills, how they became 'one soul in two bodies' and were 'equal partners in everything', 'second selves' to one another is the celebrated example here (Montaigne 1958: 97, 103). Calling it a complete and perfect bond, Montaigne admits that so many factors are required to build it up that 'it is something if fate achieves it once in three centuries' (ibid.: 92).

Lingis has observed that this emphasis on equality stems from the desire to 'rationalise' all social existence so that it becomes an exchange of complementary values; honour and affection become social currency with which goods and pleasures can be repaid (Lingis 1983: 139). There needs to be a continuous circulation of goods, pleasures and virtues, and for this, each movement of the same must be compensated for, and hence the principle of equality is salient (ibid.: 138). But is it always possible to 'equalise friendships' through proportional returns?

Aristotle is aware that there is no proper measure of returning 'proportionately' what is gained, say a benefactor's goodwill, or a philosopher's grace in sharing wisdom with us. In these cases, there cannot be friendship, because one is always in debt. We do what we can, and not what is equivalent or deserved (as towards parents and gods). If so, why should the superior become friends at all with an inferior, say a political philosopher towards the city, or a wealthy and powerful man towards a poor man, or an excellent person towards an ordinary one? Aristotle argues that benefactors love more than they are loved, just like mothers love their children more than the fathers, or as poets and craftsmen love their products. This is because they are doing what is noble, actively expending effort rather than just receiving the good. Aristotle holds that magnanimity, in terms of sharing good fortune with others, is finer than having them share our ill-fortune and suffering. In fact, a 'manly' person would not share his ill-fortune with friends, but will assist them in their ill-fortune (Irwin 1985: 264). For these reasons, Cropsey observes that the philosopher-statesman will deign to benefit the city. But such altruism and magnanimity from those in power cannot be taken for granted.

Due to the numerous equality calculations, it appears that political friendships involving rulers are doomed because of the significant power differentials. By political friendship, I mean the relations between people in power, people sharing the same partisan ideology or party identity, as well as friendships between citizens. Those in power seem incapable of rising to the demands of friendship, often betraying friends to fulfil their ambition. Machiavelli's prince has no friends. Judith Shklar echoes this when she writes, 'politically powerful people make use of or enjoy the presence of others but they are not as a rule capable of friendship' (Shklar 1984: 215). They cannot endure the frankness of friends. Ruminating on the way Hal terminates his friendship with Falstaff in Shakespeare's *Henry IV*, Allan Bloom observes,

> Hal, whose side decency forces to take against Falstaff, has the upper hand in the relationship and performs the hard deeds connected with terminating it. This shows something about politics and the essentially friendless character of the king, who has *no equals* and must subordinate the highest things to raisons d'état. (Bloom 1993: 404; emphasis added)

Then again, Pangle has noted that good people may not want to be friends with those superior in wealth or power for long, because the latter demand loyalty and gratitude, whereas the former value justice and integrity (Pangle 2003: 100).

Similar pessimism also arises with respect to political friendships between partisans, or those who share common causes. Drawing upon Stoic sources, Shklar unpacks 'republican politics where men participated in politics together as allies, friends on behalf of a common cause and who loved and hated each other passionately as a result' (Shklar 1993: 207). Friends who are willing to fight and die for a common cause are admired and suspect in all regimes. The image of a friend in extreme danger has sparked many a debate on to whom does one owe allegiance; given the acuteness of this problem during political revolution or reaction, it has also been asked: who or what is a friend? Analysing such a friendship between the American founders John Adams and Thomas Jefferson, Shklar highlights how the memory of their collaboration on the Declaration of Independence 'illuminated their friendship to its last day' (ibid.: 208). But these political friendships are often marred by competition and rivalry when disagreements arise and become acute, as happened with Adams and Jefferson. Even in ordinary times, political disagreements often drive a wedge between good friends. Hence, Shklar reminds us, 'politics and friendship do not mix, but the most complete form of friendships may well be political' (ibid.: 207).

A third kind of political friendship, pertaining to the civic bonding between citizens, has evoked much interest recently. Following another line of Aristotle's thought, John Cooper has argued for civic friendships where common benefits and advantages may be the starting point. But there is also mutual goodwill, trust, well-wishing and interest in character that is not present in purely commercial relationships (Cooper 1993: 319). Civic friendships train us in relating to and caring for others who are not blood relatives, and thus enlarge our consciousness. Such a form of caring can moderate the conflicts and resentment unleashed by justice claims in a democratic context. From an analogous perspective, Marilyn Friedman has refocused attention on friendship as offering a mode of relating to others through choice, and opines that 'it is more likely than other relationships such as family and neighborhood to be grounded and sustained by shared interests and values, mutual affection and possibilities for generating mutual respect and esteem' (Friedman 1992: 114). Jacques Derrida has been critical of this Aristotelian stress on similarity and brotherhood, which marks the modern vocabulary of sovereignty, power and representation. Recognising the seminal role of friendship and hospitality in organising the political, he espouses non-reciprocity and singularity to deepen democratic engagement with the 'other' (Bennington 1997).

But it is Cicero who questioned Aristotle's equality calculus most vigorously early on, and his lead has been followed only by Bacon. Cicero denounced limiting friendship to an exact equality in mutual good offices and good feelings, as if it were a debtor and creditor account (Cicero 1991). He claimed that true friends are generous, and unafraid of giving or receiving more than what is justly owed. In Cicero's view, there is no difference between ordinary and outstanding people in their need for friendship (ibid.: 72). This is true especially of the philosopher, who perhaps begins without equals (*a la* Socrates), and raises his friends (Plato/Xenophon) to become his equals. Cicero extolled the goodwill and constancy of genuine friends, advising us to choose friends who are frank, sociable and sympathetic. Bacon recognised that the 'ease and discharge of the fullness and swellings of the heart' that enlivens friendship is so attractive that even the wisest of princes hazard their safety and greatness by raising some of their subjects and servants to become their companions and equals (Bacon 1965: 113). He added that 'there is little friendship in the world, least of all between equals and that whatever exists is between a superior and inferior' (Bacon 1965: 172). He gives the examples of Sulla, who raised Pompey, and Caesar, who raised Brutus only to die at his hands, showing the great lengths to which we go for securing friendships. Opening the heart, getting faithful counsel, clarifying our thoughts through discoursing with one another, being rescued from error through admonition, and receiving aid in all actions from friends are so irresistible that the powerful hazard their safety and greatness for the same. In setting aside equality, Bacon recognises that rulers, unlike philosophers, are unfazed by the fear of betrayal when it comes to making friends. While Cicero and Bacon are very instructive, it cannot be gainsaid that the *Panchatantra* impresses these insights upon our minds through unparalleled entertainment.

CONCLUSION

As we saw, after highlighting the betrayal, estrangement, and separation of good friends in the very first book, the *Panchatantra* persists in showing that friendships often happen between unequals, and one's practical wisdom must be cultivated to address both the promise and the risks. Recall that the addressees were Ugra Shakti (Fierce Power), Vasu Shakti (Rich Power) and Ananta Shakti (Endless Power), who were 'averse to learning'. They must be made fluent in *niti* or practical wisdom, which is pre-eminently about steering away from extremes. Conventional *niti*, which counsels that one must follow self-interest and expediency, or make friends with equals, is questioned in favour of ethical prudence. All would be fine if we mechanically applied prudential maxims which discourage making friends with strangers or 'natural enemies'. Instead of dishing out straightforward moral maxims, the *Panchatantra* cultivates our *niti* by churning the heart, kindling the desire to be good, and shaping our emotions and sentiments.

In friendship, our practical wisdom is weaned away from narrow opportunism to caring for another who is not necessarily a blood relative. Spontaneous and disinterested goodwill towards a stranger who comes professing admiration or distress (the lion towards the bull in Book I, and the mouse towards the crow and the turtle towards the mouse in Book II) is the originary moment which sets great friendships in motion. Even for ordinary people, magnanimity towards a stranger who seeks refuge is irresistible and disrupts self-interested considerations. We come to understand and share the needs of strangers through friendship. A ruler must experience the joys of a great friendship even if he is blessed with shrewd advisors and ministers. Of course, like the mouse, we are encouraged to test those who come seeking our friendship, and not assume that all who come calling are noble and, that since we are good, no harm will befall us. There are other thumb rules, such as avoiding a loyal but foolish seeker, being circumspect about a former enemy coming as a friend, and so on.

Great friends move us to rise above utilitarian concerns and discover the joys of sharing. Good friends help us tread the path of virtue under adverse conditions through mutual aid and timely advice. Greed and self-interest are especially tamed by good friends in the *Panchatantra*. But we also neglect their counsel, involve them in trouble and cause grief. By understanding and condoning their lapses, we grasp the contingent circumstances affecting conduct and the triumph of affection over cunning reason. Most friendships are mixed up, in that we cherish mutual help and loyalty as well as wit and wisdom. We learn to balance interest and affection, loyalty and frank criticism, dependence and reciprocity, trust and good sense, and so on. M. K. Gandhi, Jawaharlal Nehru, C. Rajagopalachari and Vallabhbhai Patel were all great friends because they criticised one another on social justice, economic policy or non-violence without rancour, and without eschewing their affection for one another. Ambedkar also recognised that friendship (*maitri*) was necessary for deepening equality and freedom (Kapoor and Bhagavan 2018: 243–254).[5]

The *Panchatantra* also attunes us to the risks of friendship where the fear of betrayal is ever-present. If one is judicious, exclusive friendship will not detract one from the duties of public office. If not, there are bound to be intrigues by parasites and onlookers left out in the cold. These may be inspired either by self-interest or by 'reasons of state', or both. While all residual doubt about the other's fidelity cannot be overcome, the most important warning is about one's own proneness to rashness vis-a-vis unequal friends. We tend to judge too early, too fast, and may err greatly in the process.

Notes

1. Rajan's version concludes with Karataka's admonishment, while the Telugu translation concludes with Damanaka's advice.

2. In the *Hitopadesha*, which is more coherent, 'Winning of Friends' comes before 'Estrangement of Friends'.

3. The nobility of the pigeon in this episode is repeatedly stressed in the *Amar Chitra Katha* comic *Hitopadesha: Choice of Friends* (Pai 1975: 5–7).

4. The term *subhashitagoshti* occurs frequently in the Telugu translation of the *Panchatantra* (Reddy 1989: 260, 262, 322, 323, 336), justifying the emphasis here.

5. I am grateful to Raman Kumar for sharing with me the essay by Anjani Kapoor and Manu Bhagavan (2018: 243–254).

III

WAR AND PEACE

Dangerous Remedies and Real Success in the *Hitopadesha*

War and peace are political topics that elicit the most candid and penetrating discussions of practical wisdom in classical texts everywhere. All three texts which are treated here, *Arthashastra*, *Panchatantra* and *Hitopadesha*, provide ample material for analysis in this context. Usually, the *Arthashastra*'s political realism is the showpiece, with many scholars delighting in Kautilya's unequivocal, unsentimental and ruthless advice. Some justify Kautilya's harsh measures as dictated by the anarchy of his time, while others wonder whether his realism did not pave the way for Ashoka's idealism later (Boesche 2003: 14). Calling him the 'first great political realist', Roger Boesche observed that Kautilya recognised that every nation acts to maximise its power and self-interest, and therefore moral principles or obligations have little or no force in actions among nations (ibid.: 17). War and peace are considered solely from the viewpoint of profit; and diplomacy and foreign policy are just extensions of warfare (ibid.: 18–19). Evidence for this interpretation is overwhelming, given Kautilya's colourful use of mendicants, nuns, orphans, courtesans and wandering minstrels as spies, propagandists, poisoners and assassins.

It is not surprising that these elements were fully plumbed by literary texts like *Mudrarakshasa* to great effect. *Niti* texts like the *Hitopadesha* also suggest that the naked aggrandisement for glory and profit must be tempered by a notion of symbolic sovereignty vis-a vis other powers. They explore the right strategy for powers of equal strength, rather than for a mighty conqueror; they show wise counselors struggling to deflect proud kings from hawkish ministers and destructive wars. In the process, what do they have to say about the origins of war? What kinds of advice are peddled by ministers in the face of aggression? What desperate measures are attempted in war? What are the obstacles to peace, and which opponents are deserving of peace? What kinds of peace exist, and which is preferable in specific contexts? I track these and other questions in the *Panchatantra* and *Hitopadesha* to show how Kautilya's famous *shadgunya*, or six strategies on war and peace, were received, affirmed and modified. In the process, I flesh out ethical aspects of realist prudence that usually get eclipsed in Kautilya scholarship.

REALIST PRUDENCE

Kautilya's felicity for realist prudence is in full display in his elaboration of *shadgunya*, his sixfold policy of peace, war, neutrality, preparing to march, seeking protection and double policy. His standpoint is that of a conqueror who is seen as the hub of the wheel of states (Rangarajan 1987: 550). He begins by saying that a conqueror should always endeavour to increase his own power, which is threefold: intellectual (good counsel), physical (treasury and army) and psychological (valour and enthusiasm) (ibid.: 559). The conqueror operates within a circle of states, which includes contiguous neighbours who are natural enemies, and enemies' neighbours who are possible allies (ibid.: 555). The circle comprises twelve states: the conqueror's enemies in the front and rear; his allies in the front and rear; the friends of his allies in the front and rear; allies and friends of his enemies in the front and rear; and the middle and neutral kings (ibid.: 557). Within this system, a conqueror chooses his policy according to whether his power is in decline, progressing or static vis-a-vis the enemy. This depends on whether the enemy is equal, superior or inferior to the conqueror's own present power. To know this, one must assess the relative strengths of the *saptanga* or seven constituents of a state, including the king, groups of ministers and high officials, territory, forts and cities, treasury, army and allies. Kautilya thus exhaustively lays out the possible permutations and combinations of friends, enemies, allies and neutral kings in the front and rear, the configuration of different constituents of sovereignty within each kingdom, the right strategy for inferior, superior and equal powers, and the profit from war as well as different kinds of peace, and so on. Thus there are seventy-two elements that a conqueror must deliberate over as he applies the sixfold strategy. And, as Henry Kissinger puts it:

> [A]ll elements were relevant, calculable and amenable to manipulation toward a leader's strategic aims. Geography, finance, military strength, diplomacy, espionage, law, agriculture, cultural traditions, morale and popular opinion, rumors and legends, and men's vices and weaknesses needed to be shaped as a unit by a wise king to strengthen and expand his realm, much as a modern orchestra conductor shapes the instruments in his charge to a coherent tune. (Kissinger 2014: 197)

In principle, he must wage war against a king who is weaker rather than stronger than himself. One who fights a stronger king is crushed like a foot soldier fighting an elephant, whereas one who fights an inferior gains a resounding victory, like a stone striking a mud pot (Rangarajan 1987: 566). Enhancing the power and profit of the conqueror without endangering security is the hallmark of practical wisdom for Kautilya. It is not ideology or honour but tangible result in terms of wealth gained that underpins his discussion. Progress is measured in terms of success in building forts, irrigation works, trade routes, new settlements, elephants or productive forests, opening new mines, and so on, and also subverting similar works of the enemy (ibid.: 553). Since such progress is fragile, given that the enemy is aspiring for the same, a conqueror must be ever attentive to the dynamic changes within the circle, and calibrate his strategy accordingly. A conqueror may go to war also to help an ally or subdue a rear enemy. Besides waging direct war, he may declare war and keep quiet, or wage secret war (sudden assaults when the enemy is suffering from a calamity), or undeclared war (through secret agents and occult practices) (ibid.: 569). In fact, Kautilya's discussion of clandestine methods, such as sowing discord among the enemy's courtiers and officers, spreading propaganda, using women and mendicants as spies, using assassination as a weapon of choice, poisoning water and burning food crops, etc., demonstrates that all means were allowed for success. Even during a time of diplomacy and negotiated peace, a conqueror would be sowing dissension to weaken even allies who would be future prey (Boesche 2003: 21).

Conversely, a king who is weak and at the receiving end may decide to submit to the power of the conqueror, since the outcome of war is uncertain and the latter may gain by force anyway. Though Kautilya's discussion of *shadgunya* begins with a definition of peace and elaborates many varieties of peace agreements, it is all from the standpoint of the survival of a weaker or inferior king (Shamasastry 1919: 300). If advantages from war and peace are equal, then peace is to be preferred, since loss of power and wealth are endemic to war. Neither war nor peace can be ends in themselves within the circle of states. As Boesche notes, Kautilya did not say 'prepare for war but hope for peace but prepare for war and plan to conquer' (Boesche 2003: 19).

This has all led to the view that Kautilya's prudence is realist rather than utopian and moralistic. His advice is oriented towards survival and furthering self-interest, rather than glory. Even sanguine goals require the use of unpalatable means, not to mention predatory conquest. As R. N. Berki has observed, goodness, in the realist context, connotes sufficiency, competence and ability to get on and utilise possibilities in a given situation, rather than abstract moral virtue (Griffiths 1992: 5). There is a telling illustration of this in Vishakhadatta's *Mudrarakshasa*, where Chanakya is trying to gain intellectual power (*mantra shakti*) by co-opting the able minister Rakshasa, who is loyal to the vanquished Nanda king even after the latter's death. Knowing that the wise and astute Rakshasa would not switch sides even if one member of the Nanda family remained alive, Chanakya contrives to exterminate it to the last person, including a renunciate, Sarvarthasiddhi.

Whatever residual moral advice Kautilya may give appears to be oriented to ensuring success, rather than shaping the character of the rulers or the ruled. For instance, among targets to be attacked, if the choice is between two neighbour-enemies equally affected by calamities, of which one is vulnerable and the other is hostile, Kautilya advises that the hostile one be attacked first. This is because the unfriendly king will not help in attacking the other, whereas the vulnerable king might help in defeating the enemy. Pushing this line further, he argues that among two kings unequally affected by calamities as well, the hostile one with less trouble must be preferred over the neighbouring king, who may be seriously affected and, thus, more vulnerable. Kautilya then explicitly disagrees with his teachers, who prefer 'easy targets' (Rangarajan 1987: 573). The hostile king must be tackled early, lest his power grows. On a different subject of just and unjust kings with disaffected subjects, the unjust king must be chosen; similarly, an unjust but strong king must be chosen for attack over a just but weak king (ibid.). All this is eminently practical, for one who attacks a righteous king is hated by his own people. After conquering a new territory, a king is advised to treat the new subjects magnanimously in order to gain their loyalty (Boesche 2003: 30). Even with regard to a weak king who is an ideal target, if he is submissive in all respects, then the powerful king must conclude peace and not provoke the weak king's anger, as this may alienate him from the circle of states. Similarly, the weak and inferior king suing for peace must also assess whether the superior is just, or greedy, or demonic, and while he may seek the protection of a just superior, he is advised to fight the latter kinds through intrigue (Shamasastry 1919: 547–548).

However superficial, political prudence is not completely wrenched from ethics, to the extent that attacking and winning vis-a-vis enemies is tempered with an assessment of their justice and virtues. Kautilya also recognises that the claims of power and enthusiasm must be moderated by deliberation, and war should be the last resort. In fact, there is room for goodness in judging and offsetting gains and losses, both in the short and long term, while applying the sixfold strategy. For instance, discussing the strategy of seeking protection, he begins by saying that one may seek the protection of a king stronger than or equal to the might of the aggressor, or one who may be less powerful than the aggressor but is energetic, upright and opposed to the aggressor, depending on the circumstances. Furthermore, between two such kings, one who is immune to the intrigues of the enemy is to be preferred; between two kings equally immune to the wiles of the aggressor, one who has better counsellors and surrounds himself with 'wise elders' is preferable, and so on (Rangarajan 1987: 665). Kautilya then also hints that there is no 'greater evil' for kings than an alliance with a king of considerable power, unless one is actually attacked (Shamasastry 1919: 375).

Given the high level of abstraction and lack of historical examples, the contextual dynamics of deliberating about war and peace are obscured in the *Arthashastra*. A few scholars have cursorily discussed how the *Panchatantra* reworks the heavy and serious ideas of the *Arthashastra* for pedagogical purposes, without losing its moral compass (Gautam 2015: 11, 29, 38). But the subtle ways in which these literary texts criticise and modify Kautilya's ideas is missing. As with any compendium, it is worthwhile to ask: what elements of *shadgunya* were usually picked up, and why? What are the circumstances that defy a straightforward application of one of the six strategies? How, in fact, is the relative strength of rival powers assessed, especially their *mantra shakti*, or the power of wise counsel? What is to be done when rational deliberation is cast aside by the power and enthusiasm of kings? Is there any room for goodness in such deliberations about what is to be done?

WARMONGERS AND CAUSELESS QUARRELS

The *Panchatantra*'s third book *Kakolukiyam* (Of Crows and Owls) picks up the question of war between equals, and the *Hitopadesha*'s third book *Vigraha* (War) delves further into the conduct of war. The *Hitopadesha* is, in fact, is more complete in that it deals with war and ends with peace (*Sandhi*, the fourth book), while the *Panchatantra* concludes with 'rash deeds', and does not explicitly thematise peace. Both books espouse the standpoint of a weak or inferior power, rather than of the conqueror. Both embroider Kautilyan ideas regarding war and peace with hilarious stories, even as they differ in the details. The *Panchatantra* harps on Kautilya's 'double policy', pursuing peace while actually preparing for war, especially when an inferior power is threatened by a superior power. The *Hitopadesha* harkens to Kautilya's advice about resorting to a fort and showing valour to thwart an invader. Both books are structured in a way that deliberately plays with the reader, making her now sympathetic towards the crows, now towards the owls (in *Panchatantra*), or between swans and cranes on the one hand, and peacocks and sundry birds on the other (in *Hitopadesha*). *Kakolukiyam* is meant to push the overall moral that one must never disregard an enemy at the gates due to laziness or indifference. *Vigraha* holds that war between equals is inadvisable in general. On the surface, these books appear to set aside ethical concerns and elevate survival over honour or glory. But there is more than meets the eye in their deceptively simple narratives.

In both these texts, war is triggered between two parties due to unnecessary talk by a busybody of one group; in the *Panchatantra*, the crows find themselves being repeatedly raided by the neighbouring owl-king Arimardana (Foe-crusher), and the king of the crows asks a hereditary counsellor about the reasons for this enmity. Once upon a time, a crow chanced upon the consecration festivities of an owl, which had been chosen to be king by the birds. The birds, exasperated by their hereditary king who was busy worshipping Lord Vishnu, felt that they needed someone to more actively protect them. They brought all the waters from the sacred streams and 108 herbs; set up the lion throne; drew a picture of the earth with seven continents, seas and mountains; spread out the tiger skin; and laid out golden jars with tender sprouts and rice for offerings (Rajan 1993: 282). Bards and priests began recitations and drums were beaten to lustrate the owl, when a crow flew in from nowhere (ibid.)! Recalling that the barber is the smartest among men and the crow smartest among birds, the birds solicit the gate-crasher's views on their decision to anoint the owl (ibid.: 283).

A picture of frankness, the crow laughed at their choice and lectured them on how they could do better than elevating one who is blind by day and cruel by nature. It narrated a story about how by merely uttering the powerful name of their sovereign, Garuda, the birds can keep out of harm's way. It upbraided them on the folly of elevating a mean one to judge their disputes. Far from giving them protection, they may need to protect themselves from the new king. The crow successfully dissuaded the birds, who abandoned the consecration rite and flew away; it then repented its folly in incurring the great enmity of the owl for no reason. Defaming others in public, with no sense of place and time, is imprudent. One would not consume poison thinking that a physician is close at hand. The owl declared that since the crow had harmed him needlessly, and without provocation, there would be enmity between them henceforth.

The *Hitopadesha* also rehearses the rather unnecessary beginnings of war. Here, swans are embroiled in a war with peacocks because of a busybody crane. The crane annoys the peacocks by boasting that its swan-king was great, whereupon the peacocks retort that the crane was insulting their king while grazing in their fields, that the swan-king was meek, could not provide protection and did not deserve a kingdom, and so on. The situation spirals out of control when the loud-mouthed crane, produced before the peacock-king, further displays its valour, asserting that the swan-king is supreme and suggests that this be confirmed by a war (Chandiramani 1995: 173). Hearing this, the swan-king submits that one must know one's strengths and weaknesses, lest one be killed like the weak old donkey which was covered by a tiger skin by its kind owner and abandoned near a cornfield, and grazed happily until it brayed and was promptly killed. The swan-king's all-knowing minister does not mince words and states that the crane may have performed state affairs to the best of its ability, but to quarrel without cause is characteristic of a fool (ibid.: 180). The minister further surmises that the crane may well have been instigated by one of their own. Since the swan-king had become too complacent and meek, this move may have been intended to make it demonstrate energy and force, which are the true marks of kingship. Nonetheless, the crane is perceived as wicked by a parrot-envoy for needlessly sparking a war between two kings through mere words (ibid.: 176). It is noteworthy that virtues such as frankness and loyalty can become dangerous vices when pursued recklessly.

DOUBLE POLICY AND DANGEROUS REMEDIES

In *Kakolukiyam*, apprised of the ancient enmity with the owls, the crow-king Meghavarna, (Cloud-hued), calls for an emergency meeting with five of his ministers, all of whom have inherited office from their forefathers (Rajan 1993). Referring to Kautilya's sixfold policy, Meghavarna asks each of them, in turn, which of the following strategies they would advise: conciliation; war; indifference; prepare to march; seek protection from another; or pursue the double policy of seeking peace and waging war simultaneously.

The crow-king's first minister Ujjivin (Live Again) advises conciliation, saying that it is unwise to start a war against a powerful enemy, and that it is better in this case to make peace (*sandhi*) and gain an ally. Since the outcome of war is ever uncertain even when it is between equals, it is least advisable against an enemy who is not only stronger but knows when to strike (Rajan 1993: 268; Reddy 1989: 4). Moreover, there is nothing to be gained by war with this enemy, such as land, gold or friends. Instead, an alliance may be useful in warding off other possible invaders. Further, Ujjivin argues that when life is in danger, one must make peace even with an enemy. Like a reed that bows temporarily to the wind only to rise again, one must conciliate an immediate enemy. Like a tortoise, a wise man will retreat into his shell, only to rise again like a serpent. Just as an unbaked clay pot comes apart when it strikes a similar one, war between equals is futile. Throughout, the minister warns against 'wounded pride' and 'overbearing manners', and holds up the 'lowly reed' as worthy of emulation.

The next minister Sanjivin (Live Well) quotes other texts and aphorisms to argue that one must not make peace with cruel, unjust and greedy kings because such conciliation would be short-lived. Furthermore, such an enemy may be easily defeated, he says, and advises war (*vigraham*). Sanjivin also reminds the crow-king that the enemy has humiliated them and is seething with rage, and seeking peace will only incense his passion, just as drops of water falling on boiling butter will only make it spatter (Rajan 1993: 271; Reddy 1989: 8). Sanjivin adds that the enemy being powerful is no reason to seek peace; just as a lion, though smaller than an elephant, often kills the latter through impetuous energy, or as Bhima overpowered Kichaka dressed as a woman, so also sheer force or guile may be employed against the powerful. He closes by appealing to the valour of the crow-king, who should bring glory by drenching the kingdom with the blood of foes and the tears of their wailing wives (Rajan 1993: 272; Reddy 1989: 9).

After listening to these two extremes, Meghavarna seeks the views of Anujivin (Live Along), who counsels withdrawal (*yanam*), saying that a wise king must first secure himself, hide enmity deep within the heart and endure immediate reversals, while biding his time to launch a deadly strike later. By withdrawing, one prepares to discern the enemy's weaknesses through spies, and then waits for a propitious time to strike the enemy when troubles assail the latter. There is no shame in retreat, for even a lion crouches before a deadly leap and a ram draws back to butt more fiercely. The crow-king then asks Prajivin (Live On), who advises staying put while seeking the aid of a friend (*asana*); retreating from one's realm is never useful since one may not ever be able to enter it again. Instead, one must fortify one's realm with moats, stock food and arms, and so on. Finally, Chiranjivin (Live Long) suggests that Meghavarna seek the protection of a stronger king (*samsraya*), whose strength could offset the enemy (Rajan 1993: 276). And if a powerful king is not available, then he should band together with a weak one who is nonetheless noble and good.

Meghavarna then approaches a dear elder statesman proficient in all the *nitishastra*s, called Stirajivin (Live Firm), for advice on the best policy under the circumstances. The crow-king explains that he wanted the ministers to speak first so that Stirajivin could both test their knowledge and discern the best course, and pleads with Stirajivin to command him. Stirajivin commends the preceding discourse as being in tune with the 'authoritative' texts, but recommends duplicity and double policy as the most appropriate course under the circumstances (Rajan 1993: 277; Reddy 1989: 18). Stirajivin suggests pursuing both peace and war simultaneously by offering tempting bait to build confidence in the enemy. The wise may let the enemy flourish while dispatching secret agents to ferret out strengths and weaknesses.[1]

It is worth recalling that the above discussion parallels Kautilya's elaboration of tactics against a powerful enemy in different sections of the *Arthashastra*. In Book 7, Chapter 15, Kautilya suggests that when a weak king is attacked by a powerful enemy, he must seek the protection of a king who is stronger than and immune to the intrigues of the enemy; or band with equal powers who are immune to the wealth, army and intrigues of the enemy; or with inferior powers; or seek shelter inside a fort; or run away; or, finally, sue for peace with the enemy by surrendering himself and seeking protection (Rangarajan 1987: 665).

In Book 12, after mentioning Bharadvaja's advice that one must surrender and Visalaksha's advice that one must fight bravely, Kautilya proceeds to suggest that one who bows down to all like a crab on the banks of a river lives in despair, while one who fights a powerful enemy with a meagre army perishes; instead, one must seek the protection of a powerful king or withdraw to an impregnable fort (Shamasastry 1919: 548). Kautilya says that conquerors may be just, greedy or demonic, and hence surrender may entail mere obeisance, or the ceding of wealth and more (Rangarajan 1987: 664). He further explains that when confronted with an imminent invasion by a powerful, implacable enemy, one must avert the invasion either by seeking peace or adopting the battle of intrigue (*mantrayuddha*), or a treacherous fight in the battlefield (Shamasastry 1919: 548). While acting thus to avert war, one must sue for peace, and if the enemy continues despite his troubles, then the weak king must sue for peace by offering more than one-fourth of his wealth or army. But even then, the weak king must be adept at duplicity, and try to get away with exchanging traitors, fiery spies, uncontrollable elephants, useless land or land that can be recaptured, etc., to cut his losses.

Dvaidhibhava, or double policy, is construed as waging war with one king and peace with another in the *Arthashastra*. The sixfold policy is also anchored in the four expedients of *sama*, or conciliation or agreements, *dana*, or gifting and placating, *bheda*, creating dissension in enemy camps, or *danda*, using force. Now, Stirajivin explicitly claims that he is departing from the sixfold policy and four expedients; the first by glossing over double-dealing as waging war while appearing to befriend the powerful enemy, and the second by the use of staging dissension (*bheda*) in one's own camp. Since the owl-king is both powerful and cruel, he can be overcome only by duplicity. To this end, Stirajivin suggests that the crow-king withdraw to another hill with his retinue and allow the owls to raid and flourish for the time being. Before doing so, the crow-king is to stage a quarrel with Stirajivin, leaving him bleeding to be discovered by the owls. Thus, Stirajivin is following Kautilya's view that skill for intrigue (*mantra shakti*) is better than power (*prabhu*) and enthusiasm (*utsaha*) for overreaching others (Shamasastry 1919: 492).

Now, the owl-king Arimardana is doubly blind, literally during day and figuratively in lacking insight. Discovering a bloodied Stirajivin at the abandoned tree, Arimardana confers with his ministers about what is to be done. Here again, the most astute one, Raktaksha (Red

Eye) advises that he kill the crow right away, while the next minister suggests that one must show compassion to anyone who seeks refuge. The other three ministers provide variations of the view that one must use the enemy-refugee to one's advantage to learn the enemy's secrets, show compassion to a refugee and even befriend him.

Only Raktaksha is sharp enough to perceive the deception of the wily Stirajivin. He pleads with the owl-king not to be deceived by mere appearances and to kill the refugee immediately; he tells of a silly and greedy brahmin who is compassionate towards a gold coin-dispensing snake that kills his son (who in turn had tried to kill the snake, suspecting a treasure in the snake pit), and the prudent snake spurns the brahmin, saying that love once broken cannot be cemented (Rajan 1993: 308). Raktaksha also tells of a chariot-maker husband who is cuckolded with his own connivance, since he is only too willing to believe his adulterous wife's rhetoric of chastity. One day, sensing the husband hiding under her bed as she is about to embrace her lover, she pretends to be play-acting with another man only because a goddess assured her that her husband's impending death could thereby be displaced onto another man! Impressed, the chariot-maker regrets believing the town gossip and dances in the street, carrying the wife and her lover on his shoulders! Raktaksha warns that expecting the new refugee to reveal enemy secrets is as laughable as believing that a bird's turd can turn into gold. But the powerful owl-king is so confident of his valour that he is unmindful of the cautionary advice of his frank minister. Arimardana is moved by sentiments of pity and is too narcissistic to perceive the hidden dangers.

The crow-minister Stirajivin gloats at the idiocy of the owl-king, and recognises his 'great good fortune' (*shubham*) when Raktaksha abandons Arimardana and flies away (Rajan 1993: 335; Reddy 1989: 106). Thus rescued, pampered and ensconced right at the gate of the enemy owl's fortress (realising that he would be subject to intense scrutiny were he to live in their midst, Stirajivin had opted to stay at the gate, saying it would be 'inappropriate' for him to live inside the fortress), the crow nicely stacks a pile of wood at the gate, and then gets the other crows to burn it all one fine morning. Confidence tricks such as feigning a quarrel and infiltrating the enemy camp are prescribed by Kautilya, but it is only in the literary sources that these are fully staged. It was already mentioned how in the *Mudrarakshasa*, Chanakya/Kautilya advises his king Chandragupta to enact a quarrel to mislead the enemy's spies in one's court.

The overt lesson of the *Kakolukiyam* is that one must *always* distrust a powerful and evil enemy. This contradicts what we saw in the earlier two books of the *Panchatantra*, where a natural enemy may be embraced as a friend, albeit after some tests. This third book explicitly promotes realpolitik in statecraft as it pertains to double-dealing; where there has been a historic conflict, as between crows and owls, a former enemy coming as a friend is a cause for alarm, more so when the visitor is well-versed in *niti*, or prudence, like the old crow Stirajivin. Mere strength and enthusiasm are blind without *niti*. They induce erratic judgments, just as the owl-king is fooled by the apparent plight of the old crow and is done in by misplaced compassion. And *niti* is not learnt from texts alone, but from long experience of judicious application in actual circumstances. All the crow ministers are learned but spout one-sided advice, whereas the astute, elderly Stirajivin improvises for the circumstances. It appears that only this statesman is aware of the old enmity, which renders all options except withdrawal unviable. But the successful adventurism of Stirajivin (going off to the enemy camp in the guise of a refugee) is not prudent either, since it is equally dependent on 'great' good fortune (Rajan 1993: 355). The third book of the *Panchatantra* ends with a warning against dangerous remedies, such as frogs riding piggyback on a serpent. An old serpent, unable to fend for itself, lies down in a pool of frogs and tells a curious frog that it is cursed with carrying frogs on its back for biting a brahmin's son. The whole retinue of frogs amuse themselves on its back, until the serpent slows down due to hunger and the frog-king allows it to swallow a few frogs, only for the retinue to be exterminated without even a seed left.

This warning is also reiterated in the *Hitopadesha*, where a relatively weak king, the swan, is advised not to pursue dangerous remedies. Here, a story is told of a turtle, which hatches a plan to fly along with two swans by grasping in its mouth a stick that they would each seize on one end with their beaks, despite the swans' warning that this was a dangerous idea. As luck would have it, some cowherds who see the turtle travel in this curious fashion give chase. The turtle opens its mouth to curse them, and plummets to its death. The weak are particularly tempted to seek out dangerous means out of desperation, which is not advisable unless one is guided by an astute counsellor. Pakistan's Kargil misadventure in May 1999 was an instance of dangerous remedies, not to mention its clandestine war against India in Kashmir through supporting terror. The intrusion into Kargil, a strategic region connecting Kashmir and Ladakh through paramilitary infiltrators disguised as insurgents, came to light, triggering a full-fledged war. Coming close on the heels of a bilateral agreement to resolve the Kashmir issue amicably, this 'double policy' only resulted in Pakistan's defeat, and loss of the diplomatic goodwill it had until then. India's decisive victory through frontal battles and refusal to escalate the war by crossing the Line of Control proved to be a wise move both militarily and diplomatically.[2] Another example of dangerous remedies pursued by many powers is that of arming dissidents within a nation to carry out assassinations and suicide attacks, which often misfire against the sponsors in the long run.

REAL SUCCESS LIES IN PEACE

In the *Hitopadesha*, there are slight twists and turns with regard to both parties to a war and the actual conduct of war, while driving home similar themes as in the *Panchatantra*. As mentioned before, the origins of war are traced to unnecessary boasting by a busybody crane, which goes abroad and offends his terrestrial bird hosts. The kings on both sides, the swan-king of the aquatic birds and the peacock-king of the terrestrial ones, are only too eager to prove their mettle and thus get embroiled in a costly war. They are saved by the farsightedness of two counsellors who know when to pull back without compromising honour. Chakravaka (Ruddy Goose) is the able counsellor of the swan-king Hiranyagarbha (Golden Embryo), and must dissuade a king who is gullible and quick to take offense. Hiranyagarbha jumps to war preparations upon hearing the crane's account of the terrestrial birds' hostility, forgetting the realities of war. Chakravaka restrains him, saying that a fight against a powerful enemy is unwise, and victory in war is always uncertain. Great success through ordinary means such as agreements, gifts and dissension is the fruit of 'good counsel'

(Chandiramani 1995: 183; Reddy 1994: 141). Chakravaka then reminds Hiranyagarbha of the conduct of the 'great', who are not excited by anger, and wait patiently for an opportunity to strike at enemies. He is fortunate to have a king who is noble-minded and, though naive, willing to listen to his counsellor. The stories Chakravaka narrates to this king deal with mindless imitation. In fact, the minister mocks Hiranyagarbha as being akin to those of 'low intellect who at one time, do not suspect anything and at another time, suspect everything' (Chandiramani 1995: 261; Reddy 1994: 143). The swan-king is carried away by a spy-crow, which humiliates a parrot sent as an envoy by the peacock-king, and assumes that the crow is his well-wisher. He overlooks the fact that the crow is a terrestrial bird, and hence a 'natural enemy'.

Since war seems imminent, Chakravaka first gets Hiranyagarbha to take refuge in a fort well-stocked with supplies. This fort is built on an island in the midst of a large lake, so that the enemy will be exhausted in just reaching its gates. Hearing of the enemy marching towards the fort, the minister advises the king to send able generals to fight, and they wreak considerable losses on an army tired from the long march through forests and hills. Though sparse in detail, the minister's strategy resonates with Kautilya's advice that when no stronger protector is available, one must resort to a fort and fight, then seek peace by offering valour or asylum (Rangarajan 1987: 665, 667).

Parallelly, the enemy king's counsellor, the vulture Doordarshi (Far-sighted), also appeals to the peacock-king not to rely only on power and enthusiasm to launch a war (Chandiramani 1995: 193; Reddy 1994: 43). The peacock-king Chitravarna (Bright-hued) is drunk with power and thinks that energetic action behoves a king; he follows Vachaspati's advice that one's own elevation and an enemy's decline alone constitute policy. When instructed on how to conduct war, Chitravarna regards it as all talk and walks out to consult astrologers. Doordarshi remarks that overreaching vitality and *niti*, or policy, are like darkness and light and cannot be present at the same place and time (Chandiramani 1995: 198; Reddy 1994: 51). The *Hitopadesha* particularly argues against simple-minded and straightforward political action, anchored only in courage and strength; strength tempered by *niti* or prudence is preferred. While this overtly appears self-serving on the part of the counsellors, it is a valid comment on the impetuosity of power/strength, which overwhelms wise counsel all too often.

Only after suffering heavy losses does Chitravarna look to his minister for advice. Doordarshi upbraids him for his misconduct and agrees to find a remedy after the peacock-king pleads with folded hands for forgiveness (Chandiramani 1995: 211). Recalling wise sayings that one must restrain anger against kings, Doordarshi promises that they shall retreat with glory, and advises the immediate encircling of Hiranyagarbha's fort even as he gets the spy-crow to set fire to the fort. When Chakravaka learns of this from a spy, the swan-king's sage minister gets Hiranyagarbha to give expensive gifts to all the courageous generals and soldiers in his army. When the swan-king demurs, citing proverbs that say one should safeguard money in the face of a calamity, the minister persuades him that there is no such thing as overspending when it comes to sacrifice, marriage, calamity, destruction of enemies, glorious action, acquiring friends, dear women and aiding poor relatives (Chandiramani 1995: 212; Reddy 1994: 72). Loyal ministers and generals must be honoured forthwith to inspire them to put up a stiff resistance. As expected, the swans put up a valiant fight, but the swan-king loses and is saved by a self-sacrificing general.

Flushed with victory, the peacock-king Chitravarna is reluctant to conclude peace with the swans. His minister Doordarshi counsels that one must seek alliance with an equal, and that since they have achieved victory and fame, they should return to their own country before the rains come, lest war break out again. But Chitravarna is intent on enthroning a crow in the swan kingdom, so that he can rely on regular homage and gifts (Chandiramani 1995: 233; Reddy 1994: 95). Once again, the vulture tries to dissuade him, saying that a mean person must never be raised to an exalted position, and that obligation done to the mean only goads them to rebel against the master (Chandiramani 1995: 229).

Learning through a spy that Chitravarna is adamant, Chakravaka conspires to get an ally to lay siege to Chitravarna's kingdom while he is rebuffing his minister Doordarshi's advice to conclude peace. Hearing of this new attack, the peacock-king thunders that he would go to war on both fronts and annihilate the enemy. Doordarshi cautions him not to make loud noises, saying that a king should not fight many enemies at the same time. Doordarshi also lauds his rival Chakravaka as 'all-knowing', perhaps because the latter's plot is in tune with Kautilya's advice that when a king of equal power does not desire peace, then the same amount of vexation as he has caused his opponent must be meted out to him to compel him to enter into peace talks (Shamasastry 1919: 377).

Now, Kautilya's discussions regarding peace between conflicting powers posits a complex calculus of profits, which may be either more, or less, or proportionate to the strength of the army, or treasure, or land supplied to the enemy (Shamasastry 1919: 398). There are eleven possibilities for the weaker and five for the stronger. When the powerless king must cede part of his army, he may negotiate either to send his commander-in-chief and heir apparent, or present himself with the army, or march with his army to a specific place. When a king reaches peace through ceding wealth, it may be just what he can afford, or what he has agreed upon, or an excessive amount. And, when a king agrees to cede land, it may be just a small part (infested with troublesome elements), or all territory except the capital city, or just the produce from the land, or far more than what the land yields (ibid.: 379–380).

In contrast to these logical formulations, the *Hitopadesha* has the two counsellors Chakravaka and Doordarshi hold forth on who is deserving to be made peace with, the kinds of peace, ways of ascertaining the enemy's inclination, and so on. Doordarshi speaks of two demons who killed each other over a goddess to drive home the point that victory in war is always uncertain, more so between equals. He also reminds the peacock-king that the royal swan is noble and deserves to be made peace with. There are seven types of people deserving of peace: the truthful, the noble, the pious/just, the despicable, the powerful, the one who has many friends, and the one who is victorious in many battles (Chandiramani 1995: 237). Thus he advances both strategic and ethical considerations to bolster his views; after making an alliance, a truthful one will not be treacherous and a noble one will not be mean even if there is danger to his life, and so peace is to one's advantage. Since a just one cannot be vanquished, supported as he is by his people's affection, peace may be the best option. When destruction is imminent, peace should be made even with a despicable one. So is the case with one who has many friends, as also one who is powerful. Alliance with one who is brave is another way to bring enemies under control.

Who should not be made peace with? Chakravaka identifies twenty persons, namely one who is a child, is old, sick, excommunicated or a coward, is ill-fated, irreligious, greedy, fickle-minded, fatalist or pleasure-minded, has many enemies, has a distressed army, has cowardly or greedy servants, or one who consults many, censures god and brahmins, is struck by famine, stays away from his country or fights at an inappropriate time (Chandiramani 1995: 239). All these persons cannot be allies in war since they quickly come under the enemy's control: children, the old and the sick lack strength; one without kinsmen has more enemies than friends; a cowardly, greedy, confused or pleasure-loving king would be certainly abandoned by his servants and ministers; one who is irreligious is not reliable and may change his heart after an alliance; one who is a fatalist suffers from inertia, while one who stays away from his country or has many enemies is imprudent (Chandiramani 1995: 240; Reddy 1994: 141). By these standards, the peacock-king may appear greedy and imprudent and thus not deserving of peace, but then he has a wise and tactful counsellor who tilts the balance in his favour.

For his part, Doordarshi ascertains through spies that the swan-king is indeed noble and just, and thus deserving of peace. Gullible as he is, the swan-king tends to assess a wicked man to be as truthful as himself and thus can be easily duped. But the swan-king cannot be defeated forever, since his subjects and army are loyal and will fight valiantly. Doordarshi declares that the swan-king is endowed with many good qualities, and that real success (*karyasiddhi*) lies in peace (*samam*), especially between equals (Chandiramani 1995: 260; Reddy 1994: 141). He asserts that even though experts suggest four means, namely, conciliation, gifts, dissension and force, they are only for purposes of enumeration. Exasperated, the peacock-king withdraws, saying 'do as you please' (Chandiramani 1995: 261).

Welcomed with gifts and sweet words by the swan-king and his minister, Doordarshi expounds on sixteen different peace alliances. As victor, the peacock-king is entitled to exchange of gifts, women, army, land, military assistance, agricultural produce or wealth. But Doordarshi proposes that the two kings must conclude a 'golden peace' or *suvarna sandhi*, where there is friendship, exchange of gifts and mutual trust (as a land power, the peacock-king may have also not wanted to acquire watery realms, which would be difficult to defend) (Chandiramani 1995: 267). This kind of peace is apt for two good/noble agents (*sajjanulu*) since it allows for equal representation of interests and endures through adversity (Chandiramani 1995: 264; Reddy 1994: 147).

For Kautilya as well, golden peace involves trust and friendship cemented through gifts and marriage alliances. He admits that peace based on honesty and oath is immutable in this world as well as the next, compared to peace based on material security or hostage, which is advantageous only for this world. But Kautilya does not recommend it seriously to a victorious invader, as Doordarshi does here. Doordarshi extols a golden peace where trust matters more than material gain. He justifies this by saying that friendships between the good conduces to both religious merit and happiness (Chandiramani 1995: 267).

We already saw that the *Mudrarakshasa* mainly showcases Kautilya's ruthless and artful manipulation, rather than his ethical qualms. The stranglehold of conventional realist reading of Kautilya is most recently evident in a political novel called *Chanakya's Chant*, in which Ashwin Sanghi asserts through the protagonist that 'one should never act on principle' and that 'politics is war without bloodshed and war is politics with bloodshed' (Sanghi 2010: 53–54). That the good should form alliances with each other makes for good rhetoric in hoary texts, but the *Hitopadesha* accords it pride of place. Further, given that the *Panchatantra* does not deal with peace at all, it is significant that the hard-nosed *Hitopadesha* elevates a 'golden peace' as a worthy political goal.

RESURGENCE OF ETHICAL REALISM

To situate the above insights, it is useful to peep into the resurgence of realist perspectives in our time. Machiavelli's exhortation to princes to overcome qualms about promise-breaking, illiberality and cruelty, if needed, has been interpreted in terms of an ethical realism, one that does not reject all morals but is attuned to the necessities of public life (Berlin 1992: 224). As Isaiah Berlin notes, political goals such as glory of the patria may entail a table of values that is incommensurable with ordinary Christian morality. The 'permanent economy of violence' serves to facilitate virtues such as vitality, pride, genius, variety, firmness in adversity, self-discipline, power and success, rather than the staid morality of a private citizen or monk (Berlin 1992: 217, 219). Statesmen who are committed to these goals are not serving their self-interest as much as that of a community, and must be commended for rising above personal morality. Their actions must be judged in terms of whether social order is sustained and political glory achieved. As Berlin observes:

> The philosophy summarised by 'eat or be eaten, beat or be beaten'—the kind of worldly wisdom found in, say, Lappo Mazzei or Giovanni Morelli...is not what is central to him. Machiavelli is not especially concerned with the opportunism of ambitious individuals; the ideal before his eyes is a shining vision of Florence or Italy. In this respect, he is a typically impassioned humanist of the Renaissance, save that his ideal is not artistic or cultural but political...This is very different from mere advocacy of tough-mindedness...or of a realism irrespective of its goal. (Berlin 1992: 216)

Instead of importing yardsticks from without, this kind of realism pushes for standards internal to politics. Not just expediency, but a principled flexibility oriented to preventing great evils is one mark of ethical prudence. Opting for the lesser evil over the greatest good is not an easy, satisfying or attractive choice, but this is the call of ethical realists. Ironically, one strand of political realism has always supported war as necessary due to the anarchic nature of the international state system and perpetual conflicts of national interests. The recurring preoccupations pertain to national security and interest, force, diplomacy and state power. Reinhold Niebuhr recognised that tough-minded realism can lead to a vicious cycle of force and counter-force, and hence warned against too narrow a notion of national self-interest (cited in McKeogh 1997: 126). An example is of the United States' preoccupation with German debt repayments in the post-1918 context, while the Marshall Plan reflects 'enlightened self interest' (ibid.: 128).

Niebuhr warns that a consistent policy of self-interest may thwart the long-term interests of a nation, which may be tied up with other nations' interests. For instance, peace and justice rather than perpetual war may be in the interests of all nations. Does this mean pacifism and neutrality in the face of injustice?

Michael Walzer has revived Christian accounts of 'just war', which concerns justification for resorting to war, conduct during war and post-war settlement. Writing about the Vietnam war, Walzer has pointed out that the justice of the cause and just conduct during war are more important lessons than merely a realist prudence that tells us to avoid wars that are unpopular and costly (Walzer 2002: 931). Norms such as war as the last resort, only for self-defence, with a reasonable chance of success, and engaged with proper authority and with means that are proportional to the end, have become military necessities. But Walzer points to new problems, such as the North Atlantic Treaty Organisation's air raids in the Kosovo conflict, in lieu of ground troops. Here, the immediate effect of the air raids was an adverse intensification of war by the Serbian regime, which put Kosovans at greater risk (ibid.: 938). Walzer also thinks that justice after war must now include expansive restoration, given the extensive damage inflicted by even 'just wars'. He further argues that humanitarian wars require extensive intervention and not just stopping massacres or overthrowing a despotic regime, though the costs involved might deter realists.

Resisting this turn, Valerie Morkevičius observes that genuine realism does not support 'just wars' waged for ushering regime change or societal transformation, but recognises that wars serve a limited purpose. She cites how thirty-three scholars, including some prominent realists, published a full page advertisement in *The New York Times* on 26 September 2002 that a war in Iraq was neither necessary, nor in America's national interest (Morkevičius 2018: 3). Morkevičius warns that liberal crusading for human rights or justice can often morph into a passion to remake the world in one's own image, and thus actually fuel greater violence (ibid.: 6). Rather, she argues that realism espouses war only for self-defence and recognises, citing Kaushik Roy, that India's grand strategy has always been passive and concerned with 'internal affairs' (ibid.: 181).

CONCLUSION

However technologically sophisticated wars may have become in our time, the above discussions about realism show that they still involve ordinary men, women and expenditure of public resources. Scholarly discussions regarding whether the state apparatus is united or divided, whether institutions are designed to secure plurality or dissent on grave issues, whether national security is a choice-worthy goal or obscurantist smokescreen or whether technological equipment and training are adequate, tend to be too technical. Ordinary conversations revolve around whether a war was necessary or justified, whether the enemy is good or evil, whether the means were dangerous or moderate, whether the success was scripted only by humans or fortune or both, and whether war and peace must be tried together, and here the classics have much to teach us in nurturing our common sense and judgment.

Dangerous remedies, such as assassinating dictatorial leaders, or arming secessionists and deploying terrorists to wage clandestine wars, are favourite strategies which often backfire. This is borne out in numerous cases involving both major and minor powers in the twentieth century. The temptation to use these remedies is so high that their dehumanising impact is often overlooked; it requires 'great good fortune' not to be singed by them oneself. And great good fortune cannot be guaranteed even by the wise, not to mention hawkish, generals. Both the *Panchatantra* and *Hitopadesha* abound in stories of desperate remedies pursued by the weak that result in self-destruction.

The two texts do not also counsel indiscriminate goodwill towards all, assuming that no harm can come to one because one is so good. Weak powers must contend with the aggression of the mighty, and they are well-served by unsentimental prudence and quick wit. *Niti*, or prudence, must be calibrated afresh according to circumstances, and this goes beyond textbook learning, as demonstrated by the contradictory advice peddled by the ministers. While drawing from Kautilya, I have tried to show that the two texts move beyond doctrinal application of *shadgunya*, adapting double policy or espionage to the concrete cases at hand. Wars may be unnecessary and uncertain, but they do occur, and experts must know how to balance power, enthusiasm and wise counsel. Special alacrity about the enemy's *mantra shakti*, or deliberative strength, is needed for success. Herein lies the role of intrigue in neutralising and co-opting rival powers towards a mutually beneficial policy. Thus, the literary texts showcase a prudence that is mindful of the place of nobility and goodness, even for weak powers, a perspective that is muted in many discussions of Kautilya's realpolitik. Goodness is understood in terms of mutual trust, friendship and honesty towards the ally. The *Hitopadesha* also reaffirms, not so much peace at any cost, but peace with honour as the goal of diplomacy. What is unique here is the espousal of the perspective of relatively weak powers rather than a conqueror's viewpoint, as in mainstream realism.

Notes

1. This discussion is beautifully illustrated in the *Amar Chitra Katha* comic *Panchatantra: Crows and Owls and Other Stories* (Pai 1981: 5, 8).
2. For a detailed analysis of the latent impact of Kautilyan realpolitik, see Liebig 2013: 108–109.

IV

GAMES OF CHANCE AND STRIFE

Love and Politics in the *Dasakumaracharita*

The structure of the *Dasakumaracharita*, beginning with a sensuous depiction of the amorous sporting of a royal couple and closing with the praise of statecraft, with explicit allusions to Kautilya's *Arthashastra*, compels us to probe what may link *kama*, which is concerned with desire in general and erotic desire in particular, to *artha*, which pertains to acquiring worldly success through wealth and kingdoms. Whereas Kautilya's *Arthashastra* is sparing on *kama*, Dandin's *Dasakumaracharita* is forthcoming on their intimate and unholy coupling, raising questions about educating desire in general, and the desire for love and for kingdom/wealth/success in particular. Noting this link, Alain Daniélou observed that 'the refinements of love and the pleasures that include music and other arts are only possible in a prosperous civilization, which is why the *Kama Shastra*, the art of love is linked to the *Artha Shastra*, the rules of prosperity and the art of making money' (Daniélou 1994: 5). While this is true, there are also other less apparent affinities between the pursuits of *kama* and *artha* which strike us when we delve into the classics.

The *Dasakumaracharita* is about a deposed king's son and the sons of his various ministers, who arrive in a forest and, having 'mastered all the arts, set out to conquer the world'. Besides the customary curriculum, including the four *Veda*s and their subsidiaries, poetry, drama, music, the *Purana*s (ancient historical tales), law, grammar, astrology, logic, *mimamsa* (systematic investigation) and intricacies of the political *shastra*s (systematic studies) of Chanakya and Kamandaka, skill in using weapons, riding elephants and horses, etc., the ten *kumara*s, or young men, were also taught perfection in 'thieving, gambling, spells, medicine and magic and other crooked arts' (Kale 1986: 230). After this 'rigorous' education, they are sent deep into the Vindhya forest on an auspicious day. The crown prince vanishes in the dead of night while on a mysterious mission, which required him to help a robber-turned-Shiva devotee gain sovereignty over *patala* or the underworld, by entering a chasm. After aiding the devotee and securing a jewel that could dispel the pain caused by hunger and thirst, the prince returns to earth and wanders about looking for his companions. For their part, they go in search of him and have adventures of their own in securing love, wealth and success. They all reunite fortuitously when they converge to aid an ally-king, and recount their experiences.

Teeming with hero-mythic plots, story after story in Dandin's *Dasakumaracharita* details the intricate ways of fulfilling one's desires and earning wealth by clever means, setting aside *dharma* (ethics or duties). Interestingly, the narratives, which are supposed to educate future princes, undermine accepted ethical codes even as they showcase the practical skills of the heroes. Erotic fulfilment and the desire for wealth/fame/success, two preoccupations of the young, vivify each narrative as the heroes act out easy, cheap and sometimes desperate remedies. Of the ten adventures, only two bespeak virtue, while the rest appear to be about ingenuity and courage but involve adultery, theft, fraud, impersonation, deceit and murder to acquire princesses and kingdoms (Kale 1986: xli).[1] True, there are many other texts on erotic love, but the *Dasakumaracharita* by Dandin is unique in thematising the political implications of untutored desire in its climactic chapter, thus warranting deeper analysis.

While poets and artists wax eloquently about the agony and ecstasy of *eros* (erotic love), political philosophers are always honing their prudence vis-a-vis this ruling passion. Allan Bloom has observed that eros, as sensual desire, has engaged many Western philosophers since it was understood as life's most mysterious and exciting experience, manifesting the human longing for connectedness, beginning with a sensuous love of the beautiful and, when properly tuned, metamorphosing into the love of wisdom (Bloom 1993: 30). But eros was also a recalcitrant force, requiring great prudence and imaginative taming of the passions, giving rise to a whole array of didactic visions, beginning with Plato's *Symposium* and culminating in Rousseau's *Emile*, with Shakespeare and Jane Austen in-between. There is also Machiavelli's *Mandragola*, which mocks the high-minded cultivation of erotic desire, and celebrates its susceptibility to cheap tricks and easy solutions through a clever arrangement of appearances.

Similarly, the potential and pitfalls of *kama* as sexual desire also inspired many poets and playwrights in India, with Kalidas towering above all. *Shringara rasa*, the sentiment of erotic love, was seen as a 'lordly *rasa*', in that it encompassed all the 'emotions and sentiments of an exalted life' (Ali 2004: 209). Educating the emotions was not only about tuning them correctly, but also about 'tasting' their 'essence and flavour' fully and self-consciously (ibid.: 193). Art was supposed to evoke the experience of *rasa*, which literally meant flavour or juice, extract or essence. There were eight *rasas*, namely *shringara* (erotic love), *hasya* (humour), *karuna* (pathetic), *raudra* (furious), *vira* (heroic), *bhayanaka* (terrible), *bibhatsa* (odious) and *adbhuta* (wonderful) (ibid.: 188).[2] Owen Lynch observed that the aim of Indian aesthetics was not mimetic, didactic or cathartic, but catalytic in that it activated an emotion already present in the audience, and shaped it (Lynch 1990: 18). To this end, poets and playwrights delved into a range of emotions and sentiments in verse and prose to forge a refined sensibility. Analysing the depiction of the *shringara rasa* or erotic sentiment in Sanskrit literature, Sushil Kumar De notes that rich, idealised descriptions of sensuous beauty reflect not so much an 'all absorbing ecstasy or the state of tearing passion' as a 'balanced frame of mind and cultural aloofness, a sentiment of placid, even playful enjoyment, in which his impetuous passion itself becomes a delectable luxury' (De 1959: 16). He adds that love enthrals not in its poignancy or depth, but in its playful moods of vivid enjoyment, breaking forth into delicate blossoms of fancy.

Sanskrit poets were oriented towards two prototypical figures: the *nagaraka* (the urbane man of the world) and the *rasika* (the connoisseur) (De 1959: 18). But there were also the royalty and courtiers who patronised, consumed and produced courtly literature. Daud Ali has remarked that 'erotic love provided the palette wherein anxieties about affiliative dynamics of court such as detecting concealed feelings, use of deception, discerning strategies of others and so on are projected and thought about' (Ali 2004: 261). The *Dasakumaracharita* is stunning in its subtle, yet unmistakable delving into the myriad arrows of *kama* and many cunning ruses to acquire and tame it, especially from the standpoint of those who are partly outside conventional society, such as courtesans and thieves, as well as those who are relatively powerless, such as faithful wives.[3] This concern with rogues and rascals has led some scholars to attribute a picaresque character to the *Dasakumaracharita*, though its heroes are all of high rather than humble birth (De 1959: 124; Gray 1992: 64). Far from being immoral, as J. E. B. Gray notes, villainy is tempered with some notion of morality, or at least natural justice.

Speculating on the historical context, Robert DeCaroli spells out the political intent of the *Dasakumaracharita*. He has observed that Dandin, writing in the seventh century from the Pallava court of Kanchi, came from a family that had migrated from Vidarbha of the Vakataka kings after the latter were overthrown (DeCaroli 1995: 672). He claims that Dandin witnessed the alternation between pleasure-loving aesthetic patron-kings and energetic martial conquerors in the Pallava kingdom. The Pallava king Mahendravarman was well-known for building temples, but his lands were soon overrun by Pulakesin II, the neighbouring Chalukyan king. The Pallava lands had to be recaptured by Narasimhavarman I, after whose reign the Chalukyans again captured Pallava lands, which were then recovered after twelve years by Parameshwarvarman. As such, Dandin may be seen as constructing a political allegory, warning kings not to be complacent. DeCaroli has stressed this didactic intent from internal evidence, such as the extensive use of the prose form and extensive lectures on the danger of neglecting political activity (ibid.: 674). He points to the recurring theme that a king's worthiness, especially his ability to succeed, entitles him to rule. While ideal qualities such as self-control, vigilance, cleverness and courage are required for success, it is the 'ability to manipulate the political scene with an unwavering gaze even at the expense of personal pleasure for the sake of a secure reign' that is lauded (DeCaroli 1995: 673). Could it be that awareness of the unseemly aspects of the erotic and heroic sentiments shapes the 'unwavering gaze'?

And there are many unseemly moments: the future emperor, Rajavahana marries his beloved in a magic show, deceiving her father who is in the audience. While somewhat understandable, given that she is the daughter of Rajavahana's former enemy, this pushes the limits of deception in fulfilling *kama*. Another hero murders an usurper-cousin, marries his widow, and impersonates him. On the surface, Dandin has the main hero Rajavahana say that even adultery helped by fraud can secure *dharma* and *artha*, in as much as it serves as a means of liberating parents from imprisonment, putting to death an inveterate foe, or regaining a kingdom (Kale 1986: 300). But Dandin also raises doubts about whether such egregious violation of *dharma* would be acceptable to the people. Do ends justify means? How will the king's friends and enemies judge his conduct when the deception and fraud come to light?

LOVE AT FIRST SIGHT

Dandin portrays heroes who are extremely resourceful and highly inventive in devising ways and means of seducing the women they love. In three stories, the heroes secure princess-wives as a gift for their display of valour in helping a king regain a kingdom. In many others, they are in hot pursuit of women they have fallen for and encounter obstacles; often the moon-faced, lotus-eyed and coral-lipped beloved is either being courted or harassed by another, more powerful suitor.

The crown jewel in the set is the episode where the future king, Rajavahana marries the princess Avantisundari in a magic show right under the nose of her father, who thinks that a lookalike of his daughter has been conjured up and wedded to an illusory prince! According to M. R. Kale, this magical wedding, which is part of the *Purvapitika* (Prologue) of the *Dasakumaracharita*, may be an interpolation. The *Dasakumaracharita* 'proper' is no less sensational, in that it begins with the fawn-eyed princess Avantisundari, 'her eyes dilated through wonder after hearing the description of the universe from the prince', imploring ecstatically,

> Dearest, today my ears have been blessed through your favour; today you have set in my mind the lamp of knowledge that dispels all darkness of ignorance; today is ripened the fruit of the service of your lotus like feet. What service shall I do unto you so as to make return for this your favour... (Kale 1986: 255).

A luscious description of the 'night of uninterrupted enjoyment' follows, beginning with the princess 'resting her rounded breasts on the bosom of her husband like the monsoon spreading in the sky the train of big clouds', and 'impatiently kissing his ruby-like lower lip magnified by the stream of its spreading reddish lustre', and so on (Kale 1986: 255). In sound sleep wrought by the fatigue of enjoyment, they both dream of an old swan whose legs are bound with lotus fibres and, awakened by the vision, they find our hero's feet in silver chains! Caught red-handed, the prince is arrested and taken along in a wooden cage by the reigning surrogate Chandavarman, on an expedition against the king of the Angas, Simhavarman. When his father- and mother-in-law learn of this, they save Rajavahana from execution, but cannot free him; their son, Avantisundari's brother, who is 'doing penance so as to gain spiritual merit to rule over the whole earth in future', sends word to the reigning surrogate that the defiler must be killed and the princess must be jailed (ibid.: 258).

Chandavarman decides to have Rajavahana trampled by an elephant after the auspicious rites of his own marriage to Simhavarman's daughter are concluded. But his plans go awry when he is killed by a heroic thief, who seizes the outstretched hand of the princess Ambalika for himself. It appears that the thief is none other than one of the princely companions, Apaharavarman, who had set out to find Rajavahana. As they exchange loving words and embraces, various allies who had set out to help Simhavarman converge, and all turn out to be Rajavahana's lost companions. There is a joyous reunion.

Presenting their thrilling adventures, Dandin follows the stylised portrayals of *shringara rasa* even as he mocks the credulity inspired by our passions. He assumes that falling in love is an archetypal experience enacted in everyone's life. Given the right causes (*vibhavas*), there arise primary emotions (*bhavas*) that manifest in various effects (*anubhavas*). As Ali notes, the emotional experience of pleasure, for example, would require the presence of the beloved and the lover, various stimulants like seasons, flowers, ornaments, enjoying oneself in the garden, hearing the words of the beloved, playing, sporting, and absence of rejection. The effects include smiling faces, sweet words, clever motions of eyebrows, soft and delicate movements of limbs, and so on (Ali 2004: 186). Consider the following description of conducive conditions (*vibhavas*):

> The season of Spring now arrived—kindling the fire of love, in the hearts of persons separated from their beloveds, by means of the southern breeze, the leader of Kāma's forces, moving slowly as if under the burden of the fragrance of the sandal-trees...making the circle of the quarters resound with the sweet tunes of the bees and cuckoos with their throats rendered melodious by the feast of honey of the mango blossoms. In that exceedingly delightful season, Avantisundari, the daughter of Manasara...went for enjoying herself to the delightful garden on the border of the city... (Kale 1986: 245)

Already intimated of her presence there, prince Rajavahana enters the same garden and, enchanted by the cooing cuckoos and humming bees, the mango trees in full blossom and the ponds full of swans and ducks, he beholds the princess, who emerges glowing, having just worshipped *Kama*, the god of love, for a suitable husband. Both are instantly captivated, each seeing the other as the perfect embodiment of beauty, and give in to their intense pangs of love. These feelings (*bhavas*) give rise to effects (*anubhavas*) wherein the prince goes on gazing at her in wonder, even as she casts sidelong glances at him with her 'eyebrows a little contracted and knit'—all physical signs of their love-struck state (Kale 1986: 247). Subsequently, Avantisundari suffers and grows emaciated due to their separation, and sends Rajavahana a letter, imploring him not to be 'hard-hearted' and to quench her desire. Retorting that she had stolen his heart and mind (and so only she best knew whether it is 'tender or hard'), the prince reassures the (messenger) friend that he would devise a suitable plan to attain their union (ibid.: 252).

Love at first sight is a recurring theme, as also sleeplessness and fever due to the deferral of pleasure with various sporting and sleeping beauties. Bewitched by a dance performance where an accomplished danseuse displays all the feelings and sentiments (*rasa-bhava*) in their entirety, the dashing adventurer, Apaharavarman, goes home tormented, wondering whether her amorous side-glances and discreet smiles were due to mere chance, or coquetry, or genuine desire (Kale 1986: 275). Later, when he steals into a palace, he gazes upon a sleeping beauty, Ambalika, 'lying on a couch with ivory feet and set with precious jewels, with the upper fore-part of her left foot entwined with the inner side of her right heel, the stout long calves in close contact, her tender knees bent and thighs a little curled'. He beholds her

> creeper like arms loosely thrown over the hips, while the sprout like hand was thrown under the crown of the head, her round hips were a little curved, the fine under garment of china silk lying close to her person, the slender belly not much bent; her budlike and fully developed breasts were heaving perceptibly, her neck ornament of rubies tossed slantingly...her loosened braid unevenly tinged red due to the cluster of rays from the ear pendant not to mention an ornamental painting on her cheek by the different embroidered leaves in a mirrored canopy! (Kale 1986: 284)

Denuded of his desire to steal mere jewels, Apaharavarman thinks to himself,

> Love will not suffer me to live if I do not secure this maiden with beauteous eyes. If I touch her without previous intimation [or appointment], this extremely young girl [inexperienced in matters of love] will evidently destroy my desire by her cry of distress and then I shall have struck at myself [destroyed my prospects]. (Kale 1986: 285)

Apaharavarman departs after spit-painting a love message on the wall, only to grab Ambalika as she is being wedded to someone else.

Another hero, Mitragupta, beholds a princess playing with a ball before a goddess. He wonders whether she is the goddess herself, and rhapsodises that the goddess only holds a lotus in her hand, while this girl's hand itself is a lotus! He is enraptured by her pursuing the ball,

> now sitting, now rising, now contracting her form, now outstretching it, now standing still, now darting forward, in a manner in which her ornaments jingled in consonance with her feet, her tresses hung loosely about, her jewelled waist band jingled, her pearl necklace tossed about as she frisked up and down, while she deftly held up slipping garments and displaced ornaments. (Kale 1986: 323)

This emphasis on jewellery is in tune with what Ali has called the courtly ideal of physical beauty, where the body is strengthened, illumined and thus adorned by their effulgence (Ali 2004: 165). As Lynch noted, emotions (*bhavas*) were not just seen as psychological affects internal to the individuals, bereft of physical or cognitive aspects, as in the West. In the Indian context, they were understood as relational and cognitive appraisals of a social situation stemming from the body-mind complex; like food, emotions sustain and nourish us, and we must learn to savour and relish emotions in a mature manner (Lynch 1990: 14). Far from being smooth, it appears that there will be many bitter-sweet and hilarious moments before we get this right. While none needs to be taught to fall in love, it is for the urbane connoisseur (*rasika*) to relish the aesthetic and sensuous aspects with empathy and distance. Irony and detachment are particularly needed to mull over and digest the desperate means and ethical casuistry induced by passions.

Espousing the beloved through ingenious means, fair and foul, is a common thread in many stories of the *Dasakumaracharita*, and incites other sentiments of humour (*hasya*), heroic courage (*vira*) and odiousness (*bibhatsa*). Rajavahana's friend Pushpodbhava gets his beloved to float a rumour through her elderly and trusted relatives that a seer has announced that she is possessed by a genie (*yaksha*), and only one who overcomes the *yaksha* can marry her; she then contrives the villainous suitor to invite her to his mansion, where the hero Pushpodbhava, in the garb of a female, attacks and kills him, then flees with the beloved, only to resurface and marry her later.[4] In another variant, the hero Mantragupta wins his beloved from her royal kidnapper by pretending to be a powerful ascetic who can achieve anything; he counsels the king, who is unable to win over the princess due to her being possessed by a *yaksha*, on how to defeat the *yaksha*. The king is supposed to enter a lake in the dead of the night, lie down at the bottom for as long as he can, and emerge with reddish eyes and wet body that will frighten the *yaksha*. Mantragupta even tells the foolish king to consult his able advisors, get the fishermen to examine the lake for hidden weapons or such, have it guarded by troops, and so on, thus gaining his confidence (Kale 1986: 346). Mantragupta then hides in the lake, kills the king who dives in in the dead of the night, and impersonates the king until the time that he reveals his secret to formalise his conquests at an opportune moment.

In a more daring venture, there is Upaharavarman, who returns to his native kingdom, which was wrested from his father unfairly by Upaharavarman's cousins, and learns that it is now being ruled by an unjust king, Vikatavarman. Upaharavarman then uses a female mendicant to create hatred in the queen towards her misshapen husband, gets the queen to fall in love with his own portrait and enlists her help for a coup. She is supposed to present Upaharavarman's portrait to the king and lure him with the ruse that he too would obtain such a handsome form if he were to conduct a mega sacrifice. When the deluded Vikatavarman arrives at the appointed place, our hero traps the king and kills him, concealed by the great smoke from the burning of a hundred sandalwood and aloe logs during the sacrifice. Upaharavarman then impersonates the king, who has supposedly acquired a wonderful form, and frees his parents (it appears that the ministers see no deception since the queen is involved). Upaharavarman has some qualms about committing adultery with the queen, but reasons that if both love (*kama*) and wealth (*artha*) can be obtained, it is pardonable. Luckily, he also dreams of the god with an elephant's head (Ganesha), who instructs him not to worry since Upaharavarman is a portion of himself, cursed to be a mortal and destined to act thus! Prince Rajavahana lauds these exploits, saying that even adultery and fraud, when employed by the talented, can serve *dharma* and *artha*, in that Upaharavarman succeeded in liberating his parents from imprisonment, put to death an inveterate foe and regained a kingdom. Rajavahana remarks, 'what is there that cannot become commendable when employed by the talented?' (Kale 1986: 300).

Perhaps catering to gentler tastes, Dandin also tosses up two stories in the *Dasakumaracharita* that involve no violence and employ the least force. In one, a young man, Pramati, falls in love with a princess and, donning female garb, gets a cunning accomplice to pass him off as the accomplice's daughter, who must be protected by the king while her 'father' goes looking for a suitable groom. Thus, our gender-bending hero gets close to the princess. Then, one day, the accomplice 'father' turns up with the groom (who is our hero Pramati, now returned to true form) and, unable to find the man's daughter, the hapless king marries his own daughter to the hero. The second story concerns Arthapala, who rescues his imprisoned father and proceeds to confront the unjust king; en route, he chances upon an underground chamber where a princess has been cloistered by the paranoid grandfather, fearing danger from the unjust king (she is eventually married off to Arthapala). Remarking on these tales, the future king Rajavahana says that these would appeal to the intellect and the learned.

All the heroes are fortunate in that their beloveds also fall for them, become willing and able accomplices in their amorous ventures, and lure their credulous competitors into death traps. As Isabelle Onians has noted, women are equal partners and seduction is inevitably mutual in the *Dasakumaracharita*, if not instigated and facilitated by the women (Onians 2005: 18). Heroic actions of killing unjust kings are mainly motivated by the heroes' desire to unite with their beloveds. Dandin was certainly approving of *gandharva vivaham*, or 'secret wedding' based on mutual consent of the bride and groom, and ennobles it by alluding to their coupling in earlier births, as with the princes Rajavahana and Upharavarman. In only two stories, of Arthapala and Vishruta (the hero of the concluding story, about which more is to follow), is the love interest secondary to *dharma* as duty and right order, respectively. Hence, A. B. Keith has aptly remarked that 'love appears here in the highest and most passionate form as an affair of the senses; love at first sight which demands fulfilment without delay and despises every obstacle is the normal motif' (cited in Gupta 1970: 334). As such, Dandin embroiders it in a manner that actually evokes the sentiment of humour (*hasya*) towards the folly of amorous pursuits.

RUSES OF SEDUCTION

But what is to stop others from using the same tactics to thwart or manipulate the erotic desires and political ambitions of our heroes?

Dandin recognises the need for them to wise up to the risks of the seduction game through the adventures of Apaharavarman, the villainous hero who specialises in thieving, gambling and intrigue. Apaharavarman sets out in search of a revered sage called Marichi to ascertain the whereabouts of the missing prince, Rajavahana. Using the standard trope of a courtesan beguiling an ascetic, Dandin throws in an edifying discourse by a courtesan, Kamamanjari (Love Ornament), on the relative hierarchy of *dharma*, *kama* and *artha*. It appears that Marichi was approached by the famous courtesan, 'full of devotion and with breasts bespangled with large tear drops' (Kale 1986: 262); when asked about the purpose of her visit, she says she has come to him for protection and 'to obtain the felicity of the other world' (ibid.). Kamamanjari's relatives come chasing after her, and her mother confesses that her only 'fault' lay in performing the proper duties (*svadharma*) of her profession enjoined by Prajapati (the Creator), such as cultivating her daughter's physical beauty and nurturing it, not exposing her to others (not even to her father after the fifth year), and training her in all branches of the erotic sciences.

Rivalling the exacting curriculum of the princes, the courtesan's training included initiation into arts such as dancing, singing, painting, preparing perfumes and wreathing flowers, and learning reading, writing, simple outlines of grammar, logic and astrology. The aim was to make her adept in the art of gaining a livelihood, in sportive graces (*kridakousalam*), and in *games of chance and strife* such as cockfights and dice (Kale 1986: 66, 414). Onians translates the relevant sentence thus: 'The mother must make her intimate with the skill of earning a living, expertise in amusements, and the art of gambling, whether in live sports or inanimate games' (Onians 2005: 197).

The courtesan's practical education was geared to appearing 'carefully decorated with a large retinue at public festivals' (Kale 1986: 266), being advertised abroad through experts, palmists, astrologers, nuns, jesters and parasites, carefully choosing the objects of her favour and bestowing attention, even while remaining detached from lovers. Putting a fine point, the courtesan's mother elaborates the business plan thus:

> When she becomes the constant object of the desires of young men, then to set a very high price on her hand (or to bestow her on a youth at a

> very great price); or to give away to one who is independent (master of his own affairs) and of his own accord is powerfully affected by love for her...or to deliver her over to one who is not independent but possesses superior qualities and is extremely intelligent, even for a small sum, but giving out in public that large sums were received. (Kale 1986: 263)

In the last case, the mother adds that they would try 'to extort money from the elders related to the youth and if no money comes in, they would gain their object in the local court by winning over the friendship of the king' (Kale 1986: 263). Lest we miss the gist, she proceeds to clarify that the aim was to extract wealth by inciting the passions of men and 'unite her with rich persons, capable of giving much money, who are able to remove all difficulties, and who are unobjectionable, after duly considering all doubts about the advantages and disadvantages' (ibid.: 264).

In between, there are titbits on how to get rid of a miser (pick a quarrel), how to stimulate a liberal one (provoke his jealousy), how to dispose of a pauper (with sarcasm), and so on. After this discourse, the mother complains that Kamamanjari has transgressed the duties enjoined on her by the Creator Prajapati-Brahma, fallen for a good-looking brahmin pauper, spurned many wealthy admirers and, if allowed to continue, will spell the ruin of her dependents. The sage Marichi, unable to persuade Kamamanjari to leave immediately, consoles the mother, saying that she would return on her own once she tastes the rigours of forest life.

But the courtesan takes to the simple life, and endears herself to the sage by helping him in his daily routine of worship. Thus, as Charles Malamoud has noted, Kamamanjari fulfils the courtesan's other duty: of singing and dancing for the gods (Malamoud 1996: 138). In time, the sage's passion was kindled. Seizing the moment one evening, the courtesan engages him in a conversation about *dharma*, *artha* and *kama*, saying foolish are the worldly people who place all three on an equal footing. Urged by him to elucidate further, she demurs, ironically observing, 'it is indeed fitting Your Reverence should seek to learn of the superiority or inferiority of the three objects of worldly existence from a slave' like herself (Kale 1986: 265).[5] Then, she holds forth on how *dharma* is superior to *kama* and *artha*, in that the latter cannot come into being without *dharma*; also, *dharma* is the 'creative cause of final beatitude' (*nivruttisukham*) and is attainable only by the concentration of the mind, rather than by external means; supported by the knowledge of reality (*tattvadarshanam*), it is not affected by *artha* and *kama* and, even when affected, it can be easily set right by a little exertion; and after eradicating that defect also, it conduces to the highest bliss (Kale 1986: 265). She then proceeds to adduce the many transgressions of the gods and sages themselves, starting from Brahma's passion for Tilottama, Shiva's seducing the wives of ascetics, Krishna's amorous sports with the 16,000 wives in his harem, Brahma's inclination towards his own daughter, Indra's seduction of Ahalya, the moon's consensual violation of his preceptor's wife, the sun's 'unnatural connection' with a mare, Brihaspati's coercive violation of his brother's pregnant wife, Vayu's impregnation of Anjana, Parashara's despoiling of a fisherman's daughter, Vyasa's connection with the wives of his brother, and finally, Atri's union with a doe (ibid.: 264). Resoundingly, she is silent about Vishwamitra's seduction by Menaka and Rambha, which may have alerted the sage to his own predicament.

All of this is music to the ears of the sage, who, in the throes of desire, promptly forgets his vows. Glossing her speech as meaning that 'the *dharma* of him who knows the Truth is not obstructed by worldly enjoyment', the sage resolves upon a little dalliance to polish his spiritual radiance! Saying he is ignorant of the nature, gains and results of *artha* and *kama*, he begs for further edification. Kamamanjari obliges by duly defining *artha* as acquisition, increase and conservation (of wealth) through agriculture, trade, peace and war, etc., and states that its final aim is 'bestowal on deserving persons', or, as Onians puts it, 'endowment of worthy causes' (Kale 1986: 266; Onians 2005: 207). Incidentally, this is exactly how Kautilya also defines *artha*, as acquisition, preservation, augmentation, and bestowal on worthy or deserving recipients (Shamasastry 1919: 12).

> *Kama* is a peculiar kind of touch, yielding the highest pleasure to those who are attached to sense objects, and its fruit is highest gratification, highest delight from mutual close contact, is sweet to remember, one in which all self-conceit disappears, is supreme, is bliss directly enjoyed and felt only by one's self. (Kale 1986: 266)

Kamamanjari then concludes by saying that it is for the sake of this pleasure that men undertake severe penance, give gifts, and undertake perilous wars and voyages (Kale 1986: 266).

But wait, did she not praise *dharma* as superior to *kama* earlier? Well, her impressive list mixes up those who were arguably fortified against passion, like Krishna and Shiva, with those who capitulated to *kama* and were cursed for their illicit liaisons, either in terms of loss of spiritual merit or more. Thus, the powerlessness of ardour (*tapasya*) and knowledge (*jnanam*) in the face of overwhelming desire is resounding. Though she asserts that if one were carried away, a 'little exertion' would suffice to set things right, it means restarting the ascetic regimen yet again. Anyway, it appears that *dharma* cannot come up to 'even a hundredth part of Kāma', and thus, as D. K. Gupta remarks, the courtesan propounds the superiority of *dharma* in letter while undermining it in spirit (Gupta 1970: 292).

Dandin concedes that 'hearing this, the rishi—may be owing to the power of destiny or her eloquence or the infirmity of his own mind, became attached to her'; Kamamanjari then takes Marichi to town, and wins accolades for accomplishing what was thought to be an impossible task (Kale 1986: 267). Thus he becomes a prize exhibit (garlanded and perfumed) for the festival of *kama* at the royal court. To the befuddled sage, she clarifies that she was only play-acting to win a wager with a rival courtesan, who had chided her for being proud as if she had conquered Marichi! She implores the sage with folded hands to return to his pious duties! Recounting this saga, the sage credits her with uprooting passion and instilling disgust for worldly goods, and admits that he shall engage in ardour (*tapasya*) once again to regain his former supernatural powers.

Commenting on this episode, Malamoud has argued that seduction is an art rather than a virtue, and that it literally means to lead astray, to turn the being whom one wishes for one's own pleasure away from his or her path, or alter the will of one's prey, and thus necessarily entails a certain element of deception (Malamoud 1996: 131). He highlights that the seducer need not lie outright, but hold a discourse that is honest from beginning to end, on his own nature, a discourse he may even embellish with an honest appraisal of seduction in general, while hiding all along that the present interlocutor is the prey and not, as might seem, the confidante. While there are many such episodes of courtesans and ascetics, few are as articulate and satirical as this one in unmasking the fragility of both knowledge and austerities.

GAMES OF CHANCE AND STRIFE

Considering that this swashbuckling story comes soon after the main hero, Rajavahana, reunites with his friends and liberates an ally-king from enemy forces, there is more to be said about the context and the overall lessons for a prince than just deception in seduction. Since courtesans were integral to the royal retinue, Dandin certainly wished to instruct his princes in their wily ways. Given that princesses and queens were not averse to killing for love, the princes had to be forewarned about the risks of the seduction game; to this end, the gullibility of the villainous suitors is depicted frequently, be it the misshapen husband who believes that he can change his form through a mega sacrifice, or another who thinks he can dispel spirits possessing his indifferent beloved by diving into a lake.

However, what is more striking is that Dandin suggests a close affinity between the arts of acquiring love and acquiring wealth/kingdom, in that both involve 'games of chance and strife'—a phrase used by the courtesan's mother. Because love and war involve playing with chance and strife to win power over another, the game analogy has captivated the literary imagination. Quite literally, Kamamanjari's play-acting with the sage started with a wager with a rival courtesan, where it was agreed that the loser would become the other's slave, and ended with her winning the challenge. She is moved by another wager in the case of a wealthy but unattractive merchant, on whom she bestows favour and relieves him of his wealth, aware of his contest with a good-looking but poor friend (apparently, the town sharpers created a quarrel between them over who was more manly, and resolved that neither form nor wealth, but being sought after by Kamamanjari alone attests to manliness) (Kale 1986: 268). Be it her strategy and tactics or rhetorical word-play with double and hidden meanings, she wins the game of *kama* with ease every time.

Besides winning or losing, the game analogy also captures the non-purposive aspects of playing. Experiential aspects of playing any game, such as withdrawal from the ordinary world, entering the game world out of free impulse, transcending need, absorption in the game-space/time, repetitive improvisation of moves and counter moves, the agonistic and creative dialectic with another, and the 'playing along' of the spectator have all been recently highlighted by Hans-Georg Gadamer (1986: 23–30). Combating positivism, Gadamer's concern was to light up non-instrumental reasoning and being in the world. Kamamanjari is not needy for true love, and playfully takes up the challenge of another courtesan. During the forest sojourn, she plays the role of an aspiring initiate to the hilt, foregoing adornment and using only a couple of freshly-washed garments, watering plants, collecting flowers for worship, assisting the sage in his daily rituals, and so on. For all practical purposes, it appears as if she is not just pretending but is fully absorbed in her new life.

However, there is a deeper metaphysical significance to the game analogy that is amplified in the Indian image of divine activity as sport or dalliance. Ananda Coomaraswamy has pointed out that the Sanskrit terms '*lila*' and '*krida*' connote divine activity as moved not by interest or pleasure, but by the maintenance of order in the world. The god plays at the creative activity exuberantly, not attached to the consequences or fruits of action. And the best and most god-like way of living is to play the game wherein proficiency involves not just physical skill, but also wisdom, so that one rises above the battle and remains unaffected by the rewards of action (Coomaraswamy 1977: 150–151).

From this standpoint, Kamamanjari's rhetorical praise of erotic pleasure as well as *dharma* is imbued with deep wisdom. Recall that *kama* yields the 'highest pleasure' to those who are attached to sense objects, and its fruit is 'highest gratification', 'highest delight' from mutual close contact, sweet to remember, and one in which all self-conceit disappears, is supreme, is 'bliss directly enjoyed and felt by one's own self only' (Kale 1986: 266). If we drop the references to sense objects, the remaining description of erotic pleasure mirrors spiritual bliss. Daniélou has noted that eroticism is firstly a search for pleasure, and the goal of the techniques of love is to attain the paroxysm considered by the *Upanishads* as a perception of the divine state, which is infinite delight (Daniélou 1994: 5). Unlike the sage, Kamamanjari seems to know the close affinity between erotic and spiritual bliss.

In all of this, Kamamanjari is only fulfilling her *svadharma* of nurturing dependents and other duties of a courtesan 'as elaborated by the Prajapati', and as recalled by her mother. In the process, she is certainly cruel towards unsuspecting and gullible victims. Kamamanjari, the ornament of love, is also adept at acquiring *artha* by feigning love and beguiling the most ascetic of sages. She even connives with Apaharavarman, who espouses her sister Ragamanjari in creating an 'appearance of virtue' since the latter has resolved, unmindful of family duties (*kula dharma*) and the courtesan code (*ganika svadharma*), that she would be won by merit, not money, and that her youth will not be enjoyed by another except through marriage (Kale 1986: 86, 275). While undoubtedly self-serving and hilarious, Kamamanjari's doublespeak on *dharma* also hints at the tension between *dharma*, understood as virtuous fulfilment of one's duty, and the actual messiness of acquiring love and wealth, especially for some agents who must use fraud and deception, if not outright violence against competitors. Dandin's heroine recognises her duty to be creative and inventive in acquiring and rationalising *kama* and *artha*, even as she mocks high-minded views of *dharma*.

Finally, Kamamanjari's allusion to *dharma* as conducive to the highest bliss, independent of external means and attainable through concentration of mind, is also not just casuistry. When the mind is purified by *dharma*, she says it is not tainted by passion as dust does not taint the sky; sustained by tattvadarshanam and *jnanabalam* (strength of wisdom), a certain kind of perception or awareness about reality, one composes the mind and remains above *artha* and *kama*. Arguably, the pollution of the wives of the ascetics of the pine forest by Shiva, and Kṛishna's sporting with 16,000 *gopi*s, examples she invoked earlier, may be said to have the *jnanabalam*, or the capacity to remain detached by desire, even while playing at it. Additionally, her views resonate with the influential rendering of *dharma* in the *Bhagavad Gita* as acting without attachment to fruits of action. Clearly, Kamamanjari herself is never deluded by *kama*; she plays with it and is detached. An ornament of love in name alone, she excels at this 'jewel among games', not only in the tactics of seduction but also in the detachment with which she plays at it (Ali 2004: 242). Similarly, it was crucial for accomplished heroes not to be too attached or afflicted by the senses, since overattachment to pleasure could be debilitating for the mind and body, and endanger the capacity to act in the world (ibid.: 259).

Thus, the practical education of the courtesan bears close resemblance to the practical education of the prince, in that they both must manage appearances in public, deploy a host of advertisers (jesters, palmists, etc.) to spread rumours and intrigue, understand and manipulate people's passions, extract wealth from the rich, and nurture their dependants. While bestowing graces and gaining loyalists, they must remain independent and detached. One striking difference is that the king, unlike the courtesan, must also bestow wealth on 'deserving persons', a phrase that occurs in Kautilya's notion of *artha* and is faithfully reiterated by Dandin through Kamamanjari. This lesson is adumbrated through the roguish acts of Apaharavarman, who is aroused by these stories to enter the city and right a series of wrongs, Robin Hood-style. He befriends a gambler, becomes an expert thief, and is determined to show wealthy misers the 'transitoriness of wealth' (*arthanam nashvaratvam*) (Kale 1986: 75, 269).[6] After many daring exploits, he falls for the princess Ambalika while trying to steal from the palace, and lands up when she is about to be forcibly married to a conquering king, only to kill the latter and win her over.

Apaharavarman plays at being a thief and is as detached towards *artha* as Kamamanjari is towards *kama*. Dandin has the hero assert that he would avenge both the sage and the merchant, as well as prove to the citizens the transitoriness of wealth. He gambles and loots from the rich and the miserly, and is highly creative in games of chance and strife. He secures the loyalty of those who have been wronged by helping them overcome their difficulties. He is adept at creating appearances of virtue through spreading rumours and intrigue.

To conceal his stealing, Apaharavarman floats a rumour about a bag of treasure which replenishes itself and further, gives out that it yields treasures only to merchants and courtesans, provided the possessors give away their ill-gotten wealth in charity! He also coaches Dhanamitra, a once-wealthy man reduced to penury by his own charity, to approach the king saying that such a bag has been bestowed on him by a mendicant; knowing Dhanamitra's generous nature, the king allows him to keep the bag, and does not let anyone steal it away from him. Dhanamitra proceeds to give away wealth during the day and replenish the bag through robbery by night. Before long, Apaharavarman falls in love with Kamamanjari's sister Ragamanjari and, to obtain her, he promises the fictive bag; in preparation to receive it, she gives away her ill-gotten wealth, thus restoring wealth to the merchant she once duped. Meanwhile, the bag is given out as stolen and Dhanamitra hints to the king that Kamamanjari may have stolen it. Summoned by the king, she is advised by our hero not to betray him and cause pain to her sister, but to implicate Arthapati, a greedy merchant (who is the scapegoat in this story); when the king sentences Arthapati to death, Dhanamitra intervenes to advise banishment instead, and Arthapati is reduced to rags, his wealth confiscated. Arthapati's one vice is that he was greedy and tried to marry the girl promised to Dhanamitra.

When Apaharavarman gets arrested for killing a couple of palace guards while rushing to stage a mega-robbery in an inebriated state, he again contrives to free himself through another elaborate ruse. This time, it is suggested (by his friend Dhanamitra again) that Apaharavarman is the one who actually stole the bag and may be persuaded to part with it so that his life is spared. The chief of the city police, who is torturing Apaharavarman to obtain the bag, is deluded into believing that he bears all the auspicious marks of becoming the heir-apparent since the princess loves him; if only the chief of police could find a secret way of fulfilling the princess' desire, this good fortune would fructify. The chief of police is then advised to recruit the expert thief Apaharavarman to dig a secret passage to the palace in return for being set free, which he does, only to be killed by our hero who then escapes prison. En route, Apaharavarman encounters the royal guard, lets his older woman accomplice cry out that her 'son' is insane and is running to kill the chief of police and sport with the princess, and the guards just reprove her and let both run away! He far surpasses Kamamanjari in bold and artful deception.

Apaharavarman seems to be redistributing wealth to good persons through repeated thefts from greedy merchants. He is considerate towards his friends and accomplices, ensuring that they are not punished. Even Kamamanjari, to whom he sets out to teach a lesson, is not disgraced beyond a point. There is no moral self-righteousness here; she is to be shown the transitoriness of wealth, but not punished (though she is threatened with having her ears and nose cut off due to suspected robbery); the king even restores some wealth to her so that she can continue her *svadharma*. Among the cherished qualities of the male lover or *nayaka* (who is often conflated with the urbane man, *nagaraka*), Ali mentions the importance of being a guide and protector of women while not being subject to them, independence of means and *lack of attachment*, besides noble birth, learning, knowledge of spiritual paths, eloquence, confidence, knowledge of the arts, and so on (Ali 2004: 215). This lack of attachment was designed to attract others to attach themselves to one, thus enabling influence and control (ibid.: 249).

If Kamamanjari is playing with the erotic desires of others and Apaharavarman with their wealth, the riskiest game of chance and strife occurs in restoring kingdoms to legitimate princes, and there too Dandin hints at a certain kind of intelligence that preys upon people's desires and interests while remaining unaffected. In that context, the hero Vishruta (whose tale is the climax of the *Dasakumaracharita*) is shown to be detached towards love, wealth and power, and hence extremely successful in attaining his goals. Interestingly, this detachment is shorn of any religious basis and there is no talk of souls or gods; it appears to ensue from sheer exuberance in playing a role and the pure pleasure in exercising one's practical skills. *Jnanabalam* (strength of wisdom) or *vivekam* (discriminatory judgment) about the transitoriness of all things colours and sustains the practical wisdom of all three, and their practical wisdom has many facets, ranging from crooked opportunism, clever manipulation of other's beliefs and passions to wise resignation to circumstances. Does virtuous action have no part to play in practical wisdom? Dandin weaves a quartet of stories about women's prized virtue of chastity that contains some hints.

ADULTERATED VIRTUES

Arguably, Dandin's views about women defy easy characterisation; he presents clever older women adept at intrigue who are willing go-betweens, resourceful younger women who are determined to help their lovers, adulterous wives, murderous queens, nuns who are worldly-wise, and so on. Dandin explicates their practical wisdom through a shipwrecked hero Mitragupta, who encounters a goblin which asks him to answer the following questions: what is most cruel, what contributes to the happiness of the householder, what is *kama*, and what is the means of attaining a difficult object? Our hero, much like Yudhisthira of the *Mahabharata* or Vikramaditya in the *Vetala Panchavimshati*, answers the questions 'correctly', and is thus spared by the goblin. Mitragupta replies that a woman's heart is most cruel, the virtues of a housewife bring happiness, *kama* is resoluteness of purpose, and ingenuity is the means of attaining a difficult object (Kale 1986: 326).

Mitragupta then tells four stories to support his answers; the first one is about a cruel wife named Dhumini, who cheats and pushes her doting husband into a well before eloping with a cripple whom the husband had helped and hosted. Carrying the crippled lover on her back, she earns a reputation as *pativrata* (a chaste wife) in a new town; when she chances upon her husband again (who had survived her attempt to murder him thanks to some passers-by), she accuses him of mutilating her crippled lover and has him sentenced to death.

The second story is of a young woman named Gomini who, given some paddy by a passing merchant who requests her to prepare food, uses the occasion to display superlative virtues. She separates the bran and rice, sends the bran to the goldsmith to be exchanged for fuel, strains the scum from the rice during cooking, extinguishes the fire, sends the black coal to the market to exchange for condiments, and so on, and serves the wayfarer a four-course meal. Impressed, he marries her and then 'seemingly' attaches himself to a courtesan; unperturbed, Gomini treats the courtesan as a 'dear friend' and worships her husband 'as a god' and, subdued by her virtues, her spouse becomes entirely dependent on her and enjoys the three goals of life.

The third story, illustrating *kama* defined as 'resoluteness of purpose', is about a wife named Nimbavati whose husband, embittered by her rebuffing his advances on the nuptial night, abandons her. Nimbavati wins him back by first contriving for him to fall for her 'lookalike', and thus disguised elopes with him, then causes a rumour to be spread that he has taken back his wife out of shame and gone to another town so that his relatives do not search for him, and finally rescues him from disgrace, reveals her real identity and endears herself to him.

The final story on ingenuity is about a young man who falls in love with the portrait of a married woman, Nitambavati, and resolves to marry her. He travels to her town, becomes a fortune-teller living in the cemetery and uses a Jain nun as a go-between to entice the woman, but is rebuffed. He then tricks Nitambavati into believing that she can 'charm' her impotent husband into virility if only she were to allow a spell to be transmitted to her foot by a magician in the dead of the night! She falls for this and he steals her anklet, then tries to sell it to her husband. The latter calls for a merchant guild meeting where the con-man declares that he got the anklet from a woman who was in the cemetery at night. The chaste Nitambavati is now banished as a witch and, when she tries to commit suicide, the youth confesses his love and, after his entreaties, she resigns herself to her new situation.

True, all these stories celebrate a patriarchal set-up where women have little freedom and are constrained to be good and chaste wives trapped within heterosexual marriages. Without forgetting the misogyny, it is pertinent to note that all these ploys—murder, deception, impersonation and adultery—are deployed by the heroines as well. It appears that the women are all from privileged backgrounds, though their caste identity is unclear. But what is intriguing is that Dandin is parodying the *pativrata* ideal, and shows that unadulterated virtue does not deliver, because most men are lustful.

Dandin begins conventionally enough with a wife ready to betray her hard-working husband for her lust (harking back to Manu who 'canonised' women's uncontrollable passions), but he soon shows that it is the men who are cruel, no matter how virtuous the wife. In fact, the second story parodies the ideal of virtue in general and chastity in particular by portraying the chaste wife worshipping her philandering husband; lest we think this was 'traditional', we may note that such chaste wives were fierce, as the well-known Tamil classic *Silappatikaram* showed. This epic, dated to the fifth century CE, is a heart-rending saga about the tragic life of a chaste woman, Kannagi (Parthasarathy 1993: 1–5). After a few happy years of marriage, her husband Kovalan attaches himself to a courtesan Matavi, only to return disillusioned to his wife. Following their reunion, Kannagi and Kovalan leave for Madurai, where she gives him an anklet to sell and start afresh. He chances upon a goldsmith and requests an estimate for the price of the anklet. The latter eyes the jewel and, having stolen the queen's anklet himself, finds a good opportunity to foist his crime onto an unsuspecting Kovalan. The goldsmith informs the king that the culprit who stole the queen's anklet has been found. The king, anxious to reconcile with the queen after a quarrel, instructs the guards to go kill the culprit and fetch the anklet. Kannagi, finding that her husband has been falsely accused and callously killed due to a king's haste, without a proper trial, storms into the palace, stuns the court by producing her other matching anklet, and accuses the king of failing in his duty to dispense justice. Realising his mistake, the king dies of guilt, after which she marches through the city and, cursing it, flings her left breast into it, summons the fire god to burn down the city, then ascends to heaven, thanks to her *pativrata* powers.

In Dandin's quartet, the resemblances to the *Silappatikaram* are unmistakable. Dandin is playing with the classic trope of merchant-husbands attaching themselves to courtesans and neglecting their chaste wives, who wait for their husbands to return to them, as in the Tamil epic. Dandin's wives attempt to change circumstances in their favour and win back their husbands through their devotion, as did Gomini, or through a clever arrangement of circumstances, as did Nimbavati. The most striking resemblance pertains to the anklet-related troubles of the last wife, Nitambavati. In the Tamil classic, Kannagi burns a whole city and wreaks havoc because her husband, when going to sell her anklet, is falsely accused of stealing the queen's anklet and executed. With the story on Nitambavati, Dandin gets a lovesick hero to steal a chaste wife's anklet and present it to her impotent husband, saying that he got it from a woman who was dragging a corpse at a cemetery; the chaste wife is banished as a witch and, when she tries to hang herself, the hero surfaces, leaving her no choice but to reconcile with her new lover.

Certainly, *pativrata*-hood has lost its sheen and circumstances conspire to mute its power in Dandin's quartet, whereas Kannagi's chastity screams and burns when it is wronged. For Dandin's wives, the reputation of *pativrata*-hood is equally, if not more important, than the reality; belief in the mystical powers of *pativrata*-hood provides a perfect smokescreen for cunning and murderous acts. This is demonstrated in the climactic story, where a widow-queen, who is being courted by a stepbrother-in-law, murders the latter with a poisoned garland, which she then dips into some other solution and uses it to garland her daughter, who remains unaffected, astounding the onlookers with the queen's 'mystical' powers!

Kale has observed that Dandin's work does not teach any moral, and that he aims to please, not instruct; after all, he was mirroring the atmosphere of crime and fraud in royal successions, and the daily life of vagabonds and tramps (Kale 1986: xliv). De also concurs that the four stories show that cunning alone is the way to success (De 1959: 122). Dandin's world resonates with Machiavelli's, especially as presented in *Mandragola*. In this satire-play, Machiavelli exposes the fragility of virtues in a corrupt society, and pragmatic accommodation seems the only intelligent option. A rich young man, Callimaco is besotted by a married woman, Lucrezia's beauty and virtue, and sets out to seduce her. A big hurdle is that, though Lucrezia is married to an older man, she is honest and religious to a fault, and has no thoughts of romance. Nicia, her impotent husband, is so desperate for an heir that he falls for a fantastic scheme of administering a magic potion to Lucrezia to drink, after which she must be made to sleep with a tramp so that its fatal virulence is drawn out, and then she would be all set to conceive. Ligurio, a marriage-broker fallen on hard times, dreams up and executes the whole plot, with the lovelorn Callimaco playing both the doctor and the tramp who deals in magical potions! He is ably aided by Lucrezia's mother, who takes her to a friar who advises her as follows:

> In matters of conscience, you must accept this general truth, where there is a prospect of certain good and uncertain evil…never let the good slip for fear of bad. Here you have a certain benefit—that you will conceive, and create a new soul to praise God. The uncertain evil is that the man who lies with you…may die—but in fact they don't always die…But since the point is uncertain, it is better that your husband should not take the risk. As for there being anything sinful in the act itself, that is all nonsense. It's the will that sins, not the body. (Machiavelli 1978: 39)

The good friar further assuages her fears by pointing out that she is not sinning because she is doing what her husband wants, and that her intent is pure since she is not seeking pleasure for herself but the happiness of her husband.

The friar adds that a few drops of holy water can wash away sins, if any, incurred in all this. Lucrezia's mother reminds her that a woman without children cannot call a home her own and that, after her husband's death, everyone abandons her like a brute beast. Thus persuaded, Lucrezia acts out the plan and lies with Callimaco, after which she takes to adultery with zest. She realises that the cunning of her lover, the folly of her husband, the stupidity of her mother and the wickedness of her confessor have all led her to this; it all must be the 'will of Heaven' and she is not bold enough to refuse anything that heaven wishes her to accept; and Callimaco becomes a 'friend' who would have free access for his magical cures! This tale of 'bourgeois accommodation' is steeped in the view that the pursuit of private gain at any cost is what motivates human beings, and that one's own desire and that of others offer opportunities to manipulate circumstances to one's advantage (Martinez 1983: 20).

While Dandin may agree, he is also more optimistic about educating desire, especially sexual desire and the desire for wealth and success. For this reason, he has the heroes pursue many easy, cheap and magical tricks that quickly lead to marriage and consummation, after which they are ready to take up more 'heroic' actions, such as waging wars. Whether it is the future king marrying his bride in a magical rite right under the nose of her father, or a hero who dresses up as a female, ingratiates himself as a girl-friend to the woman he falls for and returns as the eligible bachelor to marry her, Dandin has his heroes first ascertain the women's interest (darting sidelong glances repeatedly being a surefire sign!), and then worm their way into their hearts somehow. *Kama*, or love, strikes unexpectedly, pushes heroes towards unconventional actions and plunges them into unforeseen conflicts. The hero is allowed to dream, woo and finally wed his beloved, and is thus prepared for the more serious tasks of rescuing parents, regaining kingdoms or aiding allies at war.

Analysing a similar plot in Shakespeare's *Measure for Measure*, Bloom notes that marriages, reunions with families and natural satisfactions are central to restoring justice in licentious contexts (Bloom 1993: 344). He observes that 'effective law is a delicate mixture of fear producing force, wisdom and above all, natural inclination, producing as much happiness for individuals as human society admits of', and that 'sexual satisfaction is a good thing and it does not take too much, unless there has been total emancipation, to calm sexual desire sufficiently in the name of marriage' (Bloom 1993: 345). Dandin's zeal in getting all his heroes married is intelligible from this perspective.

Even though some of these marriages were strategic alliances and extramarital liaisons were common in courtly contexts, erotic education still served to tame and tune passions and attachments to make these conducive to the exercise of authority and property, both within and outside the household (Ali 2004: 260). From this standpoint, Dandin's ambiguous and ironic presentations of a wife's fidelity or *pativrata*-hood illuminate how the practice of virtue is sustained or endangered by circumstances beyond her control. The lesson is not that one must abandon virtues, but that one must avoid extremes (a la Dhumini and Gomini), and not shy away from pragmatic resolutions (a la Nimbavati and Nitambavati). While Nitambavati's adjusting to the con-man-lover may seem self-serving, it may be noted that even Manu disapproved of an impotent husband deserting a woman, and would have regarded her compromise as driven by her extreme circumstance and hence right (*apad-dharma* or emergency ethics) (Bowles 2007: 50). When untamed, the pursuit of *kama* and *artha* can lead to the ruin of both individuals and kingdoms, and call for extreme measures to restore order. Lest we have doubt, the *Dasakumaracharita*'s climactic story vindicates this *niti* unequivocally.

POISON OF DISORDER

Anantavarman, the king of Vidarbha was addicted to pleasures and, ignoring the appeals of a prudent minister, devoted himself to gambling, hunting, drinking and womanising (as elaborated in the first chapter). Taking advantage of the king, who was untutored in the political arts, Vasantabhanu, the enemy king of Asmaka who was 'adept in policy', sent an astute minister, Chandrapalita, to wreck Anantavarman's kingdom from within, using spies, dancing girls and others. Seizing every opportunity, praising all of Anantavarman's pleasure pursuits with artful rhetoric, Chandrapalita aggravates the debauchery and causes all-round quarrels. Dandin's depiction of lawlessness and libertinage is chilling:

> The King followed his advice like the instructions of a Guru, and the people imitating the king threw off all restraint and became universally licentious....The administrators of different departments, acting in imitation of the king and the subjects, devoured the fruits of their offices...all the channels of revenue were closed, and those of expenditure multiplied...The king, under various disguises held intercourse with their wives...angry affrays proceeding from such practices became frequent; the weak were assaulted by the strong; the rich were robbed of their money by thieves; all fear of reproof being removed, the paths of sin were freely trodden. (Kale 1986: 357–358)

Horrific scenes unravel, with families reduced to penury, unjust and inordinate punishments meted out without proper trials, and the rich bent on seeking vengeance. Taking advantage of the situation, the enemy king Asmaka sends agents to poison the king and finish off the latter's army through a variety of traps such as,

> inducing some to enter mountain valleys full of dry grass...and setting fire to them...by urging some to kill tigers and letting them fall into their jaws...by extracting thorns from the feet of some with poisoned lancets...by killing with ease some when left all alone...by secretly killing those who quarrelled over ancestral property, and then casting the ignominy on their opponents...by causing consumption by inducing them to indulge day and night in the company of women whose bodies were saturated with poison...; and by many other means. (Kale 1986: 359)

That the heart of justice consists of respecting the love of one's own, starting from the family unit, is unmistakable here. When others' wives are violated by the king, there is bound to be universal licentiousness. From there on, might is right, the big fish eat the small ones, and greed reigns supreme. All classes, rich and poor, are afflicted by fear, albeit for diverse reasons. The *tejaswin*, or the aristocratic classes, are humiliated and hence indignant. As Kautilya warns, an erring king is worse than a blind king because he is bent on doing what is against the *shastras*, and thus invites calamity.

It is in this context that Dandin has an astute hero, Vishruta (the well-known one) conspire to bring back order, prudently steering Anantavarman's widow-queen towards actions that will retrieve the kingdom. Vishruta chances upon the crown prince, rumoured to be dead, and an older man in a forest, and the latter apprises him about the woes of the libidinous Anantavarman and the subsequent loss of his kingdom to Vasantabhanu, the king of Asmaka. Vishruta vows to defeat Vasantabhanu by sheer 'policy' (*naya*) (Kale 1986: 202, 361). For, Vasantabhanu not only wrecked Vidarbha from within, he also allied with enemies to invade Vidarbha and, when Anantavarman was fighting on one front, attacked him in the rear, and incited Anantavarman's feudatory allies to betray and kill him. He then tells the feudatory princes to distribute Anantavarman's wealth and vehicles according to their respective power, thus stirring a destructive quarrel among them and seizing all the wealth for himself. Given Vasantabhanu's felicity with 'policy' (*niti*), Vishruta's boast acquires salience.

First, Vishruta gets the widow-queen to float a rumour that her son was killed by a tiger, and she is now ready to wed her stepbrother-in-law, who was courting her and with whom she had sought refuge after the libertine king Anantavarman lost his kingdom. When the stepbrother-in-law shows up, she strikes him dead with a poisoned garland, with which, after dipping it in a miracle solution, she then garlands her daughter; the palace audience is astounded at her *pativrata* powers, by which the same garland can kill one while adorning another without harm! From then on, her pronouncements are taken as oracles. Vishruta has her announce that she dreamt of the goddess Vindhyavasini, who revealed that she had carried away and protected her son in the form of a tigress, and would shortly release him along with a brahmin youth to be enthroned again. In the dead of the night, after the ministers have checked the sanctum of the shrine and ensured it was empty, as rituals and loud beating of drums were apace, Vishruta emerges with the prince from beneath the idol of the goddess (to which an underground passage had been dug), and, swinging the closed door open to an expectant crowd, illustrates the mysterious ways of the goddess.

Apparently, the crown prince, now regarded as the son of a goddess, is suitably instructed in the art of ruling before being enthroned by Vishruta, who then sets about establishing order by appointing trusted ministers and officials. In the postscript, he wishes to leave to search for Rajavahana; of course, the grateful widow-queen and the subservient prince beg him to stay, until he is called upon by an allied king for assistance in Champa, where other friends of his have converged. Whether it is in steering the *pativrata* image of the queen and a goddess cult to reinstall the legitimate prince, or finding suitable moments for head-on combat with enemies and slaying them, Vishruta shows himself to be a dream counsellor. He never misses an opportunity afforded by both circumstance and his reputation for virtue to perform some unpalatable but necessary political actions. While Vishruta is also married off to the princess, and thus given personal interest in protecting the kingdom that he has secured for the prince, Dandin repeatedly presents him as a 'policy' (*niti*) expert waiting to prove his mettle, rather than a love-crazed or gold-digging hero.

Robert DeCaroli has noted that the tale of Vishruta may be building upon real historical events that concerned both the Vakataka and Pallava courts. Given that the Chalukyans posed a threat to both the Vakatakas and the Pallavas, they may have been captured in the prototype of the enemy king Vasantabhanu. He also suggests that Vishruta, as the ideal ruler, may have been based on the historical figure Subandhu (DeCaroli 1995: 677).

JUDGMENT OF FRIENDS AND ENEMIES

Notwithstanding their successes in retrieving kingdoms, Dandin and his heroes are not quite certain about how they will be judged. In fact, they all narrate their adventures to the prince Rajavahana, who offers concluding comments. After listening to Apaharavarman, the prince praises his hardy and desperate deeds, outshining even the author of a thieves manual called *Karnisuta*; hearing Upaharavarman's tale, Rajavahana observes that even fraud and adultery can serve a good cause when employed by the talented; impressed by Arthapala, who saves his father from execution by a suspicious prince, whom he in turn imprisons without shedding blood, Rajavahana says that Arthapala had done great deeds by using his intellect to the utmost. Regaled by a gender-bending Pramati, he says that such graceful sports and gentle action appeal to the learned; in the other cases, he extols ingenuity and courage. Curiously, the most complete adventure, that of Vishruta, which vindicates the importance of prudent policy (*dandaniti*), involving maximum deception and bloodshed, goes without comment. This may be partly because we have an incomplete manuscript of the *Dasakumaracharita*.

And yet, there are two contexts where the question of how one would be judged is explicitly raised. First Upaharavarman, about to execute his plan to deceive, murder and impersonate, prevaricates thus:

> This object of mine is almost achieved. But, on account of the violation of another's wife, *Dharma* may be obstructed. But it is quite allowed by writers of sacred books, if thereby wealth and love can both be secured. Again, I am going to incur sin having in view liberation of my parents; this (my motive) will extenuate the sin and will endow me with religious merit at least. But then, on hearing this, how will the prince and my friends judge of my conduct? (Kale 1986: 293)[7]

Presently, Upaharavarman is consoled by a timely dream, where the elephant-headed god reassures him that what he is about to do is destined due to some curse. His casuistry above is neither substantive nor convincing, only self-serving. Upaharavarman is motivated by pleasure and revenge, in that his father's kingdom was usurped by his elder brother and the latter's sons during Upaharavarman's absence. The elaborate stratagem through which he accomplishes his feat includes adultery and impersonation. It appears that a select few, his parents, an older nurse and his queen may know this fact and perhaps condone it. Thanks to his narration, his friends (and readers) also now know that he passed off as Vikatavarman, the usurper-villain. The approving judgment of the future king Rajavahana, that even fraud and adultery can aid good causes such as liberating parents or eliminating a foe and regaining a kingdom, has already been noted. He comments, 'what is there that is not commendable when employed by the talented?' (Kale 1986: 300). In Onians' translation, 'for thanks to these crimes, you could procure your parents' release from the oppression of captivity, slay the wicked enemy and win back a kingdom. Whatever an intelligent man does becomes a noble act' (Onians 2005: 321).

However just it might seem to friends, adultery and deceit may not be so easily condoned by the public, and so the heroes cannot come clean to the people whom they must govern. It may never come to light to the many, but a few will certainly be involved in shady acts. Then again, it is not easy to cover up the web of deceit for long. How long can a hero remain an evil king changed by an alchemical ritual? So he quickly issues amnesty and tries to rectify the wrongs of the previous ruler. And yet, he cannot be easily set apart from a tyrant who rules for his own pleasure and that of his dependents.

This predicament is reinforced in the final story of Vishruta—perhaps the complete embodiment of 'policy' or *dandaniti*—who also wonders about how he will be judged, especially by enemies; friends who are also beneficiaries and relatives may be more generous in their judgments of the dark deeds required to bring order. Why do enemies matter? We have already encountered this motif in the *Mudrarakshasa*, where Chanakya tries to win over the enemy counsellor Rakshasa. Dandin tries out a variation on the same theme towards the end of his *Kavya*.

Keen to know the enemy's opinion, Vishruta sends a spy-emissary to Aryaketu, an adept counsellor (from the queen's side) neglected by the king. Recall that leading up to this juncture in the narrative, Vishruta has caused the widow-queen to murder her brother-in-law with whom she had sought refuge, has himself killed another brother (who was to marry the princess) of the king, and restored a prince rumoured to be dead as the goddess's own 'son', protected by her and entrusted to him for care. After enthroning the prince, Vishruta also kills the main villain, Vasantabhanu of Asmaka, who had taken pride in his 'policy' by enticing the latter to fight the young prince.

To be sure, all this is possible because of willing accomplices, be they widowed or spurned queens, exiled or neglected counsellors, or unemployed and shrewd con-men and women. Not to mention a pervasive credulousness: undesired suitors who believe that they can chase away spirits possessing their indifferent beloveds by diving into lakes; chaste women who believe that estranged husbands may be 'charmed' into loving them again and fall for fantastic tricks of rakish mendicants; and people who actually believe that their cruel king acquired a charming form and good character due to a mega-smoky ritual!

However beneficial in restoring legitimate princes, rescuing incarcerated parents and besieged lovers or queens, the heroes remain anxious that their deceptive tricks may not remain 'miraculous' acts for long. Dandin recognises that even a superlative hero such as Vishruta needs to be reassured that he is not judged as a grand criminal, but as a wise statesman. Dandin builds this image by having Vishruta launch a lecture on *Arthashastra* tenets. Harking back to Kautilya, he reflects on the three kinds of strength or power (*shakti*) that sustain a kingdom, namely good counsel (*mantra shakti*), majesty or pre-eminent authority (*prabhava* or *prabhu shakti*), and energy or enthusiasm (*utsaha shakti*). Good counsel determines objects to be attained, pre-eminent strength initiates action, and energetic action effects their attainment. Describing statecraft as a tree, good counsel is akin to the root, consisting of five elements; allies, determining the right means, determining space and time, proper emergency measures, and attainment of the end itself (Kale 1986: 505). Pre-eminence is twofold: greatness in wealth and arms. Energetic action consists of employing the four means of conciliation, intrigue, gifts and force, or the exertion of mind, speech, body and action. Apart from these branches, statecraft has 'seventy-two elements for its leaves and six qualities of royalty its blossoms, power its flower and success is the fruit' (ibid.: 366).[8] Due to such complexity, 'it is very hard to make the tree of statecraft yield fruit by one who has none to back him up' (ibid.).

Reasoning thus, Vishruta tries to enlist the enemy counsellor Aryaketu to his side by sending him a spy, who disparages Vishruta and claims he is an impostor who will swallow up the prince and the state. Aryaketu then certifies that Vishruta must be descended from a noble family, has extraordinary acuteness of intellect, possesses superhuman strength, skill in the arts, nobility of mind and, most importantly, is adept in statecraft (Kale 1986: 367). Following this encomium conveyed by the spy, and after testing Aryaketu's sincerity by various trials, Vishruta co-opts him as a colleague and, with his assistance, secures good ministers and spies. Closing the work is a telling vindication of the

Arthashastra as proper policy or *dandaniti*. With the help of Aryaketu and his ministers, Vishruta claims,

> I knew which of the subjects were covetous and rich misers, which very proud, and which…refractory; and thinking that I might amass great wealth if I gave proofs of my own want of greed, inspired a sense of duty, tormented the heretics, cleared out all those who stood like thorns in the way of prosperity of the state, thwarted the secret plans of foes,… firmly established the four castes…and since all undertakings based on *policy* [*danda*] emanate from wealth [*artha*], and…*no sin would be worse than showing weakness in adhering to the principles of policy*—I zealously took all the proper measures. (Kale 1986: 367; emphasis added)

The idea that it is 'sinful' to show weakness (spelt out as *dourbalyam*, with its many connotations of impotency and feebleness) regarding *niti* harks back to *apad-dharma* (crisis or emergency ethics). For individuals, acute distress may ensue from the loss of ability to pursue one's prescribed livelihood, or when one is faced with clear and present danger to one's life. All this was tethered to the societal division into four classes (*varnas*), and dealt with when a member of one class could transgress and adopt the calling of another (Bowles 2007: 53). By linking these 'necessary transgressions' to *dharma*, or right order, their legitimacy was established. The *Dasakumaracharita* begins with the distress of a royal family, its allies and ministers who all narrowly escape capture and death, and seek refuge in a forest. All the princes have been unfairly deprived of their inheritance and must ensure their livelihood through a mixture of courage and crookedness. The climactic book elaborates on *apad-dharma* for a founding hero or counsellor intent on restoring order, or *dharma*. Here, it echoes the *Arthashastra*, which presents a more 'objective' treatment of distress situations as they impact a kingdom at large, thanks to an errant king, or a depleted treasury, or an unrighteous conqueror, rather than to individual crises. Anger and lust in the king are calamitous for the kingdom as a whole and call for extraordinary measures (ibid.: 54, 77). A graphic account of a dire crisis affecting a kingdom also occurs in the *Mahabharata*'s *Rajadharma Parva* (Book of King's Duties), where Yudhisthira asks the following:

> What way is there, Bharata, for a king who is being abandoned by his allies, who has many enemies, whose treasury is utterly depleted, whose army is weak, whose ministers and companions are corrupt and whose counsels have been made known everywhere; who, seeing no other way, is losing his kingdom; who has been attacked by an enemy's army which is strong while he is weak;...for whom peace or dissension would be untenable due to the great pressure he is under, and his life too due to his circumstances. In this case, what would be good to do? (Bowles 2007: 192)

In another variation, Yudhisthira asks thus:

> When a king is weak, procrastinating or overly sympathetic to his kin, when his citizens and kingdom are disaffected, and when there is no store of wealth, when his chief ministers are suspect and his counsels have been made known, Bharata, when his allies are not honoured, and his ministers are entirely disunited, when he is attacked by an enemy's armies which are powerful while he is weak, and when his mind is afflicted, speak! What remains to be done? (Bowles 2007: 211–212)

Bhishma, the addressee, responds that the 'right' or *dharmic* conduct in dire crisis is secret, mysterious and subtle. As Adam Bowles glosses, the linking of *niti* (conduct during political crisis) to *dharma* (as proper/right conduct) is significant in that neither Kautilya nor Manu bother to justify political expediency as *dharma*; further, that this *dharma* is 'secret' denotes that it is difficult to grasp, is potentially dangerous, has deleterious consequences, or is easily exploited. For this reason, it is also knowledge that must be kept hidden, especially from inappropriate recipients (Bowles 2007: 193). This exclusivity limits the risks and expands the privilege and responsibility of those who possess it (ibid.: 195). Bowles compares this to the secret knowledge of highly powerful weapons, which are often exclusively reserved for some people who have been trained to take risks and act maturely. Bowles also emphasises Bhishma's idea that this *dharma* is 'more subtle' than speech or wisdom, defying easy and univocal judgments (ibid.: 196). Bhishma details the acts necessary to fill the royal coffers, such as seizing wealth from the well-off and killing those who stand in the way of such procurement. Bowles adds that morally dubious acts are justified only if the ends they serve, such as stability or restitution of the kingdom, are actually met;

otherwise, the king incurs both the sin of failure in his primary duty, as well as of the various activities he performed in the failed attempt (Bowles 2007: 233).

Does this mean that the Indian texts are condoning an ends-justify-means ethic? Are they impervious to the 'problem of dirty hands', as has been discussed elsewhere? We know that the epic tradition mentions guilt and expiation, as with Yudhisthira, the epitome of *dharma* whose chariot, which always cruised slightly above ground, was grounded due to perjury during the war. Drawing from Catholic sources, Michael Walzer has recently argued that while 'dirty hands' may be justified in extreme emergency situations, good men must reaffirm the moral code by accepting punishment or doing penance (Walzer 1973: 178). He also counsels denying glory and power to the greatest liars, except in the case of the lucky few whose extraordinary achievements make us forget the lies (ibid.: 180). Taking another tack, Jean Elshtain has suggested that instead of posing 'what is the right thing for me to do', asking 'what is to come' may be more appropriate when confronted with emergency situations, such as a Nazi regime or possible terrorist attacks (Elshtain 2004: 84). She cautions that one must make emergency activities such as torture or guerrilla warfare routine, and one must still be called to account. A similar pragmatism is at work in *apad-dharma*, which 'uneasily straddles the tension between improprieties associated with ruling and the proprieties demanded by the assertion of standards of civil behaviour with which the king, too, must seek accommodation' (Bowles 2007: 234).

It is noteworthy that Vishruta is set apart from Vikatavarman who, motivated solely by pleasure and revenge, acts as if ends justify means. Vishruta's knowledge of statecraft (*niti*) is emphasised by Dandin throughout, suggesting that he is acting according to the time, place and context recognised by *arthashastra* (knowledge on acquiring wealth and ruling kingdoms) experts as requiring emergency measures. Undoubtedly, brahmin priests would have legitimised Vikatavarman's exploits through quaint casuistry and innovative atonements, since he is a royal. Vishruta is only an ace counsellor, and seeks *niti* experts for approval. In the *Panchatantra* and *Mudrarakshasa* as well, the enemy counsellor's judgment is a recurrent motif. Not moral theorists, but only a few superlative political practitioners are seen as relevant. They also happen to be ministers with integrity in all these narratives. Rakshasa is not only astute, but loyal to a fault. In the *Panchatantra* too, Stirajivin and Raktaksha lock horns, while in the *Hitopadesha*, Chakravaka and Doordarshi are mutually impressed by and approving of one another. Vishruta ascertains whether Aryaketu's praise is 'sincere' before enlisting him as an equal partner. He also adds that he gave proof of his own want of greed in the process of reinstating order. Perhaps it is the experience of acting in crises that enables them to understand the subtlety and mysteriousness of *apad-dharma*.

One final point may be made here regarding the doubling motif, that is, the Chanakya/Rakshasa, Damanaka/Karataka, Chakravaka/Doordarshi and Vishruta/Aryaketu pairs. Wendy Doniger has argued that the strategy of splitting characters in two (through sloughing and doubling) is the way myths deal with a deeply troubling paradox (Doniger 1999: 5). She shows how the shadow double allows for the original to be spared suffering, as in the case of Sita in the *Ramayana* (ibid.: 14). But the double then goes on to have a life of its own, causing confusion between the two. Though Doniger argues from mythic and epic materials and confines herself to sexuality, her argument about sloughing off to either get what one wants or avoid what one does not, is illuminating (ibid.: 305). In our context, it is clear that the authors split their characters such that Rakshasa is like Chanakya but for his humane feelings; Karataka is prudent but for his ethical compunction; Doordarshi is like Chakravaka but for his loyalty to a stubborn king; and Aryaketu is like Vishruta but for his having a dumb patron. They are impeded by loyalties and humaneness from acting ruthlessly to secure themselves during crises. And yet, their qualities are needed to restore legitimacy and trust during normal times. Though this is not immediately apparent, the recurring pattern of reconciling these characters at the end suggests that our authors grasped the chameleon-like nature of political prudence.

CONCLUSION

Recall that this book began with Viharabhadra's fulsome advice to his king that Chanakya's *Arthashastra* is demanding in its regimen and detracts rulers from enjoying what they have; by the end, the tyranny of the pleasure-loving king has been experienced in all its goriness, and an enemy expert in statecraft has plundered the kingdom. Against this context, Vishruta may be seen as a founding hero who rises above personal interest; unlike other heroes, he is not shown to be in love or pursuing his own interest; he is just keen on showing his command over *dandaniti* and subduing the king of Asmaka, who was proud of his own expertise. Vishruta is fashioned like Chanakya, except that he is married off in the end by Dandin and firmly tethered to the kingdom he secured.

Thus, notwithstanding the erotic misadventures, the *Dasakumara-charita* is so political that it is hard to read Dandin as a mere entertainer aiming to please. Dandin certainly gives us a ringside view of politics, but he also deals some lasting wounds. Even in the lives of individuals, virtue alone does not suffice for happiness and success, especially in adverse circumstances; the reputation for virtue needs to be shored up through the strategic manipulation of unfavourable conditions. But unlike Machiavelli's Lucrezia, Dandin's heroines do not give up on virtue altogether, thinking that reputation and appearances alone matter. *Pativrata-dharma*, or the virtue of fidelity, is subject to many tests by fickle and philandering husbands, and wives must manoeuvre correctly to emerge successful. Unlike epic heroines like Sita, who go through tests by fire to prove their chastity, these ordinary wives opt to convince their husbands through persistence and strategy.

There is also a deep ambivalence about attachment in love and politics; on the one hand, attachment impels action, especially heroic action; on the other hand, it compromises self-mastery and limits the agency and power of actors, especially political actors in a courtly context (Ali 2004: 251). Training in practical wisdom thus requires one to understand and cultivate detachment, just like Kamamanjari regarding love, Apaharavarman regarding wealth, or Vishruta regarding both. In all three instances, a thorough understanding of the transitoriness of the object of desire, rooted in experience, causes detachment and skilful playing upon other's desires. It is this that sets apart their detachment from that of a renouncer who shuns the world and seeks salvation. This detachment is more like that of a playwright. Alluding to the *Mudrarakshasa*, Ali notes that a courtier's skill consisted in 'sowing a tiny seed of enterprise, planning its expansion, and when the seeds have germinated, unfolding their hidden fruits, pausing skilfully and finally gathering up the results though spread far and wide' (Ali 2004: 59). In this light, Dandin's praise of the art of government (*nitishastra*, *dandaniti*) as a 'lamp' that lights up the path of action, and as a 'divine eye' that gives insight into the past, present and future, thus enabling rulers to determine desirable political ends and means, is salient. It appears that expertise in *arthashastra* bestows a 'divine eye' not only in terms of acting, but also judging; whether one has acted skilfully and well to sustain and nourish *artha* in a detached manner is appraised by rival counsellors, for only they can penetrate appearances immediately and judge the nature and scope of *apad-dharma*. The sins incurred in restoring order are bad; but it is worse to incur the sin of showing weakness in *niti*, or policy, during crisis. Dandin's achievement consists in imparting these insights, evoking the sentiments (*rasa*s) of both humour (*hasya*) and wonder (*adbhuta*) in readers.

Notes

1. Kale has noted that the *Dasakumaracharita* proper has only eight stories, and that the *Purvapitika*, or 'Prologue', and the *Uttarapitika*, or 'Epilogue', may have been added later (Kale 1986: xli). While keeping this in mind, I have not hesitated to adduce details from such interpolations wherever they agree with the dominant tenor of the main text.
2. The rise of *shanta* or serenity, the ninth *rasa*, post-dates Dandin (Ali 2004: 188).
3. For details on the nuances of prose romance and style, see Kale 1986: xi–xiii.
4. This story is from the *Purvapitika*, which Kale opines may have been an interpolation, but its theme of spirit possession occurs in the main text as well.
5. Onians translates *dharma* as 'piety' (Onians 2005: 207), but I have retained the Sanskrit term following Kale.
6. Onians also translates *arthanam nashvaratvam* as the 'transient vanity of material objects' (Onians 2005: 217).
7. Onians' translation, 'when Prince Rājavāhana or my friends hear of it, I know not what they will say', is less sharp (Onians 2005: 299).
8. The seventy-two elements refer to the elements of sovereignty of the four circles of states.

V

BEYOND *SVADHARMA*

Ethical Excellence in the *Vetala Panchavimshati*

Popularised by the Indian children's magazine *Chandamama* as well as by a Doordarshan television series, the Vikram and Vetala story-cycle is second only to the *Panchatantra* in the narrative repertoire of many Indians (Rajan 1995: xv–lxiii).[1] This story-cycle is about the encounters between King Vikramaditya and a superhuman daemon, the *Vetala*, who dwells in a corpse.[2] Through twenty-five delightful tales of conniving courtesans, famished hermits, adulterous wives, jealous husbands, ambitious merchants, virtuous thieves, foolish and fastidious brahmins, adventurous warrior-princes and wise kings, not to mention demanding gods and goddesses, the compiler Shivadasa presents ethical riddles, resolving which requires subtle reasoning and judgment. Many stories portray competing candidates for superlative courage, virtue, greatness, delicacy or fastidiousness. There are also villains and knaves who outdo one another in wrongdoing or foolishness. In each case, King Vikramaditya is called upon to judge relative merit and settle questions of superior virtue or wrongdoing.

Apart from entertainment, it appears that Shivadasa also intended the *Vetala Panchavimshati* as a *nitishastra* (expert knowledge of practical wisdom). Like the earlier texts, this work also presents erotic misadventures wherein young men and women fall head over heels in love and pine for instant gratification, failing which they feel they would surely die. The king has to settle who is the right suitor, or father, often thanks to the confusion caused by the ingenuity of the lovers. While this is already a familiar motif in the *Dasakumaracharita*, what is unique here is the concern with ethical excellence. In striking contrast to the other texts, the *Vetala Panchavimshati* explicitly asks a king famed for his virtues, 'who is greater' or 'which is nobler', showing that love's troubles do not exhaust the royal curriculum. This chapter examines ethical reasoning and judgment as they are presented in five stories about superlative nobility, magnanimity and virtue. Focusing on Vikramaditya's verdicts, I ponder over what constitutes ethical excellence and what is its relationship to *svadharma*, or proper conduct, based on *jati* (caste), stage of life, family usage or even occupational duty. When and how do virtuous acts become extraordinary acts? Why should a king being educated in *niti*, or practical wisdom, know how to judge ethical excellence?

Although the contents of these tales have an ancient provenance, they appear to have been committed to writing during the medieval period, between the eleventh and fourteenth centuries CE. Four recensions survive from this period, of which two are found in larger collections, such as Somadeva's *Katha Sarit Sagara* and Kshemendra's *Brihatkathamanjari*, and two are autonomous recensions penned by Shivadasa and Jambhaladatta (Rajan 1995: xix). Of the latter, Shivadasa's rendition is sophisticated in that it addresses

> well educated, cultivated, accomplished men-about-town with a keen interest in fine arts and beautiful women, with a lot of time on their hands and plenty of money in their purses, men who were aesthetes, dilettantes, wrote poetry, painted the pictures of their mistresses, played music, danced, told stories, understood the finer points of writing. (Rajan 1995: lxi)

While more straightforward and prosaic, Jambhaladatta's version is useful in confirming whether the riddles were preserved and retold with some consistency.

The hero of these stories, King Vikramaditya, has been famous 'down the centuries, and throughout the length and breadth of the country, for magnificence and courage, nobility and wisdom and magnanimity'

(Rajan 1995: vv). He is the ideal king, heroic, kind, benevolent and learned. Historically, we come across many kings by this name, with Chandragupta Vikramaditya (fourth century CE) being regarded as the greatest (ibid.: xxix). When Shivadasa composed his text, memories of a Malava king named Vikramaditya, who ruled around the tenth century CE, may have been fresh. But this king ruled from Ujjaini, whereas King Vikramaditya of Shivadasa's text rules at Pratishthanapura on the banks of the Godavari river (ibid.: xxxi). As such, the king of the *Vetala Panchavimshati* may not represent one historical figure as much as an archetype or 'ideal type' of wise ruler. Shivadasa describes his hero as 'never overstepping the bounds set by Law' (*dharma*), and committed to protecting the good and punishing evildoers. As an epitome of wisdom, his answers to the Vetala's ethical dilemmas provide authoritative answers worthy of special consideration.

'*Vetala*' has been variously translated as vampire, demon, goblin and spectre (Rajan 1995: lxxvii). Chandra Rajan points out that *vetala*s probably belonged to a class of pre-Vedic, non-brahmanical divinities closely associated with fertility and vegetation, and commonly referred to as *yaksha*s (ibid.: lxiv–lxv). Being associated with Shiva, the lord of destruction, these chthonic forces are believed to haunt cremation grounds, corpses and other sites of death. Like Shiva himself, these forces are regarded as both benevolent and hostile, and must be mastered with reverence and skill (ibid.: lxvi). King Vikramaditya must bring the Vetala, which inhabits a corpse hanging on a tree in the cremation grounds, to a necromancer who plans to use it for some esoteric ritual. Why is a monarch involved in one of the most humbling and degrading acts of carrying a corpse on his shoulder, twenty-five times?

King Vikramaditya is indebted to a yogi, Kshantishila, who wants the corpse for a secret ritual which would give him supernatural powers. The yogi had brought the King wood-apple fruit everyday for twelve years; and one day, the fruit slips from the King's hand, is broken by a monkey, and a ruby rolls out. It turns out that all the fruits hitherto presented, fortunately preserved and stored separately (and perhaps refrigerated for twelve years!), contained precious gems.[3] Astonished, the King exclaims that he cannot pay the cost of even one of these gems, and demands to know what the naked ascetic desired in return.

In private, the yogi asks the King to bring him a corpse that hangs from a tree, without speaking to it, for some esoteric rites. The corpse, inhabited by the Vetala, regales the King with stories and concludes by asking him to solve riddles about the just, noble or rightful nature of specific agents and their actions. If Vikramaditya keeps silent despite knowing the answer, his head will burst and he will die. If he answers correctly, the corpse is likely to return to the tree. The King's answers to a few of the twenty-five stories are the subject matter of this essay.

Of the extant renditions, Shivadasa's version carries a profound sense of the presence of evil and of moral retribution (Rajan 1995: xxxv). It alone has a preamble which shows King Vikramaditya's father Gandharvasena, due to pride, setting in motion a series of calamitous events. Once, he goes to visit a famous bark-eating hermit, Valkalasana, who, absorbed in meditation for 1,000 years, does not register his presence. Offended, Gandharvasena sends a courtesan to seduce him, who succeeds, and brings the hermit to the palace, along with their child. The king then insults Valkalasana in the royal hall, whereupon the incensed hermit dashes his child to the floor—the head falls inside the palace, the torso in a potter's house and the feet inside an oil merchant's. Three boys are born in each of these places, and the astrologer predicts that one will try to kill the other two, and that the one who survives shall be lord of the earth. The boy born in the palace becomes King Vikramaditya in due course of time; the potter's son, having heard the story of his birth and the prophecy, sets out and kills the oil merchant's son and hangs his body on the tree. The citizens find out and report him, whereupon he flees that city. Vikramaditya, who is also aware of the prophecy, concludes that his crown is secure, with one brother dead and the other in flight.

Rich in mythic and symbolic details such as the setting of the cremation grounds, the ordeal of picking up a corpse twenty-four times, tricky questions to be answered upon pain of death, and so on, this set of stories may be read as the initiation of a hero who must qualify himself as exceptionally courageous, prudent, discerning and wise. Like other mythic heroes, he must stake his life to accomplish his task, and lower himself to the level of a mere undertaker in carrying a possessed corpse. Notwithstanding these parallels with the hero myths, the King is unaware of the reward that shall accrue to him after this ordeal (Rajan

1995: lvii). This distinguishes him from mythic heroes who normally seek immortality, priceless treasures or worldwide sovereignty. The King engages in this task out of sheer gratitude to the yogi, who had for twelve years gifted him fruits laden with precious gems. In this respect, the King's conduct itself may be examined as to whether it was just ordinary, drawn from *svadharma*, or an extraordinary overreaching of what was expected of him as a king. But first, we must figure out the difference between these two kinds, using examples of the King's practical reasoning and judgment.

NOW, TELL ME O' KING...

King Vikramaditya is asked time and again to judge who or what is more noble, magnanimous, courageous, virtuous, foolish or guilty. Twenty-three times, he answers the Vetala correctly, only to fail in his larger mission of bringing the corpse to the necromancer for his ritual. The collection begins and ends with stories of kings who act in haste without due deliberation, with devastating results. In between, there are many instances of multiple suitors saving a woman, where the King must judge whose rightful bride she is, or who is more blinded by passion among three lovers who all die for one another, not to mention hilarious stories where he has to decide who is more foolish, fastidious or delicate! In this chapter, I focus on five tales where the Vetala asks the King to decide '*ko mahasattvah*' or who is most noble or glorious (Emeneau 1934: 46). The tales that follow are chosen because they explicitly raise the question of superlative nobility, magnanimity, courage or virtue. The King's answers provide considerable scope for rumination; however, they are not always consistent between different versions and, therefore, not conclusive.

Reflection upon some of these riddles must foreground the multilayered and context-sensitive nature of ethical or *dharmic* conduct. *Dharma* points in the direction of a 'situated ethics', in that what is right is informed by familial, ethnic, regional and caste norms and the conduct of good people, rather than by abstract rules or principles. J. N. Mohanty has argued that *dharma*, in the sense of ethical rules of action and moral virtues, is best understood as social ethics (a la

Hegel's *sittlichkeit*) rather than individual morality (Kant's *moralitat*).[4] As such, *dharma* includes the actual norms, duties and virtues, as well as customs of a community (Mohanty 2000: 109). What one ought to do is a function of one's caste, family usage, stage of life (student, householder, forest dweller or renunciant), and so on (ibid.: 106). *Smritis*, or canonical texts such as the *Yajnavalkya Smriti* or *Manusmriti*, also deal with one's proper duty (*svadharma*). There are exhaustive lists of common virtues (*sadharana* or *samanya dharma*), including non-injury, forbearance, honesty, cleanliness, control of the senses, charity, love, sweet temper, etc. (ibid.: 108). In cases of uncertainty or conflict, *dharma* texts themselves say that individuals must look to those respected for their wisdom and conduct (*sadachara*) in the community. Complicating matters further, the texts speak of crisis-ethics, or *apad-dharma*, in situations of extreme distress or adversity, which was referred to in the previous chapter. To protect his subjects, to be courageous or a benefactor is among the normal duties of a king; to be loyal even to the point of risking and sacrificing one's life is the duty of a servant. Is ethical excellence only about following one's own *dharma*, or *svadharma*, well?

Veeravara, a noble warrior, arrives at the city of Vardhamana, ruled by king Sudraka, seeking employment. Asked how much he expected to be paid, he replies, 1,000 gold coins per day. Intrigued, the king asks how many elephants, horses and foot soldiers he maintains. Veeravara replies that he maintains only his wife, son and daughter besides himself. Thinking that his munificence might yield fruit someday, the king retains him. Veeravara uses the extra wealth to distribute alms to brahmins, bards, dancers and others during the day and, at night, stands guard outside the king's bedroom. The king would call out at midnight, and he would respond, signifying his presence. One night, the king hears a woman wailing and sends Veeravara to investigate. Veeravara learns that the woman is a spirit who has divined that the king will die in a couple of days. The tutelary goddess may be pacified and grant the king a hundred years if Veeravara were to sever the head of his own son, himself. Blessed with a devoted wife and children who assent, Veeravara sacrifices his son. However, unable to bear the loss, the whole family (his wife, daughter and Veeravara himself) commits suicide. King Sudraka, who had followed Veeravara secretly and witnessed the gory acts, draws his dagger to kill himself, whereupon the goddess appears and restores everyone to life. Subsequently, the king gives half his kingdom to his retainer. Asked who is the 'greater hero' (*ko mahan mahasattvah*) of all the characters, King Vikramaditya replies it is king Sudraka, because he was ready to give up his life, thinking that his kingdom is not worth much (Emeneau 1934: 46–47).[5] As a master, he did not have to give up his life for a retainer, while the latter is expected to sacrifice for his king.[6] The same conclusion is reached in the Doordarshan TV serial (Episode 2), with one difference that the king remonstrates with the goddess that he cannot sacrifice a subject for his self-interest. This episode also adapts the tale by showing the goddess testing the integrity of the servant, perhaps because inexplicable demands of bloodthirsty goddesses would not appeal to modern tastes!

In another story, a Rajput princely warrior seeking employment is unable to get an audience with the king. As he is about to give up, he chances upon the king who, having gone deep into the forest leaving his retainers behind, is lost, hungry and thirsty. The Rajput follows him, fetches fruits and water for the famished king, and shows him the way back. Pleased by his conduct, the king takes him into royal service. Subsequently, he is sent on a coastal mission, and sees a beautiful lady worshipping at a shrine in mid-ocean. When she asks him about his business, the Rajput replies that he is impassioned by her; she suggests he bathe in the sacred pool nearby and enter her palace; he does so, only to find himself transported back to his own city. Astounded by this story, the king himself comes to the ocean and sees the lady. This time she falls in love with the king, and declares, 'I am yours to command, whatever you ask of me, I shall do it'. Thereupon the king asks her to marry his retainer. 'Who is the nobler one?' asks the Vetala, and the King replies it is the Rajput who rendered assistance first (Emeneau 1934: 58–59; Rajan 1995: 75). On further questioning, the King argues that applause is appropriate when one who has cause to do harm performs a noble deed, but not when a benefactor performs a good deed because the latter is expected to do so.[7] Twisting the tale slightly, the Doordarshan episode presents the warrior as more courageous, since he dives into the ocean without knowing what he would find at a mere hint from the king.

Madanasena, a beautiful maiden, was amusing herself in a pleasure grove with her friends when a young merchant Dharmadatta, who was passing by, falls in love with her. When he confesses his love to her, she reveals that she is shortly to be married to another. As he threatens to take her by force, she pleads that she is obliged to uphold family honour and vows to return to him after the marriage ceremony. The merchant relents. On her wedding night, Madanasena explains her vow to her husband, and is permitted by him to go to Dharmadatta. En route, a robber sees her and prepares to rob her of her jewels. She tells him about her date with the beloved, and he lets her go.[8] Dharmadatta is enchanted upon seeing her, but cannot recall who she is. She reminds him of the promise she had made and says that her husband has allowed her to keep her vow. Dharmadatta suddenly loses all interest in her, declares that women are fickle, vicious and not worth the trouble, and lets her go. The robber commends her highly, and also lets her go a second time. Asked which one among the three is 'most noble', King Vikramaditya replies that it is the robber, for his unexpected act of kindness (Emeneau 1934: 70–71; Rajan 1995: 83).[9] The husband perhaps let her go thinking that she loves another, while the merchant let her go for fear of reprisal; only the robber had no reason whatsoever.

Another tale revolves around a prince Jimutavahana, who has abdicated his kingdom to pursue a virtuous life and is living in a forest along with his wife and parents. One day, he encounters a weeping woman who is grieving the impending death of her son at the hands of the eagle-king, enemy of serpents and Vishnu's vehicle, Garuda. Jimutavahana offers to sacrifice himself and, despite protests from the appointed victim, Sankhachuda, he climbs the rock of slaughter and waits for Garuda. As Garuda picks him up and hovers in the sky, Jimutavahana's wife and her parents come crying loudly. The intended victim, Sankhachuda, returns to the spot and appeals to Garuda to spare Jimutavahana. Undaunted, Jimutavahana declares that a life lived only for oneself is not human but bestial and that noble men live to help others, and insists that Garuda finish the job of killing him. As he lies wounded, his wife begins to wail and Garuda hastens to bring the elixir of life and rejuvenate him. Garuda also promises to eschew eating snakes, and restores his earlier victims to life. Now the Vetala asks King Vikramaditya who is the 'more magnanimous' one, Jimutavahana or Sankhachuda, and the King replies it is the latter.[10] The King points out that the former was used to sacrificing himself due to past habits and previous births, while the latter did not allow another to die in his place even though there was a willing volunteer. Curiously, in the Doordarshan adaptation of this tale, there is a terrorising ogre which is cured of its addiction to human flesh by the king.

Yet another story is about a merchant prince who had a beautiful daughter called Unmadini, whom the prince offers in marriage to the king. The king sends experts to ascertain if she is indeed beautiful. After examining Unmadini and finding her exquisite, they fear that the king would lose all interest in the kingdom if he married her; so they report that she is ugly, whereupon the king refuses her, and the merchant marries her off to the commander of the royal forces. One day, the king chances upon her and, intoxicated with love, he is deeply disturbed. When the commander hears of the king's passion, he offers to bring Unmadini to the king. The king is incensed at this offer, and asserts that *svadharma* forbids him to possess another's wife. The commander argues that his wife is a slave to the king like himself, and should not be regarded as 'another man's wife' (Rajan 1995: 130). The king refuses to go against accepted social norms (*lokadharma*), whereupon the commander suggests that he could donate Unmadini to the temple, which would make her a courtesan (*devadasi*), and thus available for the king. The king is so far gone that he reaches the tenth stage of unfulfilled love (delighting with the eyes, constant thoughts of the beloved, birth of desire, loss of sleep, wasting away, abjuring normal pleasures, loss of shame, infatuation and obsession, loss of consciousness and finally, death) (ibid.: 131). Daud Ali has noted that approaching another's wife for the king's self-preservation in the face of overattachment was allowed by Vatsyayana in his famous treatise, *Kamasutra* (Ali 2004: 344, footnote 39). However, refusing and yet pining with love, the king expires. The commander too enters the funeral pyre, and Unmadini follows suit. The Vetala then asks the King who is the 'most virtuous' among the three, and the King replies that it is the king who preferred to die rather than accept what was offered to him voluntarily.[11]

Thus, while the kings are judged greater in the first and final stories summarised here, the Rajput warrior, the robber and Sankhachuda turn out to be greater in the other three. Except for the story of Madanasena, which involves a merchant-prince, all others involve a royal person who is ruling or fit to rule. Addressed as they are to an ideal king, it is probable that the author intended these stories for aspiring princes who must be educated about and encouraged to perform great deeds.

KEEPING THE WOMEN OUT

All the stories involve women who follow *dharma*, which lays down that they support and obey their husbands, fathers or sons. There is the devoted wife who allows her husband to sacrifice their son and commits suicide after the gory event. She even says that only a husband gives beyond all measure and is a wife's sanctuary, and that neither pious acts nor religious fasts, but unswerving devotion is the *svadharma* of a wife (Rajan 1995: 55). Then there is the woman who passionately implores the king to command her, and marries the retainer when the king so commands her. Madanasena is determined to safeguard family honour until her marriage, then marches to fulfil a vow made under duress, risking both her life and honour. More impressive is the mother who does not allow a king to die in place of her own son, who is destined to be killed. Finally, there is Unmadini, who follows her husband into the funeral pyre upon a guru's advice in an extreme show of fidelity. It is only in his last riddle to the King on who is most noble that the Vetala includes a woman as a candidate. In this instance, the King explicitly states that the '*dharma* of a wife is to follow the path of their husbands' even unto death (Emeneau 1934: 90; Rajan 1995: 132).

Thus, all the stories considered here involve heroic women, but the two men discussing virtue (the Vetala and the King) ignore women's exemplary virtues and heroism. Is this because all these women invoke family honour and may be said to act within the bounds of their *svadharma* as wives or daughters? But then, following their *dharma* does not disqualify men from being considered as candidates for ethical excellence (though they do not finally get chosen by the King). Also, not all women are rigidly bound by filial piety and pre-defined duties. The woman who sacrifices her love for the king and marries the retainer to keep her word is not considered, despite her belying the dominant view that women are slaves of their passions. Although Madanasena keeps her vow, she is not considered a candidate for superlative virtue, while the merchant who threatens to rape her is. Could it be because she is foolish enough to keep a promise made under duress to a stranger and thus willingly puts herself in danger? Then again, this reasoning would preclude the Rajput warrior or Sankhachuda, both of whom could be considered foolish (the former for not eating at least one fruit himself, and the latter for offering himself despite there being a willing volunteer).

Shivadasa's text presents women who are resolute and virtuous, but the King and the Vetala mouth the conventional view that 'women are more prone to commit evil than men for the latter are instructed in good and evil' (Rajan 1995: 48). And yet, the preamble where the King's father, offended by a hermit's indifference, sends a courtesan to seduce him, and the frame story where a naked ascetic demands a talking corpse for undisclosed reasons, reveal men to be chief evildoers. Nonetheless, the King appears to be totally oblivious to women's virtue; for instance, in the case of Madanasena, he surmises that her husband let her go thinking that she loved another man. This is peculiar since the text suggests that Madanasena had actually apprised her husband of the circumstances under which she made the vow. He allows her to go, and then takes her back (in Shivadasa's version). It is only to the robber that she may have hinted about going to a beloved. Hence, the King's reasoning appears sexist and out of touch with reality. This is also explicit in the Jambhaladatta version, where the woman, here named Lavanyawati, is abandoned by the husband who says he cannot approve of her conduct. The husband's 'sacrifice'—first in sending her to another man ostensibly to save his life, and later in giving her up despite being smitten by her beauty, thinking she had intercourse with another—is considered nobler (Emeneau 1934: 72–73)! Though both versions are titled after the heroine who keeps her promise, it is the men who are adjudged nobler (ibid.: 70–71). Clearly, educating the King about women's virtue is not the overt purpose of Shivadasa's tales.

MAKING SENSE OF THE KING'S VERDICTS

The competition being thus restricted to men, what is the reasoning underlying King Vikramaditya's judgments? It may be noted that conventional wisdom plays no role in the King's judgments regarding nobility, whereas it is critical in judging the right suitor in many cases.

In one case, a dead beloved is revived by a suitor through a magic rite. Conflict ensues over whether the man who died with her, or the lover who lived next to her cremation site, or the one who visited faraway lands and secured a magical revival rite is the right suitor; the king answers that the one who died and was reborn with her is a brother and the one who revived her is a father, hence the one who lived near her cremation site is the husband! In another case of rival claimants, both equally entitled, the king opines that a robber who publicly married the girl rather than a brahmin who had her by stealth (with her consent) is the husband.

To return to the verdicts of nobility, the king in the first story above is chosen because he is willing to lay down his life, dismayed by the sacrifice of Veeravara's family. It is not because he gave half his kingdom to Veeravara, but because he was ready to sacrifice himself that he is considered nobler than his retainer. Also, mere gratitude, as in the case of the next story where the king commands the beautiful woman to marry his retainer, does not reflect ethical greatness. Similarly, the king in the last tale is chosen because he gives up his life rather than accept the wife of the commander. If it is about a superior who gives up his life or is ready to do so, Jimutavahana who offers to die for a stranger must also be counted as great. Why is he not chosen?

The King argues that Jimutavahana was disposed to doing sacrificial acts from previous births, and such sacrifice caused him no harm.[12] As an ascetic, he is habituated to self-sacrifice, and he may be motivated by the gain of more spiritual merit (Emeneau 1934: 141–142). There is some ambiguity about whether Jimutavahana is to be regarded as a brahmin ascetic or a warrior; he begins as a prince, is married to a princess even while living in the forest, and is eventually restored to his kingdom. Garuda, as he hovers in mid-air, is troubled by the wailing below and wonders whether his prey is a brahmin or a warrior (Emeneau 1934: 140–141; Rajan 1995: 132). If we consider Jimutavahana to be a king, then he is outreaching his *svadharma* by dying for one who is not even a subject. This is how Garuda judges him, and therefore rewards him in the end.

But King Vikramaditya ignores this ambiguity and judges Sankhachuda as more magnanimous and, since the Vetala is content, we must proceed to figure out why this may be so. It appears that those who are habituated to sacrificial acts through their *dharmic* roles do not qualify even though such acts may involve extraordinary sacrifices. This is the reason why retainers like Veeravara (who distributes alms every day), or the royal commander or his wife Unmadini are not chosen even though they all sacrifice their lives for others. It appears that one must do more than what *svadharma* requires of oneself, which in the first instance counsels customary duty and in the final instance, self-preservation for all if possible, but certainly for kings.

By this logic, the king in the last tale would not qualify since he was only following his *svadharma* of protecting the social order and the sacred laws of matrimony. And yet, Vikramaditya judges him to be 'most virtuous'. Even though the royal commander is more than willing, the king refuses to violate *dharma*, which forbids adultery. The commander suggests ways around this prohibition, which are rejected by the king. After all, the commander is trying to deal with an emergency, and crisis-ethics (*apad-dharma*) allows the commander to save his king's life even at the cost of his own wife and wealth (Doniger and Smith 1991: 150). As a powerful monarch, the king chooses not to transgress the law even while dying of the pangs of love, and this elevates him over the commander and his wife. The Doordarshan episode drastically modifies this story such that the commander is only betrothed when he discovers that the king has fallen for Unmadini, and sacrifices his love, and the just king, apprised of this in the nick of time, marries her off to the commander. Perhaps because the king was not on the verge of death, as in Shivadasa's version, the commander is adjudged to be the nobler one here.

Kings qualify for ethical greatness when they go way beyond *svadharma*, or what is enjoined on them by their royal *dharma*, which is to rule over their kingdom and reward the sacrifices of their subordinates. But when they come close to sacrificing themselves or actually do so, are they not going against their kingly duties? Does going beyond involve going against our duties? Consider the king in the first story again. He follows Veeravara, who goes out to investigate the reasons for the woman's weeping, and witnesses the gory drama of an entire family dying for him. He does not interfere with Veeravara when he severs his son's head before the goddess, thinking 'whatever is going to be brings its own means as well' (Rajan 1995: 56). He could have stopped the sacrifice, but perhaps he hoped for divine intervention. Perhaps he was curious to see whether Veeravara would go all the way in fulfilling his duty. Perhaps he was just being selfish, wanting to live a hundred years. Whatever the reason, the situation puts the king in a moral dilemma. If he stops Veeravara, he would be going against his royal duty to preserve himself through the sacrifice of a retainer. If he allows him to die, he still falls short of the royal duty of protecting one's subjects.[13] By following the latter course, the king gets disillusioned and exclaims 'for my sake, this whole family has been destroyed. What use is my kingdom to me now?' (Rajan 1995: 56).

Similarly, the king in the last tale also faces a dilemma in that if he accepts the commander's offer of his wife, he would be contravening his royal *dharma* of safeguarding virtue. By not giving in to desire and preferring death, he again falls short of the royal duty of ruling the kingdom. The point is that royal *dharma* is not always clear-cut and poses ethical dilemmas. In fact, *dharma* in general is seldom unambiguous; even Veeravara and the commander had duties to their families and had to set those aside. As Bimal Krishna Matilal has observed, '*dharma*-morality is pluralistic', and demands considerable practical reason in figuring out moral priorities (Matilal 2002: 68).

Furthermore, everyone involved is going way beyond the call of mere duty in these stories. Veeravara may be bound to sacrifice himself, but not his entire family. Similarly, the commander had duties to his wife, which he set aside. So why are the kings chosen as ethically superior? King Vikramaditya highlights the fact that they subvert hierarchy by choosing to sacrifice for their retainers. But is this not because they were also in a position to do so? Kings may choose to die for their retainers, whereas the latter have no choice. True, kings are more powerful than their servants, and yet seldom do they use that power to their disadvantage; that the two kings in question did so knowing well that nothing was to be gained by their sacrifice makes them superior to their counterparts. This rationale is also reiterated in the Jambhaladatta version of these stories (Emeneau 1934: 47, 142). As the *Katha Sarit Sagara* colourfully puts it:

> But kings are inflated with arrogance, uncontrollable as elephants, and when bent on enjoyment, they snap asunder the chain of moral law.

> For their minds are overweening, and all discernment is washed out of them, when the waters of inauguration are poured...And the breeze of the waving chowries fans away the atoms of the sense of scripture[s]... as it fans away flies and mosquitoes. And the royal umbrella keeps off... the rays of truth, as well as the rays of the sun; and their eyes, smitten by the gale of prosperity do not see the right path. (Tawney 1980: 321)

MARGINALITY AND ETHICS

In posing such nuanced ethical riddles, the Vetala is testing whether King Vikramaditya can see beyond fixed roles and assigned duties. After all, Vikramaditya is dealing with these riddles as he lugs a talking corpse through a cemetery in the dead of the night. And the Vetala entertaining him is also a marginal and hybrid figure, a spirit inhabiting a corpse hanging from a tree. Thus, subtle questioning about *dharma* is not pursued within the palace but in a cemetery, a quintessentially liminal site. It appears that meting out justice toward marginal figures requires that the king cultivate an eye for the contingent factors that affect our ethical actions. The Rajput prince, the robber and Sankhachuda are all outside the pale of social order and fixed roles. The Rajput prince is bereft of money and friends and is roaming alone in the forest. Having failed to secure employment with the king, he is impoverished. The robber is obviously a transgressor of law. Sankhachuda is a 'serpent-youth', a hybrid figure from the underworld. And they all act out their great deeds in the depths of the forest (*aranya*).

As Charles Malamoud observes, 'outside the village, the world of the *aranya* is at once within and without the *dharmic* norm' (Malamoud 1996: 81). The forest is within the *dharmic* norm because the 'thieving and brigand' creatures who, were they to be caught, would be dealt with according to *dharmic* law (ibid.). Forests also represent the other world, the world of the gods and, as wilderness, they are an image of the Absolute. They represent transgressive forces that suspend, if not challenge, ordinary hierarchies and conventions. They are inhabited by irate but powerful ascetics, sages with their beautiful wives and alluring daughters, 'savage' tribes, thugs and robbers, proud demons, ferocious animals and mysterious daemons or spirits. As such, they are dangerous places where the rich and the mighty often get lost or exiled, find generous guides and patrons, listen to edifying stories, rescue and marry beautiful damsels, are humbled by 'lowly' persons, meet heavenly friends and acquire powerful weapons. In both the *Ramayana* and *Mahabharata*, the heroes must go through long exile and giant-slaying as preparation for epochal wars. Historians have noted that forests were not uncharted territory, but were very much scenes of conflict and conciliation between established settlers and forest peoples. State-building involved negotiating with forest peoples, some of whom could be gainfully accommodated while others had to be subdued (Parasher-Sen 1998: 179). Kings had to be educated about distinguishing and dealing appropriately with *aranyachara*s, or forest dwellers, and *atavika*s, or savage tribals who operated autonomously, and had to be subdued.

In our text, there is no hint of state-building or the attendant conflicts with marginal groups. What is clear is the pedagogical intent of educating the ideal king about those who have no specific *dharma*, thus forcing him to reckon with virtuous conduct that is different from what is routinely observed. But in the absence of customary norms, how do we even know that the conduct of these figures was exceptionally virtuous? That the Rajput warrior, the robber and Sankhachuda were kind is not difficult to make out. For, when the Rajput brings fruit for the famished king or the robber lets the woman go, are they not following common virtues (*sadharana* or *samanya dharma*)? What makes their conduct so exemplary that they are exalted over their counterparts such as the king, the generous husband or the royal-turned-ascetic, respectively?

Consider again the Rajput prince who follows the king into the forest. It is possible that he was looking for a chance to make an acquaintance with the king and is therefore motivated by self-interest. However, when he fetches two fruits for the king and goes hungry himself, he rises above his immediate interest. Impoverished as he was, he was not under any obligation to feed the king. In fact, it would have been proper for him to feed himself with at least one fruit according to crisis ethics. Thus, the Rajput goes far beyond the call of common virtue or *samanya dharma*, and even crisis ethics or *apad-dharma*. Having lost his retinue and his bearings in the forest, the king was at the mercy of the warrior prince. Now, the Rajput had failed to secure employment with the king, despite roaming the royal gardens, but he is generous enough to say that it was all his own misfortune. Against his conduct, the king, who later gets the beautiful damsel to marry his retainer, pales for he is only paying back his dues. Explaining his reasons, King Vikramaditya points out that the Rajput rendered assistance first, and that though he had cause to do harm, acted nobly. In the Jambhaladatta version, it is the king who sacrifices the beautiful maiden who is judged to be greater, suggesting that Vikramaditya's verdicts were probably modified and debated (Rajan 1995: 196).

The robber in the third tale need not have twice foregone the opportunity to rob the woman. The first time, he assumes that she is going to visit her beloved; the second time, he commends her highly and lets her go again. Among the competing candidates, the husband who lets his wife go to another to keep her vow and accepts her when she returns, shines out. And yet, the King only interprets it as the conduct of a husband who thinks his wife loves another man. What redeems this verdict is perhaps the fact that the robber acts altruistically, for no motive at all.

The most fascinating story is about the third figure, Sankhachuda who returns to face death even though he is now free to live, given an eager volunteer, Jimutavahana. Sankhachuda is not a saint used to doing good deeds. He is described as a 'serpent-youth' who 'comes from the underworld'. Moved by Jimutavahana's magnanimity, he argues that insignificant beings like himself must rise and fall away. Following 'virtuous people who do not wish what is hostile to oneself on others', he returns to take his place as Garuda's original victim and is ready to die. Interestingly, while Garuda is moved by Jimutavahana's magnanimity and blesses him to be a 'Paramount Sovereign on this earth', King Vikramaditya chooses Sankhachuda as the greater of the two, showing that he does not judge like the gods; he judges like virtuous people, those who are regarded as beacons of good conduct in the community. In recognising Sankhachuda, the King also shows that ethical excellence is not confined to specific caste groups.

In all three instances, Vikramaditya sets aside those who act according to *svadharma*, in that the king who reciprocates to the Rajput, or the husband who lets his wife go, or Jimutavahana are not seen as candidates for ethical greatness. Instead, those who have no specific *dharma* qualify, even though some of them like the robber only desist from non-injury to others. None of these figures are shown to be habitual do-gooders. They are ordinary human beings moved by emotions and passions. The Rajput laments his bad luck, the robber is moved by delicate feelings, and Sankhachuda is moved by Jimutavahana's magnanimity. What makes them great is that despite being worldly, they manage to rise above their immediate self-interest to help strangers. In fact, their acts are sovereign gestures in that they cannot be matched in any way; no reward can match the generosity of the Rajput, or the robber, or Sankhachuda.

These figures direct us to what may be called the contingent nature of some ethical acts; none of the actors set out seeking glory or reward. They find themselves in ethically-demanding circumstances purely by chance. They belie the general idea that ethical habituation and mature reflection upon ethical conduct are essential for ethical excellence. Ethical greatness is not only about more of the same courage or magnanimity as displayed by those who are used to fighting or giving; sometimes ordinary and oppressed persons also face ethically-demanding circumstances heroically, and prove that morality feeds upon the human spirit of self-mastery rather than selfishness.

In fact, all the agents adjudged as superior here act without any interest in rewards of action, be it Sudraka, or the king who dies for love, or the robber who refrains from robbing, or Sankhachuda, or even the Rajput (arguably less so, since he may have anticipated rewards in future). Clearly, they all had nothing much to gain, unlike their rivals, be it Veeravara or the royal commander (both of whom wished to save their kings), or Jimutavahana (spiritual rewards), or the king who sacrifices the girl (expecting fame), or Madanasena's husband (expecting love).

In the Jambhaladatta version of the *Vetala Panchavimshati*, different candidates are chosen. Not the Rajput warrior but the king, not the robber but the husband, and not the serpent-youth Sankhachuda but Garuda turn out to be nobler. The king is chosen over the warrior since he remembered the gift of fruits with gratitude (Emeneau 1934: 58). Instead of the robber, the woman's husband is chosen since his sacrifice (of letting her go to another and then abandoning her when she returns) was 'unconditioned and absolute', unlike that of the robber or merchant who may have been motivated by reward or fear, respectively (Emeneau 1934: 58). This reason is also affirmed in Garuda being chosen over the self-sacrificing king Jimutavahana, since the latter may have wanted to gain more spiritual merit, but Garuda was giving up his legitimate right to eat snakes, and thus affirming that it is going beyond *svadharma* that qualifies one to superlative virtue (ibid.: 143). Standing tall above these figures, there is King Vikramaditya himself who seems to be going way beyond what is required of him by the call of duty. But will he be able to imitate the great sacrifices of these heroes?

COMPETING FOR GREATNESS

Educating the young about unexpected sources of ethical greatness to move their hearts is a cross-cultural theme. Giovanni Boccaccio's *Decameron* is an analogous series of tales, presenting competing models of greatness pertaining to cleverness, wit, magnanimity and patience. Composed in 1349 CE, even as the Black Death ravaged Europe, *Decameron* has ten fictional characters who escape to a paradisal space where they pass the time telling a hundred stories (Rebhorn 2015: xxviii, xxxviii). For our purposes here, the stories in the tenth book provide an opportunity for comparison, being explicitly about magnanimity. In one story, a rich man Mithridanes is committed to outshining Nathan, famed for generosity in that region. No matter what his effort, he cannot match Nathan, and resolves to kill him. Mithridanes goes to Nathan's famed inn and chances upon an old man, with whom he picks up a conversation and secures a fine room. Asked who he is, the old man replies that he was an acquaintance sorely disenchanted with Nathan, whereupon the visitor confides his envy and plan to kill Nathan. The old man tells Mithridanes about Nathan's habitual walks in the morning, and the easiest way to kill and escape after his deed. As planned, Mithridanes catches up with Nathan in the morning and, on swinging his sword, discovers it was none other than the old man who had helped him! Ashamed, when he asks forgiveness, Nathan insists that he is happy to give up his life, for he does not wish anyone to depart his abode without fulfilling what they came for! After mutual praises and reconciliation, Mithridanes leaves humbled, saying he could never excel Nathan in generosity.

Another theme pertains to the magnanimity of lovers, where despite having the power to satisfy themselves, men show self-restraint. There is the lover who discovers that a married woman he loved, who was given up for dead and buried, was actually alive. He nurses her back to health and, at a party to which he also invites the husband, gets all to acquiesce that the woman belongs to him. The lover then restores her to her husband. Another narrator tells of a young man who creates a garden in winter, as stipulated by a married woman he is courting through an expert in magical arts. Constrained by her promise to the youth, her husband sends her to him, and astonished by this, the young man gives up his passion for her. Then there is a story about the magnificent king Charles who conquered Florence, being enamoured of two young nubile daughters of a noble lord who had entertained him beyond their means. Fortunately, Charles is gently rebuked by a counsellor for failing to conquer himself, and for stooping to betray a man who trusted him, thus bringing him to his senses. King Charles redeems himself by marrying off the girls to two noblemen at royal expense.

More striking is the story of a friendship between two young philosophers, one of whom gives up his betrothed bride to his friend; the latter in turn, when the friend is down and out, takes on the guilt for a crime he confessed to under duress. It celebrates friendship as the 'discreet mother of magnanimity and honour, sister of gratitude and charity and enemy of hatred and avarice' (Payne 1800: 502). The final story of a wife's virtue tells of a rich man, Gualtieri, who marries a peasant girl, Griselda, on the promise that she would be an obedient and patient wife forever. When he has two children with her, he convinces her that they have to be killed due to the taunts caused by her mean origins. She patiently bears this, and then he announces that he is about to marry again, and turns her out in a single garment. He then proceeds to recall her to prepare for the nuptials, which she does, and he presents a young woman and a boy, who are welcomed by her. Contented that she has borne all this with fortitude, he reveals that the young woman was their daughter, and that he had engaged in this elaborate charade of a trial to test her endurance!

Given the parallels with some Indian stories, be it kings and commoners who sacrifice their love or be it women's virtue, the provenance and cultural influences await future analysis.[14] Here, it is apposite to note that tutoring the young in ethical excellence is cross-cultural, and so is the attunement to unexpected sources of generosity. Boccaccio holds a mirror to a collapsing social order without imposing conventional feudal values. At the same time, Wayne Rebhorn has noted that Boccaccio makes us more adept at judging, so that we cognise the contingent nature of ethical actions (Rebhorn 2015: lvi, lix). Rebhorn also qualifies that magnanimity here is oriented to fame and is moved by the spirit of rivalry, rather than being valued for its own sake. This need not be a problem when we consider the heteronomous nature of situated ethics, where we are moved to act well through our caring for concrete others, rather than abstract categorical imperatives. In this model, we may be moved to imitate and outshine historical or mythical exemplars and desire fame and glory. There is a risk, though, that this may be carried to an extreme, as in the case of Mithridanes and Nathan, as also Gualtieri and Griselda. The multifaceted genius of this classic cannot be captured through these brief allusions; but the parallels with the Indian material cry out for a deeper probing of how virtue is shored up in the most trying circumstances in our imagination, and why it is important for us to know the limits of conventional moral standards in judging ethical excellence. The Indian text goes further in that it also shows the constraints on such excellence when it comes to the task of retaining power in the face of competition.

THE UNSOLVABLE RIDDLE

Shivadasa shows that King Vikramaditya is indeed wise, for he solves the riddle posed to him correctly twenty-three times. He is stumped the twenty-fourth time, with the tale of a king–prince duo who are out hunting and come upon beautiful footprints, and decide that the lady with larger feet will become the queen and the one with smaller feet will wed the prince. They soon catch up with the women, who happen to be mother and daughter, in exile due to their king's death. It so happens that the woman with larger feet was the daughter and the one with smaller feet was the mother. As agreed, the two men marry the two women, i.e., the king weds the daughter and the prince weds the mother. In time, the mother has a boy and the daughter has a girl, and when they grow up, they are married to each other. When asked what is the relationship between these two, Vikramaditya is speechless. This incestuous tale signals the confusing and terrible consequences of thoughtless actions, and the King's silence is telling.

Pleased with the King, the Vetala exhorts him to engage in one last deed of glory. He then reveals that the naked yogi who seeks the spirit-ridden corpse is actually the potter's son and the King's own brother who had fled the kingdom. He is now plotting to kill the King and wrest the kingdom. He will perform magic rites and ask the King to prostrate before the goddess, during which act he will behead the King. The Vetala then instructs Vikramaditya to profess that, being used to only receiving homage, he did not know how to prostrate, and to ask the yogi to show him and, when he did, he must slay the yogi. While differing in some details, the Jambhaladatta version also has the Vetala giving exactly this advice to King Vikramaditya (Rajan 1995: 233).

There cannot be a sharper contrast with the self-sacrificing kings of the tales that were narrated to him. Vikramaditya begins this quest out of gratitude towards the yogi Kshantishila, who had been presenting him gem-laden fruits. He is so moved by the ascetic's generosity that he agrees to the dangerous and demeaning task of retrieving a talking corpse for him. The King far exceeds his *svadharma* in meeting with the ascetic in private and in repeatedly risking his life for him, not heeding his minister's counsel (Rajan 1995: xxxviii).[15] Twenty-three times, the Vetala asks him questions, the correct answer to which only means walking back to the cremation grounds; not replying when he knew the answer would have meant a terrible death. Thus, the King subjects himself to considerably more than what is required of one in debt to a generous stranger.

Acting disinterestedly out of a good heart at great risk to one's life may not always have beneficial effects unless also accompanied by good judgment of character and acuity. Vikramaditya had gone out of his way for an ascetic, who had not only tricked him into service, but actually planned to kill him. Though he is good and wise, his education is not complete, for he is still vulnerable to crafty yogis (Rajan 1995: lvi). He is good at judging who or what is most noble, but not what kind of benefactor deserves such heroic service; this only happens in the last story after the Vetala reveals to him the necromancer's plans, and the means of escaping the sure death that awaits him.

Paradoxically, King Vikramaditya knows about ethical excellence, but his own 'paramount sovereignty' is a result of fratricide, albeit an unintended and perhaps justifiable one. In one sense, he did not bring about this situation and was only acting according to his *svadharma*, which is ultimately to protect himself from danger and death. But in another sense, he was also acting to secure his crown and gain the eight powers as prophesied by the Vetala, and knew fully well that he had to kill a brother. While attending to the initiatory symbolism and the tough education of a king, Rajan also highlights the faint ambiguity in the text regarding the bloodshed. For Shivadasa quotes: 'pay a man back in his own coin//do harm unto him who has done harm to you//I see no harm in that//adopt foul means towards an evil man' (Rajan 1995: xli). This adage reeks of revenge rather than justice, and hence violates the spirit of a king's *dharma*. It is soon followed by glorious verses of divine blessings on the King, that he will be 'greater than ancient monarchs and a jewel among the lineage of earthly rulers' (ibid.: 181). But the doubt is sown about whether the King acted honourably at all. One could imagine alternate possibilities, such as alerting the ministers and army so that the evil yogi could have been exposed and exiled rather than killed. But that would be to postpone the problem raised here of ambitious contenders to the throne. The problem is also that of superlative individuals in general, who may presume that since they are so good, no harm will come to them. A ruler must always be alert to hidden dangers, without compromising on ethical excellence.

Such prudence is cast aside in a companion collection of thirty-two tales of King Vikramaditya's throne—titled *Simhasana Dvatrimshika* (popularly known as *Singhasan Battisi*)—where once again his valour, wisdom and magnanimity are glorified. Composed around the thirteenth century, these tales are told to another legendary king, Bhoja, who discovers the former's famed throne with thirty-two statuettes (Edgerton 1926: liii). Each time Raja Bhoja tries to mount the throne, he is told a story by a different statuette (which are actually nymphs cursed to be such), detailing the unsurpassable generosity and heroism of Vikramaditya, and thus compelled to refrain. There are many times when Vikramaditya is ready to offer his head, and is stayed by an appeased deity. One story shows him about to sever his head for a goddess to aid a brahmin's sacrifice, mirroring the story of Veeravara discussed earlier. Another shows the King bestowing all the precious jewels gifted to him by an ocean divinity to a brahmin (Edgerton 1926: 53, 62). Yet another story is about how he is led out of a jungle by a brahmin, and the King's eloquent proclamation of his gratitude. To test him, the brahmin hides the prince in his home and makes it known that he has been killed. Vikramaditya summons the brahmin, and when he confesses, lets him off, saying he is beholden to him for a past act of kindness. In another, the King is again poised to offer his head, as a goddess demands, so that a dry pond may fill with water. He even volunteers to die for a demon who is devouring the villagers, reasoning that the body is perishable and it is better to sacrifice it for a noble cause. The recurring pattern is that of a monarch who goes out alone on dangerous missions to exotic locales (including the sun's orb and Bali's underworld), and acquires superlative charms (including the eight powers as in the *Vetala Panchavimshati* cycle), only to be waylaid by some poor brahmin who then takes away the gifts.

This text of thirty-two tales is spiritual in that it often cites the body as perishable and the immortal soul as more deserving of nurture. The King Vikrama of these narratives is either disinterested in the rewards or eager to help others who are in need. It is also suffused with the marvellous, with Vikrama always asking visitors about their adventures and being forever hungry for challenges, in pursuit of which he travels incognito so often that he is even chided by one ascetic for neglecting his kingly duties. In a stunning reversal of the Shivadasa rendition, the penultimate story in the *Simhasana Dvatrimshika* is about a King Vikrama who, after slaying the necromancer as per the Vetala's instructions, and gaining the eight powers, when asked by the Vetala what more he wants, calls for the dead ascetic to be revived and then gives away the eight powers to him! Only when Raja Bhoja says, 'I want nothing' and asks the nymphs, who are eager to bless him, that these stories be eternal upon the earth and that those who hear them may never be harmed by spirits or reptiles, thus echoing Vikrama's selfless generosity, is he at long last able to ascend the throne (Edgerton 1926: 244). Needless to say, there cannot be a sharper contrast with the *niti* nuances and intriguing aspects of Shivadasa's tales.

CONCLUSION

Even though not a canonical *dharma* text, Shivadasa's rendering of the Vikram and Vetala cycle in the *Vetala Panchavimshati* reveals that *dharmic* situatedness and *apad-dharma* did not deter ordinary beings from going out of their way in responding to challenging ethical contexts. In doing so, they often rose above their immediate self-interest without the aid of elaborate theologies or ethical theories. I have argued that judging extraordinary nobility, generosity or virtue involves seeing beyond *svadharma*. For instance, the *dharma* of servants is to sacrifice for their masters; but when masters sacrifice for their servants, they are to be regarded as greater than their retainers. But then masters or powerful people need not have a monopoly over ethical excellence, as demonstrated by the robber, the Rajput warrior and the serpent-youth, who rise above temptation and self-preservation against odds.

As we unpack the rationale of Vikramaditya's answers, we get a sense that ethical greatness is all about sovereign gestures through which one responds to the challenges posed by other's sacrifices, as against the 'what-is-in-it-for-me' calculus. In weighing and judging, we reflect upon the acts, their sources and context. We learn to distinguish between kinds and degrees of virtue, courage or generosity. More than anything, we learn with the King about seeing beyond the moral economy (structured by socially mandated roles, habits and norms) and appreciate the contingent circumstances under which ordinary beings rise to perform great actions. Through a fine-tuned ethical sensibility, we may learn about acting nobly in situations where customary duty is ambiguous or irrelevant or unattractive. As we ruminate over Shivadasa's denouement, we also see that the monarch's ethical imagination has been expanded without jeopardising the need for prudence and political necessity.

Notes

1. This chapter draws upon Chandra Rajan's insightful introduction to her translation of Shivadasa's recension of the Vikram-Vetala cycle as *The Five-and-Twenty Tales of the Genie* (Rajan 1995: xv–lxiii). However, the argument developed herein is different. I have used the Jambhaladatta version to confirm some recurrent phrases and terms, as well as key departures (Emeneau 1934). I have also noted the differences in *Vikram aur Betal*, the TV serial aired by Doordarshan in 1985, available at: https://in.video.search.yahoo.com/search/video?p=vikram+betal+doordarshan&fr=yhs-invalid# (accessed May 2021).

2. Throughout this chapter, I use 'K' for King Vikramaditya to distinguish him from the other kings depicted in the stories and, instead of 'Vetaal', I use 'Vetala' as in Rajan's text.

3. The Doordarshan series uses a papaya. The *Chandamama* series is overtly moralistic, focusing on avoiding greed, vanity of ambition, fame and physical beauty, dangers of naivety and superstition, and so on.

4. Though the word *dharma* is used to refer to disparate things such as cosmic order, natural essences, ethical duty and even laws, it is used here to refer to ethical rules of action and moral virtues (Mohanty 2000: 107–110).

5. Chandra Rajan renders the question as 'who is noblest' (Rajan 1995: 58).

6. In the *Katha Sarit Sagara* version, Veeravara is presented as a brahmin warrior who is so noble-spirited that he does not proclaim his sacrifice even when asked. And yet king Sudraka is judged to be the braver, because he was ready to give up his life (Tawney 1980: 255–256).

7. In the *Katha Sarit Sagara* version, the Rajput prince is forced to plunge into the sea to save the ship, only to find himself in a splendid city, and he voluntarily plunges mid-ocean a second time while escorting his master. For this act, he is judged the braver of the two (Tawney 1980: 271).

8. In the *Katha Sarit Sagara* version, Madanasena's virtue of keeping her word is commended by everyone, including Dharmadatta and the robber (Tawney 1980: 280).

9. In Jambhaladatta's version, the heroine's name is Lavanyawati (Emeneau 1934).

10. Jambhaladatta's version has '*ko mahayasah*', which Emeneau translates as who is 'more glorious' (Emeneau 1934: 142–143).

11. Jambhaladatta's version has '*kim mahasattvah*', which Emeneau translates as who is 'most noble' (Emeneau 1934: 90–91).

12. Jimutavahana is portrayed as a *bodhisattva* (one on the path to Buddhahood) in the *Katha Sarit Sagara* version (Tawney 1980: 314).

13. Of course, the king could have stopped one or all the three suicides (Veeravara's, his wife's and his daughter's), though it is questionable whether that would have mitigated the dilemma.

14. Rebhorn has noted the possible, though remote, influence of the *Panchatantra* in the technique of using a frame story based on a Latin translation, which was drawn from a Hebrew translation, that was in turn drawn from an Arabic translation, which was based on a Persian one (Rebhorn 2015: xxxiii)!

15. This is explicitly picked up in the first episode of the Doordarshan TV serial, where Vikramaditya's minister says he will not allow the King to go anywhere without bodyguards, and the King brushes him aside, saying he has already given his word.

CONCLUSION

As the welcome chorus for liberal arts grows louder in India, we must engage in boundary crossings, overcoming disciplinary constraints and historicist timidity. In a modest way, I have tried to show that premodern secular sources can be instructive and enriching if we steer away from doctrinal approaches that often preach and rationalise exotic notions like the divine king, or subordinating temporal power to spiritual authority. By now it should be clear that classics like the *Panchatantra* or *Vetala Panchavimshati* were neither meant solely for children nor illiterate folk. They were meant for princes and courtiers who are still amidst us, albeit in disguise, with the same ambitions and expectations. They were also addressing the experts and their penchant for peddling knowledge as a panacea for political ills. While questions regarding the relevance of specialised knowledge traditions still resonate with us, their insights about the difficulties and risks involved in transmitting expert know-how are not so apparent today. Teasing out the sparse but telling resistances and responses to the *Arthashastra* shows that then, as now, there were hilarious objections to studying and teaching politics as causing mental strain, anxiety and confusion. There is an aversion to bookish learning among those who are ambitious and intent on seizing opportunities for 'real' action. Like Vishnu Sharma, experts must devise jazzy formats to impart their know-how, online courses and video games being the latest craze. The demand for abridgement has only gotten worse with Twitter and soundbite-driven media spaces which demand instant solutions. Winning elections, managing public opinion and simplifying policy initiatives are all creating a clamour to distil knowledge into mere information couched in artful rhetoric. For instance, we find that many experts in our time echo Damanaka's words that the 'policy of rulers is protean, appearing true but actually false, appearing compassionate but actually cruel and appearing sweet but actually harsh', and so on. Racing to simplify *nitishastra* can often lead to sycophantic opportunism, superficial success and populist acceptability as the only test of useful theory.

Seasoned politicians need not be tutored in expediency or self-interest by political theorists. Dandin's Viharabhadra is right in saying that this comes 'naturally' to them. It is their hard-nosed realism that needs to be prised open to accommodate a sliver of ethics. This is often done through ideological preaching in our time, which gives political 'theory' its reputation for 'la-la landism'. Lured by the desire for fame, or inducing change, or both, some experts, like the bull Sanjivaka, venture too far, imparting esoteric knowledge only to be undermined by clever courtiers who promise immediate results. Against this tide, our authors proffer a more nuanced prudence, one that preserves the 'swellings of the heart', as Francis Bacon put it. Being attracted to those who come professing admiration, or seeking refuge without applying the equality calculus enriches our lives in multiple ways. It is not just that everyone, even a little ant, may help in future that inspires such magnanimity, but also the disinterested joys of friendship. One is hailed by strangers and unequals, and one's workaday prudence not to trust strangers is tested, disrupted and strengthened by the experience. This is possibly why the *Panchatantra* repeatedly showcases friendships among unequals without bowing down to the fear of betrayal, as would have been the case if *niti* was only about self-preservation.

Today, the language of 'contacts and networking' on social media pages elevates sameness and mere liking over serious and robust discussions. And if the media is anything to go by, political friendships, whether of people in government or business (including the entertainment industry) are all about mutual benefits and utilitarian exchanges. We do not hear of powerful people who befriend philosophers and, if and when they do, we do not hear of ethical dilemmas and intellectual disagreements. False friends abound, and there is neither truthful nor frank criticism of political agendas or goals. Even among ordinary people, friendships between unequals (whether in wealth or power or caste) seem to be getting rarer, though not as frowned upon as love and marriage between unequals. Or if they exist, they have become invisible in the media space, which provides a window into the political realm. Is this not why we no more hear of extraordinary stories of affection and betrayal that compel us to debate who is a real friend, or whether *niti* is only about expediency?

That *niti* is not just about brute assertion of strength was further evident in the discussions of war and peace in the *Panchatantra* and *Hitopadesha*. There is perhaps no better illustration of how the *shadgunya*, Kautilya's sixfold strategy, can be applied mechanically or innovatively, depending on the experience of the advisors. While considering dangerous remedies such as war or political assassination, these authors are also acutely aware of the uncertainty of results and the great good fortune required to gain success. Above all, they capture ordinary ways of reasoning about war and peace, and the need to tame enthusiasm and bravado through deliberative counsel, one that is relevant for us today, given the hawkishness of both populist politicians and their bloodthirsty fans at times. Scholarly theories of war and peace, based on the relative strengths of different wings of the army, or state departments such as the ministries of home, defence and external affairs, and international geopolitical compulsions are too technical and speak to the experts. Popular conversations (say on social media) about these matters still revolve around the common sense and judgment of the leaders, their vanity and integrity, the courage of the soldiers, the justness of the cause, relative benefits for the strong and the weak, and emotional rhetoric of self-assertion. The uncertainty of wars is still a fact, notwithstanding sophisticated technological strikes and guerrilla resistance which make us wonder, for instance, whether the 'War on Terror' is over and, if so, who won it. The *Hitopadesha*'s assertion that 'real success' lies in achieving peace, especially between relatively weak and equal powers, is quite relevant given how globalisation has made all nations dependent and vulnerable, thanks to flows of capital, products and services, and arms. Without losing sight of the power play, the *Hitopadesha*'s idea of using intrigue to forge peace between 'good' rulers is also a reminder that realist thought need not be impervious to virtue politics.

Dandin unveiled the games of chance and strife involved in love and politics, further sharpening *niti* as discriminating judgment. By portraying the cunning ruses of desire in general and desire for wealth and power in particular, he evokes both empathy and distance toward the sentiments of love and heroism. The satirical antics of the courtesans and heroes not only induce laughter but also make us reflect on the transitoriness of desire and thus become somewhat detached. Love at first sight, seducing the beloved (often the girl) by hook or crook, ingenious thrashing of rivals, not to mention magical weddings, are thriving in the Indian film industry; what needs to be recalled is the intelligent irony of Dandin, be it in presenting the credulousness of the lovers or the detachment of the successful players. We now oscillate between shrill moralism and perverse relativism, either piously repressing or irresponsibly inflaming the passions, ignoring that emotional sophistication must be the aim of good art and liberal education. Like Dandin, one must know about the art of ruling in general to excel at the art of taming the passions. Mere cinematic wizardry that induces paradisal pleasure-seeking is hollow, without practical wisdom about the limits of such pursuits. There is much that feminists can learn about the nuances of women's sexual agency and ruses of seduction, which are seldom straightforward, so that we become more sophisticated regarding the problem of sexual harassment. Similarly, conservatives may also learn about the fragility of women's virtues in a world of philanderers and moderate their tirades against women's freedom.

Lest we think that Dandin's politics was confined to kings and courts, we may recall that attracting the rich and the powerful, influencing the talented, and manipulating public perceptions are still mainstays of politics. Defecting to the winning side and deceiving the public with buzzwords are so rampant that one wonders whether there is any honesty at all. Noble declarations of intent, and tall promises of wiping out corruption, unemployment or terrorism obscure structural obstacles to such radical transformation. Given the expenses of campaigning on diverse media, the relentless technological advances towards automation and artificial intelligence, and the seething resentments unleashed by poverty and identity politics, it is not clear how corruption can be weeded out, jobs can be increased, or the appeal of terror can be superseded. Many politicians would chime with Dandin's views on *apad-dharma*, claiming that they need extreme measures such as suspending due process to 'eliminate' terror suspects. But it is well known that crisis ethics (sidestepping legal procedures, eliminating rivals when gifts and intrigue fail, and embezzling temple treasures), is rampant for promoting self-interest rather than the public good. As such, they would not have the gumption to seek independent judgments; in fact, there is little evidence that anyone is troubled by such egregious acts at all.

In contrast, our authors are disturbed by the paradoxes intrinsic to political prudence; while it is theoretically anchored in the limits of human knowledge and action, its pre-eminent experts often act as if they are omniscient and other humans can just be means to their ends. This is true of Chanakya in the *Mudrarakshasa*, Damanaka and Stirajivin in the *Panchatantra*, Chakravaka in the *Hitopadesha*, and Vishruta in the *Dasakumaracharita*. Their doubles, namely Rakshasa, Karataka and Raktaksha, Doordarshi and Aryaketu, respectively, all represent what is repressed—the humane side of practical wisdom. Rakshasa has friends and family that he cares about, which endears him more than the austere Chanakya. Karataka has an ethical side, which makes him more wary than wily. Raktaksha, Doordarshi and Aryaketu are all less successful than their counterparts, either due to circumstances, or luck, or both. And yet, their favourable judgment and cooperation are sought after by the heroes. This is perhaps because prudent statecraft so closely resembles opportunism and villainy as to be virtually indistinguishable from tyranny during some critical moments, and only the most subtle experts of *niti* can gauge what is *apad-dharma* at all.

Since *apad-dharma* or stooping to survive can become a routine habit, Shivadasa educates the king in ethical excellence before preparing him for extreme acts of self-preservation. One must know what it means to go beyond *svadharma* in trying circumstances, though one may not always be able to act nobly. Judging unconventional gestures of magnanimity expands the moral imagination of rulers and moderates their pursuit of self-interest. When a young girl saving money for her surgery donates that amount for flood victims somewhere else, she suspends self-interest and exhibits a disinterested virtue that no reward can match and no theory can enframe as realpolitik. There are still poor beggars who return a lost wallet, and it is they, more than preachy patrons, who sustain and nourish everyday moral sensibility.

My comparisons throughout have aimed to explicate the common concerns of those who study, teach and do politics everywhere, especially as it pertains to the quintessentially political capacity of prudence. By fleshing out aspects of practical wisdom and persistent dilemmas which these comparisons attest to, I show that they elicit further inquiry into old questions. Thus I agree with Michael Freeden, who argues that 'when we study political thought from a comparative perspective, we study above all the nature of politics' (Freeden, cited in von Vacano 2015: 471). Even though these texts mainly addressed kings, courtiers and the leisurely class with a taste for ethical discourse, their insights about friendship and equality, war and peace, ethics and political necessity still sparkle, and startle us with their wit and wisdom.

BIBLIOGRAPHY

Primary Sources

Dandin. 1986. *Daśakumāracarita of Daṇḍin*. Trans. M. R. Kale. New Delhi: Motilal Banarsidass.

Jambhaladatta. 1934. *Jambhaladatta's Version of the Vetālapañcavinśati: A Critical Sanskrit Text in Transliteration*. Trans. and ed. M. B. Emeneau. New Haven: American Oriental Society.

Kautilya. 1919. *Kautilya's Arthashastra*. Trans. R. Shamasastry. Mysore: University of Mysore Oriental Library Publications.

———. 1987. *The Arthashastra*. Trans. and ed. L. N. Rangarajan. New Delhi: Penguin.

———. 1999. *Kautiliyam Arthashastram*. Trans. Pullela Ramachandrudu. Hyderabad: Jayalakshmi Publications.

Narayana. 1994. *Nārāyana Pandita Rachita Hitopadesamu*. Trans. G. Reddy Bala Chenna Reddy. Hyderabad: Samskruta Bhasha Prachara Samiti.

———. 1995. *The Hitopadesha: An Ancient, Fabled Classic*. Trans. and ed. G. L. Chandiramani. New Delhi: Jaico Publishing House.

———. 1998. *Nārāyana Hitopadesa*. Trans. A. N. D. Haksar. New Delhi: Penguin.

Shivadasa. 1995. *The Five-and-Twenty Tales of the Genie*, Śivadāsa. Trans. Chandra Rajan. New Delhi: Penguin Classics.

Visakhadatta. 1923. *Visakhadatta's Mudra-Rakshasa or The Signet Ring: A 4th Century CE Sanskrit Play on Chanakya and Chandragupta*. Trans. and ed. K. H. Dhruva. With Sanskrit text, English translation & Notes. Second edition. Poona: The Oriental Book-Supplying Agency. Available at: https://archive.org/details/Mudrarakshasa-Vishakhadatta-SanskritTextTranslation/mode/2up (accessed May 2021).

Vishnu Sharma. 1989. *Pancatantram*. Trans. G. Reddy Bala Chenna Reddy. Hyderabad: Samskruta Bhasha Prachara Samithi.

———. 1993. *The Panćatantra*. Trans. Chandra Rajan. New Delhi: Penguin Classics.

———. 1997. *The Pañcatantra: The Book of India's Folk Wisdom*. Trans. Patrick Olivelle. Oxford: Oxford University Press.

Secondary Sources

Ali, Daud. 2004. *Courtly Culture and Political Life in Early Medieval India*. Cambridge: Cambridge University Press.

———. 2010. 'The Subhasita as an Artifact of Ethical Life in Medieval India'. In *Ethical Life in South Asia*, pp. 21–42. Eds. Anand Pandian and Daud Ali. Bloomington: Indiana University Press.

Alphonso-Karakala, John. B. 1975. 'Facets of Panchatantra'. *Indian Literature* 18(2): 73–91, April–June. New Delhi: Sahitya Akademi.

Altekar, A. S. 2001. *State and Government in Ancient India*, pp. 1–25. New Delhi: Motilal Banarsidass.

Apte, Vaman Shivram. 1987. *The Student's Sanskrit-English Dictionary*. New Delhi: Motilal Banarsidass.

Aristotle. 1985. *Nicomachean Ethics*. Trans. Terence Irwin. Indianapolis: Hackett Publishing Company.

Bacon, Francis. 1965. 'Of Friendship'. In *Francis Bacon: A Selection of His Works*, pp. 112–118. Ed. Sidney Warhaft. Toronto: Macmillan.

Badhwar, Neera Kapur, ed. 1993. *Friendship: A Philosophical Reader*. Ithaca and London: Cornell University Press.

Bennington, Geoffrey. 1997. 'Politics and Friendship: A Discussion with Jacques Derrida'. Centre for Modern French Thought, University of Sussex, 1 December. Available at: http://livingphilosophy.org/Derrida-politics-friendship.htm (accessed April 2019).

Berlin, Isaiah. 1992. 'The Question of Machiavelli'. In *The Prince*, pp. 206–236. Trans. Robert Adams. New York: W. W. Norton & Company.

Bloom, Allan. 1993. *Love and Friendship*. New York: Simon and Schuster.

Boesche, Roger. 2003. 'Kautilya's *Artha Shastra*: War and Diplomacy in Ancient India'. *The Journal of Military History* 67(1): 9–37, January.

Bowles, Adam. 2007. *Dharma, Disorder and the Political in Ancient India: The Āpaddharmaparvan of the Mahābhārata*. Leiden: E. J. Brill.

Burrow, T. 1968. 'Canakya and Kautilya'. *Annals of the Bhandarkar Oriental Research Institute* (Golden Jubilee Volume 1917–1967) 48/49: 17–31.

Chakravarti, Uma. 2004. 'Women, Men and Beasts: The Jataka as Popular Tradition'. In *Subordinate and Marginal Groups in Early India*, pp. 210–241. Ed. Aloka Parasher-Sen. New Delhi: Oxford University Press.

Cicero, Marcus Tullius. 1991. *Cicero, On Duties*. Trans. and ed. M. T. Griffin and E. M. Atkins. Cambridge: Cambridge University Press.

Chandiramani, G. L., trans. and ed. 1995. *The Hitopadesha: An Ancient, Fabled Classic*. New Delhi: Jaico Publishing House.

Coomaraswamy, Ananda K. M. 1977. *Selected Papers: Metaphysics*, Volume 2. Ed. Roger Lipsey. Bollingen Series 89. Princeton: Princeton University Press.

Cooper, John. 1993. 'Political Animals and Civic Friendship'. In *Friendship: A Philosophical Reader*, pp. 303–326. Ed. Neera Kapur Badhwar. Ithaca: Cornell University Press.

Coulson, Michael, trans. and ed. 1981. *Three Sanskrit Plays*. Great Britain: Penguin Classics.

Cropsey, Joseph. 1977. 'Justice and Friendship in the Nicomachean Ethics'. In *Political Philosophy and the Issues of Politics*, pp. 252–273. Chicago: University of Chicago Press.

Dallmayr, Fred. 2010. 'Beyond Monologue: For a Comparative Political Theory'. In *Comparative Political Theory: An Introduction*, pp. 7–20. Ed. Fred Dallmayr. New York: Palgrave Macmillan.

Daniélou, Alain, trans. 1994. *The Complete Kāma Sūtra*, Vatsyayana, pp. 1–12. Rochester: Park Street Press.

De, Sushil Kumar. 1941. 'The Prose Kavyas of Dandin, Subandhu and Bana'. In *A Volume of Studies in Indology*, pp. 112–145. Eds. S. M. Katre and P. K. Gode. Poona: Oriental Book Agency. Available at: https://archive.org/details/in.ernet.dli.2015.31864/page/n3/mode/2up?view=theater (accessed May 2021)

———. 1959. *Ancient Indian Erotics and Erotic Literature*. Calcutta: Firma K. L. Mukhopadhyay.

DeCaroli, Robert. 1995. 'An Analysis of Daṇḍin's Daśakumāracarita and Its Implications for Both the Vākāṭaka and Pallava Courts'. *Journal of the American Oriental Society* 115(4): 671–678.

Dhruva, K. H., trans. and ed. 1923. *Visakhadatta's Mudra-Rakshasa or The Signet Ring: A 4th Century CE Sanskrit Play on Chanakya and Chandragupta*. With Sanskrit text, English translation & Notes. Second edition. Poona: The Oriental Book-Supplying Agency. Available at: https://archive.org/details/Mudrarakshasa-Vishakhadatta-SanskritTextTranslation/mode/2up (accessed May 2021).

Doniger, Wendy. 1999. *Splitting the Difference: Gender and Myth in Ancient Greece and India*. Chicago: University of Chicago Press.

Doniger, Wendy and Brian K. Smith, trans. 1991. *The Laws of Manu*. London: Penguin Classics.

Edgerton, Franklin. 1926. *Vikrama's Adventures or The Thirty-Two Tales of the Throne*. Cambridge, Massachusetts: Harvard University Press.

Elshtain, Jean. 2004. 'Reflection on the Problem of "Dirty Hands"'. In *Torture: A Collection*, pp. 77–89. Ed. Sanford Levinson. Oxford: Oxford University Press.

Emeneau, M. B., trans. and ed. 1934. *Jambhaladatta's Version of the Vetālapañcavinśati: A Critical Sanskrit Text in Transliteration*. New Haven: American Oriental Society.

Freeden, Michael. 2012. 'Interpretative Realism and Prescriptive Realism'. *Journal of Political Ideologies* 17(1): 1–11.

Friedman, Marilyn. 1992. 'Feminism and Modern Friendship'. In *Communitarianism and Individualism*, pp. 101–119. Eds. Shlomo Avineri and Avner De Shalit. Oxford: Oxford University Press.

Gadamer, Hans-Georg. 1986. *The Relevance of the Beautiful and Other Essays*. Trans. Nicholas Walker. Ed. Robert Bernasconi. Cambridge: Cambridge University Press.

Ganguli, Kisari Mohan, trans. 2004. *The Mahabharata of Krishna Dwaipayana Vyasa, Book 12: Santi Parva*. U.S.A.: Kessinger Publishing.

Gautam, P. K. 2015. *Kautilya's Arthashastra: Contemporary Issues and Comparison*. IDSA Monograph Series 47. New Delhi: IDSA Press.

Ghoshal, U. 1923. *A History of Hindu Political Theories: From the Earliest Times to the End of the First Quarter of the Seventeenth Century A.D.* London: Oxford University Press.

Goodwin, Robert E. 1998. 'The Divided World of the Mudraraksasa'. In *The Playworld of Sanskrit Drama*. New Delhi: Motilal Banarsidass.

Gray, J. E. B. 1992. 'The Daśakumāracarita as Picaresque: Some Reflections on Standard Approaches'. In *The Indian Narrative: Perspectives and Patterns*, pp. 61–80. Eds. Christopher Shackle and Rupert Snell. Germany: Otto Harrassowitz Verlag.

Griffiths, Martin. 1992. *Realism, Idealism and International Politics: A Reinterpretation*. London: Routledge.

Gupta, D. K. 1970. *A Critical Study of Daṇḍin and His Works*. New Delhi: Meharchand Lachhmandas.

Heesterman, J. C. 1985. *The Inner Conflict of Tradition: Essays in Indian Ritual, Kinship and Society*. Chicago: University of Chicago Press.

Irwin, Terence, trans. 1985. *Nicomachean Ethics*, Aristotle. Indianapolis: Hackett Publishing Company.

Jackson, William J., ed. 1992. *J. L. Mehta on Heidegger, Hermeneutics and Indian Tradition*. Leiden: E. J. Brill.

Kapoor, Anjani and Manu Bhagavan. 2018. 'Beyond the Nation: Ambedkar and the Anti-Isolation of Fellowship'. In *The Radical in Ambedkar*, pp. 243–254. Eds. Anand Teltumbde and Suraj Yengde. New Delhi: Penguin.

Kale, M. R., trans. 1986. *Daśakumāracarita of Daṇḍin*. Delhi: Motilal Banarsidass.

Kissinger, Henry. 2014. *World Order: Reflections on the Character of Nations and the Course of History*. United Kingdom: Penguin.

Liebig, Michael. 2013. 'Kauṭilya's Relevance for India Today'. *India Quarterly* 69(2): 99–116, 8 June.

Lilla, Mark. 2001. 'The Lure of Syracuse'. *The New York Review of Books*, 20 September.

Lingis, Alphonso. 1983. *Excesses: Eros and Culture*. Albany: New York State University.

Lynch, Owen, ed. 1990. *Divine Passions: The Social Construction of Emotion in India*, pp. 3–35. Berkeley: University of California Press.

Mackenzie Brown, D. 1953. 'The Premises of Indian Political Thought'. *Western Political Quarterly* 6(2): 243–249, June.

Machiavelli, Niccolo. 1978. 'Machiavelli: The Mandragola'. In *Five Italian Renaissance Comedies*, pp. 15–58. Ed. Bruce Penman. London: Penguin.

Malamoud, Charles. 1996. *Cooking the World: Ritual and Thought in Ancient India*. Trans. David White. New Delhi: Oxford University Press.

Manu. 1991. *The Laws of Manu*. Trans. Wendy Doniger and Brian K. Smith. London: Penguin Classics.

March, Andrew. 2009. 'What is Comparative Political Theory?'. *The Review of Politics* 71: 531–565.

Martinez, Ronald. 1983. 'The Pharmacy of Machiavelli: Roman Lucretia in "Mandragola"'. *Renaissance Drama*, New Series 14: 1–43.

Matilal, Bimal Krishna. 2002. *Ethics and Epics: The Collected Essays of Bimal Krishna Matilal*. Ed. Jonardon Ganeri. New Delhi: Oxford University Press.

McClish, Mark and Patrick Olivelle, ed. and trans. 2012. *The Arthashastra: Selections from The Classic Indian Work on Statecraft*, pp. ix–xlv. Cambridge: Hackett Publishing.

McKeogh, Colm. 1997. *The Political Realism of Reinhold Niebuhr: A Pragmatic Approach to Just War*. Great Britain: Palgrave Macmillan.

Mehta, J. L. 1992. 'Krishna: God as Friend'. In *J. L. Mehta on Heidegger, Hermeneutics and Indian Tradition*, pp. 121–136. Ed. William J. Jackson. Leiden: E. J. Brill.

Mehta, V. R. 1996. *Foundations of Indian Political Thought*. New Delhi: Manohar Publishers.

Mohanty, J. N. 2000. *Classical Indian Philosophy*. Lanham: Rowman & Littlefield Publishers, Inc.

Montaigne, Michel De. 1958. 'On Friendship'. In *Michel De Montaigne: Essays*, pp. 91–105. Trans. and ed. J. M. Cohen. London: Penguin.

Morkevičius, Valerie. 2018. *Realist Ethics: Just War Traditions as Power Politics*. Cambridge: Cambridge University Press.

Naik, Ashay Deepak. 2016. *Natural Enmity: Reflections on the Nīti and Rasa of the Pancatantra [Book 1]*. U.S.A.: Create Space Independent Publishing Platform. Kindle edition.

Olivelle, Patrick, trans. 1997. 'Introduction'. In *The Pañcatantra: The Book of India's Folk Wisdom*. Oxford: Oxford University Press.

Onians, Isabelle, trans. and ed. 2005. *What Ten Young Men Did*, Dandin. New York: New York University Press and the JJC Foundation.

Pai, Anant, ed. 1975. *Hitopadesha: Choice of Friends*. *Amar Chitra Katha* 556. Bombay: India Book House.

———. 1981. *Panchatantra: Crows and Owls and Other Stories*. *Amar Chitra Katha* 561. Bombay: India Book House.

———. n.d. *Hitopadesha: How Friends are Parted and Other Stories*. *Amar Chitra Katha* 185. Bombay: India Book House.

Pangle, Lorraine Smith. 2003. *Aristotle and the Philosophy of Friendship*. Cambridge: Cambridge University Press.

Pantham, Thomas and Kenneth Deutsch, eds. 1986. *Political Thought in Modern India*. New Delhi: Sage.

Parasher-Sen, Aloka. 1998. 'Of Tribes, Hunters and Barbarians: Forest Dwellers in the Mauryan Period'. *Studies in History* 14(2): 173–191.

Parthasarathy, R., trans. and ed. 1993. *The Tale of an Anklet: The Cilappatikāram of Ilanko Atingal*. New Delhi: Penguin.

Parekh, Bhikhu. 2008. 'Friendship in Classical Indian Thought'. *Indian International Centre Quarterly* 35(2): 152–167.

Payne, John. 1800. *Stories of Boccaccio (The Decameron)*. London: The Bibliophilist Library. Available at: https://archive.org/details/storiesboccacci00boccgoog/page/n11/mode/2up (accessed May 2021).

Prabhupada, A. C. Bhaktivedanta Swami. 1977. *The Summum Bonum, The Life of Sri Krishna, Srimad Bhagavatam*, Canto 10, Chapter 80, Verse 19. Bhaktivedanta Book Trust. Available at: https://www.vedabase.com/en/sb/10/80/19/ (accessed May 2021).

Prabhupada, Swami. n.d. *Bhagavad Gita As It Is*. Available at: https://asitis.com/2/11.html (accessed May 2021).

Rajagopalachari, C. 1980. *Ramayana*. Bombay: Bharatiya Vidya Bhavan.

———. 1999. *Mahabharata*. Bombay: Bharatiya Vidya Bhavan.

Rajan, Chandra, trans. 1993. 'Introduction'. In *The Panćatantra*, Viṣṇu Śarma, pp. xx–lv. New Delhi: Penguin Classics.

———. 1995. 'Introduction'. In *The Five-and-Twenty Tales of the Genie*, Śivadāsa, pp. xv–lxiii. New Delhi: Penguin Classics.

Rangarajan, L. N., trans and ed. 1987. 'Introduction'. In *The ArthaShastra*, Kautilya, pp. 13–98. New Delhi: Penguin Classics.

Ramachandrudu, Pullela, trans. 1999. *Kautiliyam Arthashastram*. Hyderabad: Jayalakshmi Publications.

Rebhorn, Wayne, ed. and trans. 2015. `Introduction'. In *The Decameron*, Giovanni Boccaccio, pp. xxiii–lxvi. New York: W. W. Norton & Company.

Reddy, G. Reddy Bala Chenna, trans. 1989. *Pancatantram*, Vishnu Sharma. Translated into Telugu, with Sanskrit text. Hyderabad: Samskruta Bhasha Prachara Samiti.

———. 1994. *Nārāyana Pandita Rachita Hitopadesamu*. Translated into Telugu, with Sanskrit text. Hyderabad: Samskruta Bhasha Prachara Samiti.

Salkever, Stephen. 2009. *The Cambridge Companion to Ancient Greek Political Thought*. Cambridge: Cambridge University Press.

———. 2014. 'Teaching Comparative Political Thought: Joys, Pitfalls, Strategies, Significance'. *Political Science Faculty Research and Scholarship* 26. Available at: http://repository.brynmawr.edu/polisci_pubs/26 (accessed May 2021).

Sanghi, Ashwin. 2010. *Chanakya's Chant*. Chennai: Westland.

Sarkar, Benoy Kumar. 1918. 'Democratic Ideals and Republican Institutions in India'. *American Political Science Review* 12(4): 581–606. Cambridge: Cambridge University Press.

Shamasastry, R., trans. 1919. *Kautilya's Arthashastra*. Mysore: University of Mysore Oriental Library Publications.

Shklar, Judith. 1984. *Ordinary Vices*. Cambridge: Belknap Press.

———. 1993. 'Politics and Friendship'. *Proceedings of the American Philosophical Society* 137(2): 207–212, June.

Siegel, Lee. 1989. *Laughing Matters: Comic Tradition in India*. Delhi: Motilal Banarsidass.

Sokolowski, Robert. 2002. 'Phenomenology of Friendship'. *The Review of Metaphysics* 55(3): 451–470, March.

Sternbach, Ludwik. 1956. 'Cānakya's Aphorisms in the Hitopadeśa (1)'. *Journal of the American Oriental Society* 76(2): 115–130, April–June.

Strauss, Leo and Joseph Cropsey, eds. 1987. *History of Political Philosophy*. Chicago: University of Chicago Press.

Strauss, Leo and Alexandre Kojeve. 1991. *On Tyranny*. Chicago: University of Chicago Press.

Tawney, C. H., trans. 1980. *The Kathá Sarit Ságara or Ocean of the Streams of Story*, Vol. 2, Somadeva Bhatta. Delhi: Munshiram Manoharlal.

Totton, Mary-Louise. 2003. 'Narrating Animals on the Screen of the World'. *The Art Bulletin* 85(1): 6–24, March.

Trautman, Thomas. 2016. *Artha Shastra: The Science of Wealth*, pp. 1–27. The Story of Indian Business Series, Ed. Gurcharan Das. New Delhi: Portfolio, Penguin.

von Vacano, Diego. 2015. 'The Scope of Comparative Political Theory'. *Annual Review of Political Science* 18: 465–480.

Valdes, Mario J., ed. 1991. *A Ricoeur Reader: Reflection and Imagination*. Toronto: University of Toronto Press.

Walzer, Michael. 1973. 'Political Action and the Problem of Dirty Hands'. *Philosophy and Public Affairs* 2(2): 160–180, Winter.

———. 2002. 'The Triumph of Just War Theory (and the Dangers of Success)'. In *International Justice, War Crimes, and Terrorism: The U.S. Record, Social Research* 69(4): 925–944. Baltimore: Johns Hopkins University Press.

West, Thomas and Grace West. 1984. *Four Texts on Socrates*. Ithaca and London: Cornell University Press.

GLOSSARY

adbhuta: astonishment or wonder, one of the nine *rasa*s in Indian aesthetics.

Amar Chitra Katha: an Indian children's magazine that has popularised Indian classical literature, mythology and epics.

Amara Shakti: 'eternal power'; the king in the *Panchatantra* who employs Vishnu Sharma, the compiler of the *Panchatantra*.

Ananta Shakti: 'endless power'; a dull son of Amara Shakti.

Anantavarman: the pleasure-loving king who neglects policy in the *Dasakumaracharita*.

Angirasa: an expert in *arthashastra*.

anubhavas: consequents/effects of the *rasa*s, such as smiling at the sight of a beloved or speaking sweet words, which manifest the *rasa* of love.

Anujivin: 'live along'; a minister of the crow-king in Book III of the *Panchatantra*.

apad-dharma: emergency or crisis ethics.

Apaharavarman: a hero who plays at stealing in the *Dasakumaracharita*.

Aparikshitakarakam: 'Rash Deeds', title of Book V of the *Panchatantra*.

Arimardana: 'foe-crusher'; the owl-king in Book III of the *Panchatantra*.

artha: wealth; kingdom; worldly success in gaining land, wealth, power or fame.

Arthapala: a hero in the *Dasakumaracharita*.

Arthashastra: expert knowledge tradition on acquiring wealth and ruling kingdoms; also the title of Kautilya's magnum opus.

Aryaketu: a minister in the climactic book of the *Dasakumaracharita*.

asana: staying put while seeking a friend's aid, one of the six strategies of Kautilya's *shadgunya*.

Avantisundari: a princess, and beloved of prince Rajavahana in the *Dasakumaracharita*.

Bahu Shakti: 'great power'; a dull son of Amara Shakti in the *Panchatantra*.

balam: strength; power.

Bharadvaja: a political thinker mentioned by Kautilya.

bhavas: in Indian aesthetics, emotional states corresponding to pleasure, sorrow, laughter, anger, courage, fear, disgust and surprise, of which eight are permanent.

bhayanaka: fear, one of the nine *rasa*s in Indian aesthetics.

bheda: creating dissension; one of the four expedients suggested by Kautilya.

bibhatsa: disgust, one of the nine *rasa*s in Indian aesthetics.

Brahma Prajapati: creator; god, lord of all creation.

brahmins (also *brahmanas*): in Hinduism, members of the caste charged with imparting learning and conducting religious rites.

Chakravaka: ruddy goose; the able counsellor of the swan-king in the *Hitopadesha*.

Chandamama: an Indian children's magazine.

Chandanadasa: a friend of Rakshasa in the play *Mudrarakshasa* by Vishakhadatta.

Chandavarman: a villain in the *Dasakumaracharita*.

Chandragupta: a character in the play *Mudrarakshasa* fashioned after Chandragupta Maurya, a legendary Indian emperor who ruled around 321 BCE.

Chandrapalita: a shrewd minister of Anantavarman's enemy in the *Dasakumaracharita*.

Chitravarna: 'bright-hued'; the peacock-king in the *Hitopadesha*.

Chitragreeva: 'bright-necked'; the pigeon-king in Book II of the *Panchatantra*.

Chitranga: 'speckled'; a deer in Book II of the *Panchatantra*.

Chiranjivin: 'live long'; a minister of the crow-king in Book III of the *Panchatantra*.

dana (*danam* in Telugu): gifting; one of the four expedients suggested by Kautilya.

Damanaka: wily; a jackal in Book I of the *Panchatantra*.

danda: force; punishment; one of the four expedients suggested by Kautilya.

dandaniti: proper application of force; systematic study of the art of government.

Dandin: author of the *Dasakumaracharita*.

Dasakumaracharita: 'Adventures of the Ten Princes', by Dandin.

dhanam: wealth; property; gold.

dharma: ethics; duties; virtues; familial, ethnic, caste norms and customs; religion.

Dharmadatta: a merchant who falls for Madanasena in the *Vetala Panchavimshati.*

Dhumini: 'the smokey one'; an adulterous woman in the *Dasakumara-charita.*

Doordarshan: Indian state-controlled television channel.

Doordarshi: 'the farsighted one'; the peacock-king's minister in the *Hitopadesha.*

dvaidhibhava: double policy, one of Kautilya's sixfold strategies.

Gomini: worshipper; the superlative wife in the *Dasakumaracharita.*

goshti: salon-like gathering for entertainment and conversation.

hasya rasa: humour or levity, one of the nine *rasa*s of Indian aesthetics.

Hiranyagarbha: 'golden embryo'; the swan-king in the *Hitopadesha.*

Hiranyaka: 'goldy'; a prudent mouse in Book II of the *Panchatantra.*

Hitopadesha: 'Beneficial Advice', a popular collection of stories on practical wisdom compiled by Narayana Pandita.

Jambhaladatta: the compiler of a second recension of the *Vetala Panchavimshati.*

jati dharma: occupational or caste duty.

Jimutavahana: a prince-turned-ascetic in the *Vetala Panchavimshati.*

jnanam: knowledge; wisdom.

Kakolukiyam: 'Of Crows and Owls', Book III of the *Panchatantra.*

kama: love and desire, especially sexual desire.

Kamamanjari: 'ornament of love'; a courtesan in the *Dasakumaracharita.*

Kannagi: heroine of the Tamil epic *Silappatikaram.*

Karataka: 'the prudent/wary'; a jackal in Book I of the *Panchatantra.*

karma: action; deed.

karta: doer; agent.

karuna: compassion, one of the nine *rasa*s in Indian aesthetics.

karyasiddhi: success in action.

Kautilya (also Chanakya and Vishnugupta): a famous Indian realist and political thinker, and a character in Vishakhadatta's play *Mudrarakshasa.*

krida: sports; games of chance.

Kshantishila: a yogi in the *Vetala Panchavimshati.*

Kuchela/Sudama: a childhood friend of Krishna.

kula: lineage.

kula dharma: family duty; lineage duty.

Labdhapranasham: 'Loss of Gains', Book IV of the *Panchatantra.*

Laghupatanaka: 'light-wing'; a curious crow in Book II of the *Panchatantra.*

lokadharma: socially accepted norms and practices.

lila: play; sport; drama; divine play.

Madanasena: a woman who abides by her vows in the *Vetala Panchavimshati.*

mahasattvah: the nobler, greater or more glorious hero.

Mahilaropya: a city ruled by Amara Shakti in South India, and the setting for some stories in the *Panchatantra.*

Malayaketu: the discontented ally of Chandragupta in the *Mudrarakshasa.*

Manthara: 'slowcoach'; a turtle in Book II of the *Panchatantra.*

Mantragupta: a hero in the *Dasakumaracharita.*

mantra shakti: deliberative power; power of wise counsel.

mantrayuddha: battle of intrigue.

Marichi: a sage who is outwitted by a courtesan in the *Dasakumaracharita.*

Meghavarna: 'cloud-hued'; a crow-king in Book III of the *Panchatantra.*

mimamsa: systematic investigation; one of the six Vedic schools.

mitra: friend; ally.

Mitra-bheda: 'Estrangement of Friends', Book I of the *Panchatantra.*

Mitragupta: a hero in the *Dasakumaracharita.*

Mitra-prapti (also *Mitra-samprapti*): 'Winning of Friends', Book II of the *Panchatantra.*

nagaraka: urban sophisticate; man of town.

Nanda: the king who is defeated by Chandragupta Maurya.

naya: policy; prudence; political wisdom; foresight; a scheme or design.

nayashastra: expert knowledge on policy and prudence.

nayika: heroine; female protagonist

Nimabavati: 'the bitter one'; a female character in the *Dasakumaracharita.*

Nitambavati: 'she of the beautiful hips'; a female character in the *Dasakumaracharita.*

niti: practical wisdom; guidance; direction; conduct; course of action; propriety; policy; prudence; a contrivance or scheme.

nitishastra: expert knowledge traditions on the art of ruling in general, as also practical wisdom.

Panchatantra: 'The Five Treatises' (or Principles), a famous collection of tales on prudence by Vishnu Sharma.

Pataliputra: a city in the *Hitopadesha*; ancient name for present-day Patna.

pativrata: a chaste wife.

Pingalaka: 'tawny'; the lion-king in Book I of the *Panchatantra.*

prabhu: power or strength; the lord/divine.

Prajivin: 'live on'; a minister of the crow-king in Book III of the *Panchatantra.*

Pramati: a hero in the *Dasakumaracharita.*

purohita: royal priest.

rajadharma: royal duty.

rajarishi (or *rajarshi*): a sagely king.

Rajavahana: the hero-prince who is the addressee of the stories in the *Dasakumaracharita.*

rajniti: royal policy; political science; statecraft.

Rakshasa: minister of the deceased enemy king Nanda in the play *Mudrarakshasa.*

rakshasa, *rakshasi*: demon, and demoness.

Raktaksha: 'red/blood-eyed'; a minister of the owl-king in Book III of the *Panchatantra.*

rasa: literally 'juice, essence, taste, flavour', *rasa* is a key concept in Indian aesthetics pertaining to the aesthetic flavour of any visual, literary or musical work that evokes an emotion or feeling in the reader or audience; the emotional flavour/essence crafted into the work by the creator/writer/artist and relished by a 'sensitive spectator' or *sahrdaya*, one who can intuitively connect to the work with emotion. *Rasa*s are created by *bhava*s; there are nine *rasa*s (only eight are discernible in the *Dasakumaracharita*).

rasik/*rasika*: connoisseur (male and female).

raudra rasa: rage or fury, one of the nine *rasa*s in Indian aesthetics.

sajjan (*sajjanulu* in Telugu): good or noble people.

sakhya: friendship.

sama: conciliation or agreement; one of Kautilya's four expedients.

samana (*samanam* in Telugu): equal; on par.

samanya/sadharana dharma: common virtues; humane virtues.

samsraya: seeking protection of a stronger king, one of the six strategies of Kautilya's *shadgunya*.

sandhi: conciliation, peace.

Sanjivaka: 'lively'; the wise bull in Book I of the *Panchatantra*.

Sanjivin: 'live well'; a minister of the crow-king in Book III of the *Panchatantra*.

Sankhachuda: a serpent-youth who is ready to sacrifice himself in the *Vetala Panchavimshati*.

saptanga: the seven constituents of a state, namely the king; groups of ministers and high officials; territory; forts and cities; treasury; army; and allies.

shadgunya (*shadgunyam* in Telugu): the sixfold policy as suggested by Kautilya.

Shakatadasa: an agent of Chanakya in the *Mudrarakshasa*.

shakti: power, energy, strength.

Shanti Parva: Book XII of the *Mahabharata*, in which Bhishma lectures on statecraft, *dharma*, *artha* and *kama*, among others.

shastra: expert knowledge traditions; systematic studies.

shringara rasa: erotic love, one of the nine *rasa*s in Indian aesthetics.

Siddharthaka: an agent of Chanakya in the *Mudrarakshasa*.

Silappatikaram: literally, 'the tale of an anklet', it is a famous Tamil epic attributed to the prince-turned-monk Ilanko Atingal, with roots in the ancient Tamil bardic tradition, which tells the tragic love story of a chaste wife Kannagi and her husband Kovalan.

Stirajivin: 'live firm'; a minister of the crow-king in Book III of the *Panchatantra*.

*subhashita*s: literally, 'well-spoken', witty aphorisms and paradigmatic verses in Sanskrit.

Sudraka: a king ready to sacrifice himself for a servant in the *Vetala Panchavimshati*.

suhrd: intimate friend; bosom pal.

Shukra: an expert in *arthashastra* and composer of the *Shukraniti*.

suvarna sandhi: 'golden peace'; one of the types of peace discussed by Kautilya, and in the *Panchatantra*.

svadharma: one's own calling or duty.

tapasya: ardour or asceticism.

Ugra Shakti: 'fierce power'; a dull son of king Amara Shakti in the *Panchatantra*.

Ujjivin: 'live again'; a minister of the crow-king in Book III of the *Panchatantra*.

Unmadini: a beautiful married woman with whom a king is besotted in the *Vetala Panchavimshati*.

Upaharavarman: a hero who succeeds through fraud and adultery in the *Dasakumaracharita*.

utsaha: enthusiasm, one of the components of a king's power.

Vachaspati: a political thinker mentioned by Kautilya.

Vasantabhanu: enemy king adept in policy in the *Dasakumaracharita*.

Veeravara: a hero-warrior in the *Vetala Panchavimshati*.

vetala: spirit inhabiting a corpse in the *Vetala Panchavimshati*.

Vetala Panchavimshati: 'Five and Twenty Tales of the Vetala', by Shivadasa.

vibhavas: determinants or causes which give rise to emotions (*rasas*), such as the presence of the beloved in the context of love.

vigraha: war, one of the six strategies of Kautilya's *shadgunya*.

Viharabhadra: 'pleasure-seeker'; a flatterer in the *Dasakumaracharita*.

Vikatavarman: 'crooked man'; a character in the *Dasakumaracharita*.

Vikramaditya: a king famed for his wise judgments, and hero of the *Vetala Panchavimshati*.

Vindhyavasini: a form of goddess Durga.

vira rasa: courage, one of the nine *rasas* in Indian aesthetics.

Vishruta: 'the eminent one'; a hero skilled in *niti* in the climactic book of the *Dasakumaracharita*.

vyasanas: vices; afflictions.

yanam: withdrawal, one of Kautilya's sixfold strategies/policies.

INDEX